The Scott and Laurie Oki Series
in Asian American Studies

Imprisoned Apart

The World War II Correspondence of an Issei Couple

Louis Fiset

University of Washington Press
Seattle and London

| For Joni, in all seasons

This book is published with the assistance of a grant from the Scott and Laurie Oki Endowed Fund for the publication of Asian American Studies, established through the generosity of Scott and Laurie Oki.

Publication was supported in part by The Civil Liberties Public Education Fund.

LIBRARY OF CONGRESS CATALOGING-IN-PUBLICATION DATA

Fiset, Louis.
   Imprisoned apart : the World War II correspondence of an Issei couple / Louis Fiset.
      p.   cm.—(The Scott and Laurie Oki series in Asian American studies)
   Includes bibliographical references and index.
   ISBN 0-295-97645-4 (pbk. : alk. paper)
   1. Matsushita, Iwao, 1892–1979.   2. Matsushita, Hanaye, 1898 or 9-1965.   3. Japanese Americans—Correspondence.   4. Japanese Americans—Evacuation and relocation, 1942–1945.   I. Title.
II. Series.
D769.8.A6F49   1998
940.53′089956—dc21   97-29984
                                                                CIP

The fields under snow
Have withered, but unwithered
Are the asters.

no wa yuki ni
karuredo karenu
shion ka na

—Sengin,
17th-century Japanese poet

CONTENTS

ILLUSTRATIONS

I FIRST "MET" Iwao Matsushita some fifteen years ago when I read his papers—mostly letters and documents from the World War II era—in the University of Washington archives. Impressed by their richness and the humanity they displayed I used excerpts from them in my book *Asian America* and intended to publish a small edition of his letters at some time in the future. Some years later, Karyl Winn, the UW curator of manuscripts, wrote me that a younger scholar, Louis Fiset, was interested in doing something with the letters. He and I corresponded, met, and became friends. At some point in this process I decided to waive my own interest in the Matsushita letters in favor of Fiset. My project had never gotten off the ground, and Fiset was on the spot and ready to go ahead.

It is now clear that this was a wise decision. Fiset devoted years to this book and has gone far beyond anything that I would have done. He has skillfully given us a rare glimpse of two Japanese American immigrant lives. Iwao and Hanaye Matsushita were Japanese nationals and, like all Asians in 1941–42, ineligible for naturalization. Unlike most Japanese Americans who were incarcerated in camps under the authority of Executive Order 9066, Iwao was subjected to internment by the Immigration and Naturalization Service as an enemy alien. There had been more than 90,000 Japanese nationals in the continental United States and Hawaii in 1940, and perhaps 8,000 of them—fewer than 10 percent—

were interned during the war. Iwao was snatched up shortly after Pearl Harbor and sent to an INS-run facility at Fort Missoula, Montana, while Hanaye remained in Seattle for months, alone, and then was transported first to the fairgrounds at Puyallup, Washington, and then to the camp at Minidoka, Idaho. Their understated letters show us the pain of the separation inflicted on them.

It is because of this wrenching experience—the separate government confinement of a couple who had never been parted since their 1919 marriage—that we have this wartime correspondence. *Imprisoned Apart* is both a moving human interest story and a significant addition to our knowledge of some of the circumstances of wartime internment. The INS camps have been little written about and are thus largely unknown. Few of the other Japanese internees were as acculturated as Iwao Matsushita, and his physical environment at Fort Missoula was superior to that of most other internees. Iwao and Hanaye, both Christians and of middle-class economic status, were far from typical of their generation of Japanese immigrants.

Fiset has blazed a trail which, one hopes, others will soon follow by giving us accounts of other prisoners and other camps. The little-known internment story is a small but significant aspect of the wartime ordeal of more than 125,000 Japanese Americans, citizen and alien. Fiset has shown us new aspects of that ordeal.

Unlike the incarceration of most Japanese Americans—two-thirds of them native-born United States citizens—the internment, after all, did conform to the usages of nations. American internment practices generally observed the forms of law, and the record of the United States was significantly better than those of its sister democracies, Great Britain, Canada, and Australia. But, while there were undoubtedly some enemy aliens who should have been interned, Iwao Matsushita and the majority of the other internees were in no way a threat to the public safety. They were detained in part to satisfy public opinion, for the public had been frightened by fears of an imaginary "fifth column." Both the internment of a small percentage of Japanese Americans and the incarceration of almost all the rest of those living in the continental United States were the result of what a recent Presidential Commission judged to be "a failure of political leadership." Only when we keep in mind the attitudes engendered by a devastating war for survival, and understand that the officials concerned with national security in times of crisis tend to become what one scholar investigating internment in Great Britain has called "professional witch-finders," can we even begin to imagine either why so many were interned or why so many federal officials and the public-spirited citizens who assisted them expended time and scarce resources keeping such persons under guard.

The World War II internment policies constitute a relatively dark page in the history of civil liberty in America. Not the least virtue of *Imprisoned Apart* is that Fiset shows us, at the human level, just how unnecessary and cruel those policies could be.

Roger Daniels
Cincinnati, June 1997

ACKNOWLEDGMENTS

S EVERAL INDIVIDUALS PROVIDED essential assistance throughout this six-year project. Professor Roger Daniels originally intended to publish a collection of Matsushita's wartime correspondence but graciously stepped aside to allow me to take on a project of greater scope. He reviewed both major drafts, for which I am grateful. An anonymous second reviewer also provided important suggestions from a different perspective. Two professional philatelists, Richard W. Helbock and L. Dann Mayo, Jr., provided me access to important postal documents related to World War II censorship and offered helpful comments on relevant portions of the manuscript.

Miss Teruko Inoue visited me in Seattle on two occasions from her home in Fukuoka, Japan, bringing family photographs, stories, and valu-able information concerning her uncle Iwao and Hanaye's family. Carol Zabilski shared her interview notes and impressions of Matsushita from a dozen visits with him twenty years ago, then caringly and skillfully copyedited the manuscript.

Because it proved impossible to write this book while simultaneously doing dental research and providing clinical care, I took a year's leave of absence from the University of Washington Dental School in 1993–94. My colleague and former mentor, Professor Peter Milgrom, not only encouraged me to pursue this year of writing but took over my clinical duties at the Dental Fears Research Clinic without complaint. Later, a Centrum Foundation Artist in Residency Award in 1995 provided me with the month-long tranquil environment in a natural setting I needed in which to revise the manuscript.

Finally, Joan Fiset read every word—both the discarded and the salvaged —and lived with me through every day of this experience.

PART ONE

THE

AMERICAN

EXPERIENCE

"Mountain Lake," one of many pictorial photographs exhibited by
Iwao Matsushita during the 1920s and 1930s.

ONE

Establishing Roots

Island soul of me
Cast off to cross the ocean.
Ah, the world is big!
—Issa[1]

O N A DRIZZLY LATE summer morning in 1919, the passenger freighter
S.S. *Suwa Maru* nudged its hull against the pilings of a familiar berth
at the Great Northern Railway pier in Seattle's Elliott Bay, bringing a
collection of people and cargo from Asia. The ship, one of four British-
built vessels owned by the NYK (*Nippon Yusen Kaisha*) shipping line, was
completing the North American leg of the company's twenty-five-year-
old route between Seattle and the Asian Pacific.

Shortly after the lines were secured, a first-class passenger, Dr. Toma
Inoue of Tokyo, appeared on deck attired in a deep blue-black silk
kimono with "a touch of white at the throat." One of 500 licensed
female physicians in Japan, Dr. Inoue had received her training in Western
medicine, with a specialty in internal medicine and diseases of children.
She was en route to New York at the invitation of the international
YWCA to attend a conference on education in health and social morality.
Following an interview with the press, the assistant manager of NYK
escorted her off the ship for a tour of the city; his instructions from
his superiors were to attend to her welfare during her twenty-four-hour
stay in Seattle.[2] The ship's passenger list recorded this as her sixth journey
to America.[3]

Among the 325 other passengers on board (233 of them Japanese subjects) were twenty-seven-year-old Iwao Matsushita and Hanaye Tamura

Matsushita, his twenty-one-year-old bride of seven months. They had boarded ship at Yokohama, the last of several scheduled stops prior to the Pacific crossing. Although the majority of the Japanese passengers were returning to the United States, the Matsushitas, having booked one-way passage, were traveling abroad for the first time. They planned to make Seattle their home for as long as five years.

The year 1919 saw 10,064 Japanese immigrant arrivals in America,[4] many of them came as sojourners with dreams of accumulating wealth to take back to the homeland for a better life. The Matsushitas also arrived with dreams of riches, but they sought a wealth of a different kind. Iwao's passport bore a student visa,[5] which gave him entreé to a culture that would enable him to pursue fluency in the English language, to acquire familiarity with its literature, and, he believed, "to become a better man."[6]

Iwao Matsushita was born on January 10, 1892, in Miike, Hiroshima-ken (Hiroshima prefecture), on the island of Honshu.[7] He was the second son and third of five children of Isao and Hana Matsushita. A sister, Toku, and a brother, Sekio, were four and two years older. Sisters, Tonomi and Fumi, followed three and five years later. The Matsushita family members were among a minuscule group of people practicing the Protestant faith in Japan at that time. Earlier, following the Meiji Restoration, Methodist missionaries had converted the elder Matsushita to Christianity; he later became a proselytizer.[8]

Isao Matsushita's superiors sent him to engage in mission work in Tonomi, a small fishing village near the seaport town of Mitajiri. Immediately, the Matsushitas became a curiosity to the non-Christian villagers, a curiosity that quickly turned on the newcomers and led to persecution of the children. Spreading the word of Christ among a Buddhist majority proved burdensome enough for Isao, but the lives of the Matsushita children became unbearable after the parents enrolled the two eldest children in the primary school. Years later, as an adult, Toku revealed in her diary the story of her early persecution at the school:

A few days after our arrival [at] Tonomi, father took me to the primary school for admission. The teachers and children received us with looks of surprise. Many children at once crowded around and stared at us very wonderfully as if we Christians were visitors from a distant foreign country or rather something not human. Though I was able to pass my first day at the school without suffering any mischief because my father was with me, some mischievous boys would not let any other day pass without teasing me in some way or other. The very next day, some boys came near me and by turns pulled my hanging braided hair crying, "Why did you Christians come to this village? What did your family come here for? We guess you've come to destroy our Empire, you hateful foreign girl!"[9]

Despite the early cruelties suffered by each of the children, young Iwao's upbringing in a Methodist household exposed him to Western culture and awakened a keen interest in the English language, one shared by his parents and all his siblings.[10] Following graduation from Kobe's *Kwansei Gakuin* high school in 1911, he entered the prestigious Tokyo Foreign Language College to study English language and literature. During summer breaks, his eagerness to learn led to employment at the British Embassy tutoring an attaché in Japanese. After three years of study in the Department of Education, he received a certificate to teach English in Japan's high schools. From 1914 to 1919 he drilled students in English grammar at a high school in Fukuyama, Hiroshima-ken. His principal there, Mr. Tamura, was the father of the woman who later became his wife.

Hanaye, six years younger than Iwao, was born March 9, 1898, in Okayama, Okayama prefecture, on Honshu Island. Her parents, too impoverished to provide for their children's basic needs, eventually turned her and her siblings over to an orphanage. In time a home was found for Hanaye. Her adoptive parents, the Tamuras, possessed sufficient means to support a child; they raised Hanaye in the Protestant tradition and sent her to a private Christian school in Tokyo for a portion of her education.

As was the custom, the Tamuras planned to arrange their daughter's marriage. The intention was to adopt a boy whom Hanaye would marry and who would eventually inherit the family property. The adoption took place; however, the marriage plan dissolved after the spirited young Hanaye balked. According to surviving family members, she simply did not like the boy and refused to go along. Therefore, at twenty she remained unwed. Still determined to find a match for their only daughter, Mr. Tamura turned to Matsushita, the eager and promising young English

5

| Iwao Matsushita, as a young high school teacher, poses before emigrating to the United States.

teacher at his high school. A traditional go-between helped arrange a match, this time successful, and a marriage took place on January 22, 1919. Hanaye viewed this relationship not only as an opportunity to be rid of her "brother" but also as the beginning of an exciting life with an educated man whose sights were beginning to focus eastward on America.

It is not clear when Matsushita first considered coming to the United States. Certainly his upbringing and professional interests influenced his developing vision, but his marriage to Hanaye also must have contributed. Dr. Kyo Koike, an old friend of Mrs. Tamura's whom Hanaye fondly called Uncle, the customary address for familiar elders, was a Seattle physician who had emigrated from Shimane prefecture in 1917. Koike's

6

medical practice, which included surgery, was located in the heart of the city's Japantown, the Nihonmachi, where he served the immigrant population living there and in the surrounding farm communities.[11] Longer established in Seattle was Katuichi Katayama, a relation of Koike's, who served the Japanese business community as an interpreter. These familial links led Matsushita to look to Seattle too, where the University of Washington might be the means of achieving his intellectual goals.

The encouragement of Katayama and Koike, the frugality that enabled Matsushita to save the necessary capital for a comfortable oceanic journey and adjustment period in America, and the adventurous spirit of a young wife led to passport applications and booking on a trans-Pacific steamer in the summer of 1919.

| THE CROSSING

The Matsushitas arrived at Yokohama at least a week prior to the scheduled departure of the S.S. *Suwa Maru* for America in order to validate their passports and receive the obligatory medical examination. On August 12 they presented their papers to the American Consulate General. Iwao's passport stated the purpose for their travel to America—"for scholarly pursuits and research" (*gakujutsu kenkyuu*).[12]

On August 19 the ship slid from its berth in Yokohama harbor to begin the crossing, the trip having originated in Hong Kong and made stops at Shanghai, Nagasaki, and Kobe. Matsushita's savings enabled them to avoid the discomforts of third-class passage endured by many married couples and picture brides of that era. One third-class passenger who paid the $75 booking later remembered: "Of course the trip was third class, and there were miserable things about it. There were four people in one cabin with four small silkworm-type shelf-bunks. On the floor was cargo with canvas spread over it, and sitting on that we third class passengers had our meals."[13]

Following sixteen days on the high seas and a twelve-hour stopover in Victoria, British Columbia, the *Suwa Maru* headed southward into Puget Sound. Hours later she entered Seattle's Elliott Bay. At 11:00 a.m. on Wednesday, September 3, under a pewter sky, the Matsushitas' trans-Pacific journey ended beside the long finger pier at Smith Cove, nestled

Iwao Matsushita's 1919 passport states that he is traveling to the United States of America for scholarly purposes. It also indicates that he sailed aboard the S.S. *Suwa Maru,* which docked in Seattle. Washington, on September 4, 1919.

between Magnolia Bluff and Queen Anne Hill. Adjacent to the pier another frequent visitor, the *Azumasan Maru*, awaited her scheduled departure date for the return voyage to Asia.[14]

Although the Matsushitas' passport status and ship accommodations made their voyage much less exhausting than most immigrants', it still took many hours to clear immigration and customs.[15] Only the next morning were they able to leave the wharf and shuttle southward toward Japantown, likely under the escort of Katayama. Europeans of their status would have walked right through.

For the young couple, Seattle was part of a strategy for furthering Iwao's professional life as a teacher in Japan. They had no intentions of making Seattle their permanent home. Fate, however, would intervene. Hanaye would never return to her homeland, and neither one would see his parents again.

| SETTLING INTO SEATTLE LIFE

The Matsushitas arrived in America with $450 in cash, an ample sum to tide them over for several months until they acclimated to the strange country. This amount far exceeded the traditional $50 per capita of most immigrants. With this cushion they could afford to rest for the first days or perhaps weeks without Iwao's having to seek immediate employment. They stayed with Katayama at his house for the first month, and there Matsushita met Koike, who had stayed with Katayama upon his own arrival two years earlier.[16]

Few immigrants spoke English adequate to facilitate adjustment into the mainstream. Seattle's Japantown provided a welcome transition. In 1919 the Matsushitas and their fellow passengers found 7,484 people there, 2.5 percent of the city's total population.[17] The Nihonmachi extended some blocks from its business center at Sixth Avenue and Main Street, below Skid Road and south of the city's main downtown area. The area bustled with 1,489 business of all kinds.[18] Japantown consisted of a mélange of small groceries, restaurants, apparel shops, barbers, dye works, and many other small operations serving the needs of arriving immigrants, resident Japanese, and nearby working-class whites as well.

Following their stay with Katayama and his family, the Matsushitas moved to their first housekeeping address, 1032 Main Street. This rental house was situated several blocks east of the heart of the Nihonmachi business district and faced southward toward majestic Mount Rainier, a fourteen-thousand-foot peak that would play a spiritual role in their lives in later months and years. Iwao soon found temporary employment as a cook in a Japanese-run restaurant.

An active community religious life awaited the couple, for both Buddhist and Protestant churches were well rooted in Seattle by the time of their arrival. The Japanese Methodist Episcopal church, which they soon joined, had its own permanent building on Washington Street.[19] Their affiliation with the church (which later became Blaine Memorial Methodist Church) would bring them spiritual fulfillment throughout their lives.

The stay on Main Street and Iwao's career as a cook proved brief. On January 7, 1920, the census taker recorded the Matsushitas as on-site managers of the Chester Lodging House at 1322 Old Fifth Avenue (Fifth-and-a-Half Street).[20] Eight working-class boardinghouses lined the two-block street, in reality a wide alley sandwiched between Fifth and Sixth avenues and hardly a legitimate thoroughfare. The Chester's thirty rooms earned it the reputation as the largest residence along the row.[21] The lodgers included twenty-three men, of whom eleven were European immigrants and the remainder, an assortment of migrants from other parts of the country.[22]

The Chester was among the numerous lodging places in the district that catered to whites who toiled in the shipyards or worked other blue-collar jobs; other establishments provided accommodations for Japanese immigrants, Issei, many of whom were recent arrivals. The grueling physical labor associated with the couple's new work countered Iwao's preference for intellectual toils. A contemporary described a typical workday as an immigrant hotel manager of a larger residence:

My Pacific Hotel had sixty rooms, and I hired two whites, but as I was the manager, I did everything from chambermaid work to being a porter, clerk, bellboy and telephone operator. I went the rounds at 6 a.m. beginning to awaken the guests. Then I took a short rest at 10 a.m. I continued a very

| Iwao Matsushita on duty as manager of Seattle's Chester Lodging House, ca. 1920

irregular life until midnight every day, getting up, and going to sleep, and getting up again.[23]

In addition to the large number of Nihonmachi businesses catering to Seattle newcomers, there was a Japanese-language school founded in 1902 to provide immigrants' children with education in the culture and language of their parents' native country. As second-generation—Nisei— children came of school age, administrators developed curricula to bridge the gap between the generations. The Matsushitas were never to have children of their own because of Hanaye's inability to conceive and because of their apparent decision not to adopt, despite her own family history. However, Iwao would oversee the weekly lessons of Seattle's Japanese children many years later as principal of the Japanese-language school.

By spring of 1920 the Matsushitas had left the hotel business,[24] but Iwao's plan to enter the University of Washington to study English failed to materialize. He likely overestimated his proficiency in English and, thus, his ability to handle the anticipated workload. No surviving evidence exists to document official class enrollments during the 1920s, although Matsushita did take language classes there on an informal basis.[25] Whatever the reason, the couple's anticipated return to Japan after a five-year sojourn was postponed. In fact, twenty-nine years would elapse before Iwao would finally begin his American college education at the university.

Matsushita's attention now turned away from menial hotel work toward permanent employment. Through connections in the Japanese community, possibly with the aid of Katayama or Dr. Koike, he found a white-collar position at Mitsui and Company (*Mitsui Busan Kaisha*), a major Tokyo-based trading firm, with branch offices in New York, San Francisco, Portland, and Seattle. Mitsui happily hired this college-educated immigrant for $150 per month.[26] Over the ensuing years, the city directory listed Matsushita as company clerk, cashier, and secretary.[27] His actual duties expanded to include larger responsibilities. Soon the firm charged him with interviewing prospective employees and entertaining important guests from Japan, as well as other public relations. Eventually he became involved with the company's overall affairs. An escalating salary with yearly $25-per-month raises and year-end bonuses reflected his managerial value to the firm.[28]

Matsushita's growing income made unnecessary Hanaye's entry into the workplace. Following her experience at the Chester Lodging House, she never again worked for wages. However, had she sought employment during the 1920s, her limited proficiency in English, race, and gender would likely have limited her opportunities to domestic service.[29]

| Hostility and Exclusion

Matsushita's status at Mitsui and Company brought him into contact with numerous Americans wishing to do business with Asia. As a result, his English improved, along with his ability to navigate Seattle's social and economic terrain. However, neither the couple's increasingly secure financial status nor Iwao's intellectual bearing insulated them from a long-simmering hostility toward the Japanese community as a whole, which re-erupted just before their 1919 arrival.

| Portrait taken several years after Matsushita's arrival in the United States.

With the armistice in November 1918, wartime shipbuilding in Seattle had slumped, for the government canceled its contracts en masse. Simultaneously, what started as a local shipyard strike grew into the nation's first citywide general strike, idling sixty thousand workers for four days.[30] In Seattle as elsewhere, the economy faltered; the glut of returning war veterans could not immediately be absorbed into the work force. A three-year postwar recession enveloped the country. On the West Coast, many fingers pointed toward the Japanese community as a cause of the worsening conditions.

Americans had long made scapegoats of Japanese immigrants. As early as 1900 the Japanese had taken over the role of the Chinese as racial targets for a citizenry that perceived itself economically threatened. A 1906 attempt by the San Francisco School Board to force Japanese pupils to attend a segregated school for the Chinese created such a furor that Japan, whose military was now emerging as a power in Asia, lodged official protest, and President Theodore Roosevelt became personally involved. What resulted was an executive arrangement known as the Gentlemen's Agreement of 1907–1908, by which Tokyo agreed to issue no more passports to "laborers" attempting to enter the United States, in exchange for the objectionable school order being rescinded.[31]

The agreement, however, failed to stem the flow of immigrants because of a loophole permitting issuance of passports to the parents, wives, and children of laborers already living in the country. Immigration actually increased as husbands sent for wives and children and bachelors returned to their native villages to find brides.[32] Alarmed citizens in the western states gave in to racial, cultural, and economic bias, and in 1913 California lawmakers responded to their constituents' anger with legalized discrimination: they barred land ownership by immigrants, especially farmers. In the next decade anti-alien land laws followed in other states, including Washington, modeled after the California measure.

Despite occasional eruptions of hostility along the west coast, the period between 1914 and 1919 was relatively quiescent. Citizens occupied themselves with the war in Europe. Japan played an opportunistic role against Germany by helping to defend Allied shipping against German raiders in the North Pacific. Moreover, the California anti-alien land law on the books seemed to satisfy the exclusionists.

A wave of anti-Japanese feeling suddenly arose shortly after termination of the war, however. Inflamed by political rhetoric, California residents began to accuse the Japanese of living comfortably as a result of Americans going to the front. The movement started in March 1919, exploding onto the Seattle scene four months later, on July 26, just forty days before the Matsushitas' arrival in America. On that day, the front page of the Seattle *Star* proclaimed: "DEPORT JAPANESE Demanded by Secretary of Veterans' Commission."[33]

The secretary of the Veterans' Commission was Miller Freeman, a former state legislator and local publisher, who would militate against Japanese residents until after World War II. His crusade was backed by many Washington businessmen, farmers, and trade unionists. The real goal of the state anti-Japanese movement, like the one in California, was to cripple Issei agriculture. The anti-alien land laws passed by the legislature in 1921 and 1923 managed to do some damage but failed to achieve their ultimate goal.

Nevertheless, building on state-sponsored anti-alien land acts in California, Oregon, Washington, and elsewhere and on a 1922 Supreme Court ruling that upheld the constitutionality of determining citizenship eligibility on racial grounds, Congress in 1924 denied immigration quotas to any foreigners who were "aliens ineligible to citizenship." The Immigration Act of 1924 slammed the door on Japanese immigration, isolating the Japanese in America.[34]

| JAPANTOWN BETWEEN THE WARS

Although the Matsushitas lived in the hostile climate and may have experienced personal affronts in the 1920s and 1930s, Iwao's lucrative employment insulated them against its potential economic effects. His association with Mitsui and Company provided a social buffer and material comforts, but it failed to stir a creative spirit residing within him. Photography and poetry writing suited his temperament and intellectual interests, avocations he shared with Koike, who had led him on his first outing to Mount Rainier, his muse, during the couple's stay with Katayama.[35] They shared their creative lives until Koike's death in 1947.

Matsushita's senior by eleven years, Koike had preceded the couple to Seattle by two years. He brought with him a medical degree, years of medical experience employing Western methods, and, like most immigrants, hope for a richer life. Soon after his arrival he established his residence and 9 a.m.–to–8 p.m. office hours in the Empire Hotel Building, at 422½ Main Street, in the heart of Japantown. He treated fellow immigrants and their families from the city, as well as Issei from outlying truck farms who sought care from a doctor with whom they shared culture and language. In 1920 Koike was one of nineteen Issei physicians and surgeons serving the Seattle Japanese population.[36] Within walking distance of his office,

| His salary at Mitsui and Company enabled Matsushita to afford a car as early as 1929.

other professional men maintained offices, including nine dentists and five interpreters, as did six real estate and investment companies. In addition, four Japanese-language newspapers and five Japanese banks had rooted in the self-sufficient community.[37]

Dr. Koike was a competent physician, but he is remembered today for his artistry and leadership in the arts community. In late 1923 he co-organized the Seattle Camera Club, and eleven years later, a haiku society, the Rainier *Ginsha*.[38] Shortly after his arrival in America, Koike had acquired a Kodak camera and began photographing natural images. Success came quickly. Within a few years he was internationally recognized as a pictorialist photographer. Pictorialism had emerged as a worldwide movement in the late nineteenth century and was popular among the immigrant Japanese. As a genre it was a "conscious attempt to turn beautiful objects and experiences into beautiful images, and thereby to assure the position of the medium in the hierarchy of art."[39] Pictorialism was well suited to Issei photographers, who brought a unique visual style

16

| On a snow skiing trip with Dr. Kyo Koike, ca. 1935.

steeped in Japanese traditions of arts and crafts. Koike suggested to his peers that "we must be the best interpreters for both nations because we are not free of Japanese ideas, and yet at the same time we understand Western ways."[40] At his peak of success he was inducted into the Royal Photographic Society of Great Britain.

Like Koike and Asakichi (Frank) Kunishige,[41] a mutual friend, Matsushita was a charter member of the Seattle Camera Club. And like them, he received peer recognition as a pictorialist. However, he was less gifted than others, an artist whose hybrid style encompassed elements borrowed from numerous colleagues, especially from Koike, whom he considered his mentor. Nevertheless, he enjoyed modest success, exhibiting prints in numerous salons throughout the United States and abroad. In 1927, six of his evocative images hung in four salons in the United States and Great Britain.[42]

The Seattle Camera Club, one of many artistic organizations to develop in Washington State between the wars, arose during a prolific period in the local artistic community, a time when other immigrant artists also

Hanaye, holding the camera, and Iwao at Alki Beach in West Seattle, ca. 1930.

made their appearance in Seattle. Notable among them were Kenjiro Nomura, Takuichi Fujii, Shiro Miyazaki, Kenjiro Miyao, and Kamekichi Tokita. Together they were known as the Sunday Painters, one of the strongest groups of "progressive" painters in the Northwest.[43] Nomura brushed dark oils into unsentimental street scenes of early Seattle, earning him national recognition and the company of his fellow Northwest artists Kenneth Callahan, Mark Tobey, Morris Graves, and Guy Anderson.[44] Later Nomura canvases encapsulated the life of the Japanese during their incarceration at the Puyallup Assembly Center and the Minidoka Relocation Center.[45]

The six-year existence of the Seattle Camera Club coincided with the city's rebound from the postwar downturn. Much of the new activity was along the waterfront. World War I had made Seattle the leading shipping port on the Pacific Coast, and now, in the mid-1920s, it boasted forty-seven piers and wharves. Waterborne commerce, domestic and foreign, prospered. Imports from Asia, primarily Japan, accounted for 70 percent of the total value and 40 percent of the total tonnage, of which nearly 60 percent was in raw silk. Exports to Asia through the 1919 Seattle waterfront accounted for 75 percent of total shipping.[46]

The number of shipping lines calling at Seattle increased steadily during the war years and beyond. In 1915 OSK (*Osaka Shosen Kaisha*) expanded its operations, and the Suzuki Company moved its shipping and commercial firm from Portland to Seattle, augmenting the world's largest vegetable oil terminus. By 1920 thirty steamship lines sailed regularly to Seattle. To serve the Asian trade, thirty-five Japanese importers and exporters operated on the Seattle waterfront.[47] With Mitsui and Company doing business in the heart of waterfront commerce, Matsushita's white-collar status was secure.

From 1921 to 1929 Seattle's Japantown grew along with the rest of the growing city. The number of Japanese residents in 1920 stood at 7,874, 24 percent of whom were native born. In 1930, the population reached 8,448, with 47 percent native born, reflecting the long-term impact of the Gentlemen's Agreement.[48] The bulk of the *nihon-jin,* or Japanese, population began an eastward shift up Yesler Way, scattering northward and southward into previously Jewish, Italian, and working-class white neighborhoods.[49]

In 1925 the Matsushitas followed the outward movement to a clapboard rental house on 29th Avenue South. Two years later they settled closer to the Nihonmachi business district, at 905–24th Avenue South. This small brick bungalow, which they leased from its Italian American owner for seventy-five dollars per month, remained their permanent home for the next fourteen years. There Hanaye kept house with an omnipresent population of pet cats, and from there she went with Iwao, Koike, and their mutual friends on skiing, hiking, and photography outings into the mountains.

Hanaye's athleticism in the presence of male Issei reveals an adventuresome spirit that appears to have set her apart from other, more traditional, Issei women of her era. Surviving family photographs frequently portray her outfitted in contemporary Western fashion, always sporting headwear, at times splashy, such as Garbo-like wide-brimmed hats; one Nisei, a young adolescent at the time, later recalled her in turbans. If not eccentric, she was outspoken in her adopted language, and he remembered her as a cigarette smoker. In his words, "She was her own woman."[50]

Shortly after the couple's move to the brick bungalow, Matsushita began a new professional affiliation, with the University of Washington.

The Matsushitas rented this bungalow on Twenty-fourth Avenue South from 1927 until April of 1942.

| Hanaye with a feline friend in 1927, one of the many cats the Matsushitas owned during their prewar years in Seattle.

His friend, Eldon Griffin, assistant professor in the Department of Oriental Studies, arranged a temporary teaching opportunity after encouraging him to pioneer a Japanese-language course complementary to the Chinese-language courses then being offered by the department. The university was searching for a qualified instructor, but no state funds had yet been appropriated for the position. Hoping his informal demonstration course would eventually lead to a permanent appointment, Matsushita taught evening classes through the university's extension service without compensation for the fall, winter, and spring terms. The position, however, failed to materialize, and other salaried professional opportunities lacking, he continued his employment with Mitsui and Company.[51]

21

Iwao Matsushita, 1933.

Hanaye Matsushita, 1933.

Hanaye and Iwao enjoy a Sunday afternoon in one of Seattle's parks, ca. 1930.

| On a hike in bear grass
and alpine fir country,
Mount Rainier, ca. 1935.

| Hanaye Matsushita rests
during a summer
mountain hike, ca 1939.

Predictably, the Seattle Camera Club disbanded with the onset of the Great Depression in 1929. Most club members were employed as store clerks, salesmen, tailors, barbers, and grocers or eked out their living in other low-paying occupations and were unable to sustain the cost of materials, postage for mailing photographs abroad, or even the expense associated with the simplest of club activities.[52] Because their professional salaries could absorb the costs, Koike and Matsushita continued joint outings to their "holy mountain," Mount Rainier, throughout the 1930s, where Koike made more than one hundred "working visits." Matsushita himself would later recall 190 visits to that spiritual source. Hanaye was a constant companion on these excursions, donning backpack during the hiking season and skis in winter. The binding friendship of the two men would later play a role in her welfare during the war brooding on the horizon, a war that began with Japan's 1931 incursion into Manchuria.

| RESIGNATION FROM MITSUI AND COMPANY

Matsushita reached his zenith with Mitsui and Company by 1940. A steady increase in Asia trade had brought regular raises and year-end bonuses, so that by the beginning of the year he was earning the equivalent of a manager's salary of $530 per month.[53] He had accumulated nearly $10,000 in U.S. savings banks, and more than $12,000 in Seattle branch Japanese banks.[54] Matsushita was a wealthy man. In addition, 1940 brought an offer from management to transfer to the home office in Tokyo. Such an offer was unusual and may have indicated his status in the firm. At least one large Japan-based trading company, *Mitsubishi Shoji Kaisha,* refused entry of any employees hired overseas into even the bottom ranks of top management, regardless of whether they were Japanese born. These *yoin,* or "hired employees," were individuals to whom no permanent commitment had been made, as distinguished from *seiin,* or "formal employees," persons to whom the firm had made a lifetime commitment. Matsushita, it appears, had reached exalted *seiin* status.[55]

24   Nevertheless, on August 31, 1940, after twenty years with the firm, Matsushita submitted formal resignation to company officials. His accompanying letter cited an undying desire to fulfill his original purpose

for coming to America, to study English and English literature at the University of Washington. He further stated:

> I enjoy my life in Seattle. I have so many happy memories with nice people—both Japanese and Americans. Especially I enjoy photography and mountain climbing. I have visited Mt. Rainier, my lover, more than 190 times. I cannot leave Seattle when I think of the beautiful views of Mount Rainier.[56]

Matsushita must surely have had mixed motives for his decision to leave the firm. Pressure brought by his employers for him to transfer, first to their New York office and later to their headquarters in Tokyo, was certainly a factor in his walking away from such lucrative employment. But he could also see the war clouds gathering in the Pacific and anticipate the inevitable toll it would eventually take on Asia-Pacific commerce. His resignation came in the face of dwindling trade with Japan, a result of American responses to Japan's increasing militarism in Asia. In July 1939, the United States terminated its existing commercial treaty with Japan and a year later declared an embargo of all iron and steel scrap.[57] In December 1941, the government would shut down operations at Mitsui and Company altogether.

"Autumn Clouds," exhibited at the Internacional D'Art Fotographic, Barcelona, 1933.

Listening to the Sound of Shoes

The time has come
For my arrest
This dark rainy night.
I calm myself and listen
To the sound of the shoes.
—*Sojin Takei*[1]

MATSUSHITA HAD LONG AGO abandoned his plan to return to Japan to teach English language and literature. Because there was no actual need now to enroll at the University of Washington, he sought other employment. The job market for *kaisha,* or "corporation," workers, however, had shrunk by the autumn of 1940 as a result of increasingly strained relations between the United States and Japan. Finding the equivalent of the job he had left was impossible. Instead, in October the Seattle Japanese Chamber of Commerce hired him to compile trade statistics for the benefit of the American public. The chamber of commerce, a loose association of Seattle businesses, aimed at maintaining positive trade relations with Japan. Although well qualified for this line of work, Matsushita held a rather lowly status within the organization, in both responsibilities and salary ($150 per month), and the job, with its emphasis on statistics, must have been dulling to his creative leanings.

Unknown to Matsushita and other chamber of commerce employees throughout the country, statistics of another kind were quietly being collected by the FBI and the Office of Naval Intelligence (ONI) in preparation for a possible Pacific war. As early as 1932, mainland U.S. resident Japanese with suspected close ties to Japan, or whose high regard for her culture was publicly known, came under surveillance as potential saboteurs.[2] Included were members of scores of Japanese clubs and organizations in the U.S.

27

promoting cultural and business ties with Japan, as well as the various Japanese chambers of commerce throughout the country.

By mid-1939 the government's need for a sophisticated information-gathering capability had increased significantly, but because of agency competition and a lack of coordinated effort, intelligence operations were inefficient and inadequate. Thus, on the eve of the outbreak of World War II in Europe, President Franklin Roosevelt assigned control of all espionage, counterespionage, and sabotage investigations to the FBI, which was part of the Justice Department, the Military Intelligence Division of the War Department, and the Office of Naval Intelligence. All investigations involving civilians in the United States and its territories fell to the FBI a year later.[3]

Along with this reorganization came the Alien Registration Act, passed by Congress in 1940, authorizing collection of background information on nearly five million aliens from all countries of the world living within U.S. borders. Data gathering on citizenship status, organizational affiliations,[4] and "activities" such as employment was designed to ease the FBI's task of monitoring more than one million alien Japanese, Germans, and Italians who would be proclaimed "enemy aliens" by December 8 of the following year. Resident aliens were required to report changes of address within five days of a move, and all aliens temporarily in the country had to report every three months, regardless of residency status.

In 1940 Matsushita dutifully registered his residence, his recent change of employment, and other background information on him and Hanaye. These data were mingled with those on 47,305 foreign-born Japanese falling under the authority of this legislation.[5]

Whether an undifferentiated mass of data collected in an era preceding powerful mainframe computers was of actual use to the FBI is questionable. Nevertheless, the FBI began building dossiers on Japanese residents in the country and, by early 1941, had created personnel files for more than two thousand individuals, most of whom were male community leaders perceived as a potential threat to the nation's security. Individuals were assigned to three hierarchical categories according to this perception. The first category, Group A, included suspects "known dangerous" and who had been the subject of individual investigations. Because these persons were influential within the Japanese American community or had jobs that placed them in strategic locations or situations in which espionage or sabotage was likely, they required continuing, intense observation. Thus, fishermen, produce distributors, Shinto and Buddhist priests, farmers, influential businessmen, and members of the Japanese Consulate were listed as Group A suspects.

Group B suspects were presumed to be "potentially dangerous" but had not yet been fully investigated. Other Japanese, because of their pro-Japanese leanings and propagandist activities, made the C list. Among the B and C listees were Japanese-language teachers, the Kibei (Nisei who received a part of their education in Japan), martial arts instructors, community servants, travel agents, social directors, and editors of the vernacular press.[6]

For most, it was "guilt by association." Matsushita's name was added to either the B or C list because of his long-term professional ties to Japanese trade. An anonymous informer had earlier reported him to the FBI as an "agent of a foreign principal."[7]

Although intelligence-gathering sources reported the existence of small numbers of Japanese residents who might commit acts of sabotage or espionage, wholesale evacuation of the whole population was not then considered. Summary action would be taken on an individual basis.[8] The job of handling the two thousand Japanese on the so-called ABC list, in the event of war, would fall to the War and Justice departments. On July 18, 1941, the secretary of war, H. L. Stimson, and the U.S. attorney general, Francis Biddle, entered into an agreement regarding responsibilities for the apprehension, temporary detention, and permanent internment of enemy aliens. They determined that the Justice Department would make the arrests using the arm of the FBI. The Immigration and Naturalization Service (INS), also part of the Justice Department,[9] would then provide temporary detention and establish loyalty hearing boards responsible for recommending disposition of individual detainees. The War Department, specifically the U.S. Army, was charged with the permanent custody of all deemed too dangerous to release.[10]

On December 8, 1941, within an hour after Congress declared war, the attorney general brought to the president a proclamation prepared the night before declaring "that an invasion has been perpetuated upon the territory of the United States by the Empire of Japan" and that all resident Japanese nationals over the age of fourteen in the United States and its possessions are immediately "liable to restraint, or to give security, or to remove and depart from the United States." This and two additional restraint-and-removal proclamations declaring Japanese, German, and Italian nationals to be enemy aliens, derived their authority from the first Enemy Alien Act of 1798, as amended in 1918, which gave the president absolute power over such persons in time of war.[11]

With regard to the Japanese, the attorney general issued a verbal blanket warrant to arrest those on the ABC list. The FBI director, J. Edgar Hoover, then teletyped instructions to the head of each of his fifty-six field offices throughout the United States and its territories, who had been awaiting instructions for weeks: "Immediately take into custody all Japanese who have been classified in A, B, and C categories in material previously transmitted to you. . . . Persons taken into custody should be turned over to nearest representative of Immigration and Naturalization Service."[12]

In Seattle, FBI agents armed with three-by-five cards containing data on each individual to be apprehended, and assisted by nearly a dozen police officers who had received previous training in search-and-seizure methods, moved systematically through the Japanese community, making arrests and confiscating cameras, shortwave radios, firearms, personal papers, and other belongings.[13] Similar raids occurred in all FBI jurisdictions throughout the U.S., Alaska, and Hawaii; hundreds of arrests were made up and down the Pacific coast and in Hawaii during the first hours of the war.[14]

The earliest arrests came without warning. Takeo (Tom) Matsuoka, a farmer in rural Bellevue, east of Seattle, was a member of the Japanese Association of America, an organization included among those on the ONI's list of the twenty-two groups alleged to be the most actively subversive.[15] He also had assumed a leadership role in the Bellevue Vegetable Growers' Association. Either membership may have cost him his freedom on December 7.

That night after we were in bed the FBI came and picked me up. Three of them. You had better take at least a tooth brush, but you won't need your clothes. You won't stay long. That's what they said. Don't take nothing; no suitcase, no nothing. Well, then I went outside the door; there's a couple more cars waiting by the gate—thought maybe I was gonna run away, you know. As soon as the car pulled out the guy watching outside, they pulled out too. Then they took us to the immigration office in Seattle.[16]

Heiji (Henry) Okuda, a septuagenarian, was one of the older Issei living in Seattle. He was prominent in the community as a result of his early association with the Oriental Trading Company, a supplier of immigrant Japanese labor to the railroads. In addition, he operated both a fishing tackle business and a transfer company that hauled merchandise for the trading companies on the waterfront, including Mitsui and Company. He also held numerous leadership positions in community organizations, including the kendo society, which alone extended his reputation from Vancouver, B.C., to San Diego. His authority brought frequent opportunities as a go-between for marriages as well as requests to entertain visiting delegations from Japan. This community visibility brought the FBI to his door.[17]

Matsushita also answered a knock at the couple's front door on the evening of December 7. Like the Matsuoka and Okuda families, the Matsushitas had little warning before arresting officers hustled him off to the jail at Seattle's immigration station on Airport Way, less than three miles from their home. Although the FBI's interest in Matsushita stemmed largely from his association with organizations that the ONI had listed as subversive, his bilingualism, his reputation as a teacher, and his various memberships in Japanese organizations, including the haiku society, identified him as a community leader and intellectual elitist whose loyalty was therefore suspect.

As news of arrests spread, Issei families jumped at every knock on the door. After the war Monica Itoi Sone recalled her mother's fears associated with the sudden disappearance of her friends' husbands. She packed a small bag for her husband, containing a change of clothes and toilet articles, and kept it near the front door of their Beacon Hill home. For the Itoi family, however, the dreaded knock never came.[18]

By December 9, the INS had 1,792 enemy aliens in custody, of whom 1,212 were resident Japanese nationals. Arrests continued into 1942. By mid-February the FBI had apprehended 3,021 Japanese in the continental United States and Hawaii.[19]

Of the resident Japanese nationals under INS control on December 9, each suspected of "advocating the overthrow of the government of the United States,"[20] 116 were in Seattle, causing the immigration station's jail to bulge.[21] Tom Matsuoka, the Bellevue farmer, noted that by the time he got there late on the night of December 7, most of the Seattle "big shots" were already locked up. Though it soon became clear that their stay was to be short, none of those jailed knew their ultimate fate, let alone where they would be sent next.

Most of the detainees established contact with their families from behind bars. During the indefinite wait, each was permitted once-a-week family visits, limited to ten minutes of English-language-only conversation. In addition, the inmates could send and receive letters, although only if written in English, and all were subject to censorship by local INS personnel.[22]

Hanaye Matsushita went to the station to drop off bundles of comfort items and to visit with her husband whenever permitted. In the interim, day-to-day minutia, such as B.V.D.'s, socks, and bromo-quinine, provided a focus for three penciled notes he mailed to her during his eighteen-day incarceration in the INS jail. In the first, written four days after his arrest, he reassured her that he was among many friends and being nicely treated but admitted truthfully that he knew nothing about his fate.

Matsushita's last letter from jail, posted December 26, reported "a swell turkey dinner on Xmas day" and a succinct, "We are leaving Saturday morning for probably Montana." His prediction, ultimately proven correct, was based upon an earlier group of detainees who had left Seattle for Fort Missoula on December 18. "God be with you till we meet again," Matsushita concluded his last note from Seattle. He could not have known that two years would pass before this meeting would take place.

| SEATTLE'S JAPANTOWN AFTER DECEMBER 7

The Issei elders detained at the Seattle Immigration Station and other INS facilities throughout the country represented the leadership of Japanese culture in America. According to one writer, elimination of the ABC suspects, totaling nearly 10 percent of all alien Japanese residents in the country, deprived "the community of its financial hierarchy, religious leaders, social promoters, and enlightenment advocates." Thus, the government's program of custodial detention "not only strip[ped] the Japanese of spirit and self-esteem" but effectively eliminated the ability of the community to function normally.[23] Leadership in this now foundering community passed from fifty- and sixty-year-old parents to the oldest of their Nisei children, few of whom had reached their midtwenties. Most Nisei had no experience as leaders. In Seattle, only one hundred Nisei had their own businesses or professional offices.[24] A longtime Nisei Seattleite remembered the anxious Nihonmachi residents as "leaderless, frightened, and confused."[25] The community was virtually rudderless.

The Treasury Department further crippled the Japanese American community by canceling the licenses of all shipping companies still operating between Japan and the U.S., including Mitsui and Company, Matsushita's employer of twenty years, shutting down Japanese banks doing business in the country, and impounding all Japanese investments. It revoked individual Issei business licenses and blocked the bank accounts of all Issei. Travel restrictions were imposed, and ticket sellers at Seattle's King Street Station and elsewhere asked persons who appeared to be Japanese to demonstrate their citizenship.[26] Compliance with the so-called Trading with the Enemy Act meant that lodgers, regardless of ethnicity or race, were forbidden to pay rent to their Issei landlords. Although Japan-born domestic servants could remain on the job, their employers were forbidden to pay their wages.[27] The cumulative effect brought business involving the Issei to a temporary halt.

Early arrests were widely publicized in order to propagandize the effectiveness of antiespionage and antisabotage efforts by government organizations and to urge a public calm in the face of growing hysteria.[28] Public officials heeded a directive of the attorney general to take no direct action against the Japanese in their communities, but to consult with the FBI. Although individual Japanese were insulted, threatened, and beaten, and rocks were thrown through some windows and graffiti scrawled on others, most Japanese Americans did not experience violence.

The press, with the notable exception of the Los Angeles *Times*,[29] urged fair play during the first four weeks of the war, reminding the citizenry of the loyalty of the American-born Japanese as well as the principles of democracy. The Seattle press urged its citizens to set examples of good citizenship by behaving with restraint. The Seattle *Times* asserted: "It is not the part of private citizens to heckle or harass these or any other nationals. If there are aliens to be watched, undoubtedly the government bureaus have been advised, and will do the watching effectively."[30] The *Northwest Enterprise*, a widely distributed Seattle African American newspaper, warned its readers to avoid mob mentality against the Japanese in the name of patriotism: "The same mob spirit which would single them out for slaughter or reprisal has tracked you through the forest to string you up at some crossroad. The Japanese [in the U.S.] are not responsible for this war."[31]

The Seattle press also conveyed local politicians' statements. Mayor Earl Milliken called for tolerance toward American-born and -educated Japanese who, he said, were loyal to the United States, and whom "we don't want to cut . . . adrift from us in this crisis."[32]

Civic groups sent clear messages of tolerance to the Seattle community. For example, the Seattle Council of Churches and Christian Education issued a statement to the press on December 8 calling for "sane thinking and a sober, prayerful attitude," and it urged Christians to avoid discrimination against Japanese in the community, especially in employment.[33] The King County superintendent of schools insisted on the "fair play" of Japanese children attending schools outside Seattle. "Every child born under the American flag is an American citizen and is entitled to protection and consideration."[34]

Although many Seattleites, both private citizens and public figures, no doubt viewed the Japanese population as treacherous,[35] the public voice of the people was silent during the four-week period following the bombing of Pearl Harbor. Only a single letter to the editor appeared in the *Post-Intelligencer* on the subject of the Japanese in Seattle.[36]

Despite a public calm, the Treasury Department's economic stranglehold on the alien Japanese was beginning to disrupt commerce, with a resulting negative effect on the overall citizenry. Especially vulnerable was the movement of fresh vegetables and other foods to meet civilian needs in Pacific Coast markets. The inability of Japanese nationals to withdraw funds would soon place cruel hardship on their innocent American-born

New arrivals at Fort
Missoula. Through
March of 1942, most
Japanese aliens held
at Fort Missoula were
from West Coast
homes and came
in groups, by train.
Matsushita arrived
there in December
1941.

children. Within a few days, restrictions on financial transactions between citizens and resident Japanese nationals were modified to permit rents and wages to be paid and produce to move. Issei depositors could now withdraw up to one hundred dollars per month for living expenses.

TRANSFER TO FORT MISSOULA DETENTION CAMP

The loosening of restrictions in the Japanese community had little effect on the jailed Issei, including Matsushita, who were about to experience changes of their own. On December 14 the Justice Department announced its plan to transfer all enemy aliens in its custody to inland detention camps. The Japanese contingent was assigned to Fort Missoula; German nationals would go to Fort Lincoln in Bismarck, North Dakota.[37] Four days later, a government-requisitioned train snaked its way northward from Los Angeles through the major urban centers of Japanese population and into Seattle, picking up jailed Issei along the way. On December 18, following an overnight journey from Seattle, the INS agent Ed Kline telephoned his superior, Superintendent W. F. Kelley, from Fort Missoula to report that he had discharged 364 Japanese and 25 Italians "without untoward incident" and was soon departing for Fort Lincoln with 110 Germans.[38]

On December 27 a second government train repeated the northward journey from California to Seattle, where Matsushita and sixty-one fellow Issei inmates huddled, awaiting its arrival. The Seattle contingent completed the manifest of the second Kline party, which totaled 213. As the train departed King Street Station, few if any of the weeping family members and friends who came to see them off knew exactly where the prisoners were being sent.[39]

During the journey the detainees were permitted to carry no money; suitcases carefully packed with their meager possessions were taken from them and replaced with paper sacks containing personal comfort items, such as towels, a toothbrush, simple snacks, and tobacco. Matsushita surrendered a key container and his house key, his fingernail scissors, and his shaving kit, which included a Gillette razor and blades.[40]

In a letter written upon his arrival at Fort Missoula, Iwao reported to Hanaye "a wonderful trip and nice meals on the N.P. train." Having repeatedly suffered the experience of handing over his outgoing mail to censors, he may not have conveyed the entire truth in his statement. As one detainee who accompanied Matsushita on the overnight journey later remembered:

> The view outside was blocked by shades on the windows, and we were watched constantly by sentries with bayoneted rifles who stood on either end of the coach. The door to the lavatory was kept open in an attempt to prevent our escape or suicide. . . . there were fears that we were being taken to be executed.[41]

"Lake Wilderness," 1925.

Incarceration

Ants climbing up my foot—
I don't begrudge anymore
The time I spend
Just watching them.
Such is my life nowadays.
—Sojin Takei[1]

As EARLY AS DECEMBER 1939, the Immigration and Naturalization station at Ellis Island, New York, was used to detain nearly seventeen hundred seamen from Axis countries who had been trapped in neutral waters or in neutral ports at the outbreak of the war in Europe. In order to relieve the strain imposed by the number of captives and to prepare for a possible U.S. involvement in the war, the Justice Department initiated a plan in January 1941 to construct three inland detention camps for the incarceration of merchant seamen and resident aliens "with something in their record showing an allegiance to the enemy."[2]

The INS acquired rights to a former Civilian Conservation Corps (CCC) site near Fort Stanton, New Mexico, and converted it into an enclosed detention camp for German seamen. Later in the year the INS expanded two existing facilities acquired from the War Department— at Fort Lincoln, near Bismarck, North Dakota, and at Fort Missoula, on the outskirts of Missoula, Montana—anticipating that each could accommodate up to two thousand Axis seamen and resident enemy aliens if needed. On December 1, 1941, Fort Stanton's population included 425 German seamen from the scuttled liner S.S. *Columbus*.[3] Fort Lincoln held 285 seamen from other German vessels. Fort Missoula took in all the Italian seamen captured up to that time and would eventually incarcerate the largest number of detainees overall. By mid-September 1941, in the months before the U.S. entry into the war, its resident population reached 982, including 912 seamen and 70 employees from the Italian pavilion at the 1939 New York World's Fair.[4]

| ## FORT MISSOULA DETENTION STATION

Fort Missoula was constructed in 1877 to house an army garrison assigned to protect local settlers from the neighboring Flathead Indians. It operated as a training center during World War I. In the peacetime that followed, it became the Northwest Regional Headquarters for the CCC. Built on the north bank of the Bitterroot River before it joins the Clark Fork River, four miles southwest of Missoula, the fort sat on the dry bed of Lake Missoula, a mammoth Ice Age glacial lake. This prehistoric ice-dammed body, at times a thousand feet deep and the size of modern-day Lake Ontario, filled and drained three dozen times during the last Ice Age. In the process, distinct geologic fingerprints were etched on the surrounding landscape, many of which are visible today.[5] To the east of the site rise the high, timbered, sedimentary Rattlesnake Mountains, the taller peaks rounded by Ice Age glaciers. To the north, 7,996-foot Squaw Peak stands guard, and in the Bitterroot Range to the west, the 9,075-foot granite batholith Lolo Mountain eclipses Blue Mountain in the foreground. The spectacular scenery inspired the first Italian arrivals in the spring of 1941 to exclaim, *Che bella vista!* The camp's nickname, Bella Vista, endured until the Italians left in 1944.[6]

On Sunday morning, December 28, many of the Italian detainees turned out for the arrival of the 213 West Coast detainees, among them Matsushita and his Seattle comrades.[7] Others gathering near the gate entrance to witness the event included many of the 398 Issei who had arrived in earlier parties. The curious onlookers stared through chain link fence at the shivering new group, poorly clothed to face the marrow-chilling Montana weather. The new recruits were quickly escorted to quarters to receive army winter issue and to join ranks with other Issei comrades.

Thirty army-design wooden barracks, erected the previous spring and summer, were designated for use by the Japanese prisoners. These temporary, but weathertight and well-insulated structures were built to supplement the existing twin two-story stucco buildings that housed

| Aerial view looking northward of the World War II Fort Missoula Internment Camp and surroundings. The Bitterroot River is at left, and a public golf course can be seen at the bottom of the picture. The Japanese were housed in the long barracks to the right.

some one thousand Italian nationals. Each barracks enclosed twenty-four-hundred square feet, accommodating up to thirty-eight men. Lit by seventeen overhead lights, each had central steam heating and an auxiliary coal-burning stove. Dormitory-style spring cots, with a cotton mattress and cover, lined the walls. Inmates received two woolen blankets, a comforter, one pillow, and a weekly change of linen. The new occupants found hot and cold well water, baths and showers, flush toilets, and locker space.[8] In addition to their living quarters, the men were provided an assembly hall, mess hall, kitchen, storehouse, and canteen.

The theater of operations barracks and permanent administrative and service buildings were situated within a rectangular fort enclosure, completely surrounded by high chain link fence topped with barbed wire and complemented by a guardhouse positioned at an iron gate entrance. Two compounds were fenced off within the outer enclosure, creating separate communities for the Italians and the Japanese. Floodlights ensured twenty-four-hour surveillance.[9]

Outside these inner compounds was a permanent fifty-bed hospital of concrete and steel, staffed by both detainees and U.S. Public Health Department employees. The medical staff included two public health physicians, an Italian surgeon, and three Japanese physicians. Inmates filled the ancillary positions and also ran the infirmaries, two twelve-bed facilities located within each compound.[10] Other health services included a pharmacy run by a Japanese pharmacist and dentistry provided by a public health dentist and a contract dentist from Missoula. Several Japanese detainee dentists also volunteered their services, although the dental procedures made available were limited to extractions and dentures.[11]

The beauty of the Fort Missoula area beyond the fences soon became apparent to the Japanese, and Matsushita himself found the surrounding geography and its accompanying severe weather frequent subjects to write about.

A frozen moon, round and pale
Sinks beyond the western hills.
Mountain peaks in greater haste
Awake in purple and pinkish tint.[12]

| THE GENEVA PRISONER OF WAR CONVENTION OF 1929

The political status of the inmates remained unresolved even as the INS facilities filled because no precedent existed from previous conflicts to guide government decision makers. At the moment of their arrests, Matsushita and all Issei apprehended under the presidential restraint-and-removal proclamations assumed the interim status of detainee until the attorney general could determine whether each should be released, paroled, or interned as a prisoner of war.[13]

All belligerent nations had imprisoned enemy alien noncombatants during the First World War. However, no contemporary international rules existed to guide either their conduct or that of the inmates themselves. Nevertheless, humanitarian motives dictated that provisions be made for civilian enemy aliens caught in areas under enemy jurisdiction. As a result of the lessons learned in the First World War and with a conviction that retaliation against prisoners of war for acts by their governments should be forbidden, many nations ratified the Geneva Convention of 1929. This document provided a model for the protection of civilians.

The Geneva accord laid out the rules of conduct for both prisoners of war and the belligerent powers. It covered all general contingencies of capture and their aftermath. As later adapted to civilians, the rules called for individuals to be interned in enclosed camps, lodged in buildings or barracks but not behind bars. There should be guarantees of food, hygiene, healthfulness, and medical treatment for all those needing it, as well as the freedom to express religious beliefs. Prisoners were to be allowed access to authorities, including local camp administration, international relief societies, and their own governments via neutral countries representing their interests. Correspondence with friends and relatives, although subject to censorship, should be permitted, and sports and intellectual recreational diversions encouraged.

Conditions of work were spelled out as well. Inmates could be required to maintain their camp without pay, but other work was to be voluntary and compensated for at a rate of pay equal to the rate in force for soldiers doing identical work.[14] The Geneva Convention further provided for representatives of the protecting power to visit the camps in order to assure compliance with its provisions and for the International Red Cross to carry out humanitarian work in the camps.

In an effort to motivate agreement among the belligerents on the status of interned civilians, Cordell Hull, the secretary of state, on December 18, just eleven days after the attack on Pearl Harbor, communicated to the Japanese government, through Swiss diplomatic channels, the U.S intention of applying the provisions of the Geneva Prisoner of War Convention to any civilian enemy alien taken into custody, to the extent that the provisions were adaptable, and requested Japan to do likewise.[15] Thus, persons confined under U.S. jurisdiction were to be accorded the same rights and privileges as prisoners of war "until a contrary course is indicated."[16] The governments of Japan, Italy, and Germany subsequently agreed to these terms, even though Japan had never ratified the original accord.

Employing these guidelines, the Fort Missoula camp superintendent Nick Collaer[17] instructed the first Issei arrivals of December 18, 1941, to begin organizing themselves through election of leaders and assignment of duties. Two weeks later, on December 30, Yahei Taoka, the new "mayor" of the growing Japanese population, reported significant progress on the various phases of camp organization.[18] Collaer, anxious from the outset to monitor detainee morale, ordered his staff to examine all outgoing English-language correspondence for references to camp conditions. Such mail surveillance was justified under the provisions of the Geneva Convention even though by year's end the belligerent nations had not yet formally agreed on protection of civilians held under their jurisdiction.

The detainees, having just left crowded conditions and restricted movements in jails and various immigration stations designed for smaller populations, were eager to report to their loved ones the improved conditions at their new location. The following comments typified the dozens that were recorded: "The officers of the camp treat us very kind and the camp, bed, sheets, and towels all new. . . . our daily life very pleasant and happy"; "Ample to eat, warm and comfortable. We are grateful to the U.S. government"; "Enjoying our freedom, better food, better quarters than in San Francisco. Letters and things from home o.k." Matsushita himself provided a testimonial when he recorded his first impressions for Hanaye, on December 28: "Arrived here Sunday morning. This place is much more comfortable, every convenience, spacious dining room, and better food."[19]

Collaer was apparently pleased with the abundance of positive comments culled by the censors. Two days later he reported to his superiors that "I have no complaint whatsoever to make with regard to these Japanese detainees. They are willing and eager to comply with all suggestions and commands."[20]

| DISCORD

The snows piled deep during the winter of 1942, and the temperatures below zero kept the detainees close to their coal-burning stoves. Beyond the few assigned chores that made the small community operate as smoothly as conditions would allow, there was little to do. Matsushita worked as a waiter in the dining room and helped out in the laundry plant as part of his rotating duties under self-government rule. Mostly he read or composed poetry, while others played *go* and other quiet games. Iwao's cheerful letters to Hanaye bore no hint of the discord developing at Fort Missoula.

Despite a well-organized camp and the presence of a congenial spokesman for the group, peaceful conditions for the 633 Issei at Fort Missoula began to deteriorate almost immediately. Early in 1942 a report of potential violations of the Geneva Convention pertaining to Japanese nationals at Fort Missoula reached the Spanish foreign minister, whose government represented Japan's interests in the continental United States. The plaintiffs alleged that the government violated convention rules prohibiting compulsory labor and physical and verbal abuse. Some of the Japanese complained through their spokesman, Taoka, that they were required to perform "upkeep and maintenance" of the camp outside the enclosed compound and without compensation of any kind. This included shoveling the stables maintained for the U.S. Border Patrol's four horses, cleaning up the gymnasium, and maintaining the grounds beyond the confines of their own area. There were also charges that ill-tempered immigration officials had kicked and beaten several detainees and at times had withheld food in attempts to extract confessions. "Insulting treatment" by interpreters of Korean ancestry, on whom the detainees were frequently dependent during the ongoing loyalty hearings, was also alleged. Taoka himself was threatened with detention in isolation if he did not curtail his requests on behalf of the inmates for more humane treatment by INS officers.[21]

Some of the allegations may have been fueled by a meeting between administration officers and camp spokesmen in which the responsibilities for work were outlined. A written summary of that meeting appears to reflect an incomplete understanding of the articles of the Geneva Convention. The administration insisted that uncompensated camp maintenance was not confined to the actual detention area "but involved the upkeep and maintenance of the entire detention station, without regard to the confines of the actual detention compound."[22]

Following transmittal of the allegations to the State Department, the Justice Department initiated an investigation resulting in a formal hearing at Fort Missoula presided over by the INS director for the Spokane District. In the aftermath, two Border Patrol officers were dismissed from the service, and their superior was reassigned. Border Patrol personnel were required to undergo a detailed review of convention rules, and copies were translated into Japanese for use by the detainees.

No further incidents were reported to the Spanish foreign minister, and subsequent visits to the Japanese compound by Red Cross officials in 1943 failed to uncover similar problems.[23] The muffling effect of mail censorship kept these incidents from gaining life beyond the compound fence.

| Alien Enemy Hearing Boards

During the First World War, many German enemy alien civilians held in U.S. Army camps never learned the reasons for their incarceration. Formal charges were never brought, nor did a formal appeal process exist to permit them to defend themselves and offer evidence of their loyalty, evidence that might have led to their release. Moreover, it was five months after the war ended, in April 1919, before any of these prisoners were set free.[24]

In contrast, the presidential proclamation of December 7, 1941, provided for detained enemy aliens to be able to plead their case for release. The mechanism consisted of hearings before Alien Enemy Hearing Boards set up by the attorney general. The purpose of the hearings was to record evidence and make recommendations to the attorney general about whether a detainee should be released outright, paroled, or interned for the duration of the war. The hearings were to be provided, "not as a matter of right, but in order to permit enemy aliens to present facts in their behalf."[25] These facts would be weighed against the evidence gathered in each case, and the decision made by the attorney general to release, parole, or intern would reflect the individual's perceived loyalty. Such proceedings, the reasoning went, might serve to placate the Japanese government and avoid reprisals by Japan against Western civilians within its sphere of influence.

On December 13, 1941, the Department of Justice distributed the first set of guidelines for judging the loyalty or disloyalty of enemy aliens. A week later, on December 20, the first twenty-two of an eventual ninety-two boards were established, representing all of the judicial districts in which arrests were being made. The number of boards within each district varied according to the number of people arrested there. Membership of each board consisted of representative civilian members of the community, one of whom was to be an attorney appointed by the attorney general. All members served as dollar-a-year employees. Representatives from the INS, the FBI, and U.S. attorney's offices were also instructed to attend each hearing. Each detainee was to be heard by the board representing the judicial district in which he was apprehended; he was permitted to present witnesses, documents, and personal testimony and to have an adviser. The adviser, however, could not provide legal counsel.[26]

Frequently, hearings were hampered by language barriers made worse by translation services involving Korean interpreters. At times Korean nationals, whose countrymen remained subjugated during the Japanese occupation of their homeland, may have expressed their outrage toward Japan by attempting to sabotage a detainee's hearing by inaccurate translation. Some Issei refused their hearing if a Korean national was to be present. This situation was a problem for the INS, which had succeeded in recruiting few Nisei or Kibei interpreters.[27]

A partial solution to the problem was provided by former missionaries to Japan, who were among the few non-Japanese in the U.S. fluent in Japanese at the time. Among them were Herbert Nicholson, a Quaker, and Dr. Frank H. Smith, superintendent of the Japanese Methodist churches. They, along with Floyd Schmoe of the American Friends Service Committee, other Quakers, and church leaders representing many denominations, spent much of the war attending to the physical and emotional needs of the Japanese American community. Nicholson interpreted for the ongoing hearings of fifty-two Nevada Issei laborers and, with Smith, for men who came before the two California boards.[28]

The Washington board was chaired by the Seattle attorney Francis Holman, whose wife was a Quaker, and whom Schmoe had known for many years.[29] In a private conversation with Schmoe, Holman predicted that nearly half the detainees would be released and that, in cases where the board and the assistant district attorney agree, "the man will without doubt be freed."[30]

Matsushita went before Holman's board during the second week of February.[31] The members asked questions arising out of the summary of findings in the FBI's report on him[32] and, satisfied with the responses, recommended parole without bond. A favorable decision by the attorney general, based upon the outcome of this hearing, would result in reunion with Hanaye in Seattle. Inexplicably, more than nine months would elapse before a decision was issued on Matsushita's case. In the meantime, he remained in INS custody.

No transcript of Matsushita's hearing has come to light. About what may have transpired, a portrayal of the Nevada cases is instructive. Nicholson described the questioning as farcical, and it failed to resolve the question of the men's threat to national security. Questioning usually began with a detainee being asked if he knew why he had been arrested, with a predictable response of "I don't know." Follow-up questions about the detainee's philosophy of life were meaningless to "these poor uneducated *sake* drinking gamblers."[33] Board members peppered detainees with other questions: Did you send your children to Japan? to Japanese-language school? Who do you want to see win this war? Are you loyal to Japan or the USA? Did you attend welcoming parties for Japanese government officials, military officials, or Japanese training ships? Were you a member of the Japanese Association?[34]

Nicholson's assessment of the Nevadans' hearings apparently was not unique; following multiple complaints by interpreters and detainees alike, in August 1942 the Department of Justice organized an appeal system to permit the rehearing of cases in which the decision for internment appeared to be arbitrary. Inmates awaiting hearings and those awaiting transfer to internment camps following decisions on their hearings were informed of the new policy:

> It is proper to consider the fact that the early cases were heard before experience and information had clarified the extent and nature of the danger to be anticipated from certain recurring types of individuals or organizations. This situation not infrequently has resulted in a lack of uniformity in the treatment of the earlier and later cases. Such lack of uniformity should be cured by rehearing where it appears.[35]

48 Edward Ennis, director of the Alien Enemy Control Unit, advised internees and their families that a case could not be reopened unless the application and supporting papers clearly disclosed new evidence

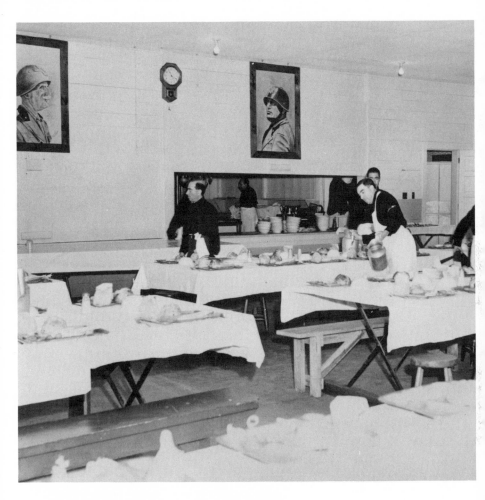

The Japanese and Italian inmates maintained separate eating facilities. In October 1942, however, the Italians far outnumbered the Japanese, making practical a switch in mess halls to allow the Europeans more elbow room. The Japanese contingent easily fit into the 100-seat dining area shown here prior to the exchange. Note the portrait of Il Duce and one of his field generals bracketing the wall clock, which announces late morning.

or pointed out important aspects of the case not considered at the first hearing.[36]

For the most part a decision for internment was based upon guilt by association. Because so many men arrested were community leaders, membership in ethnic organizations tied to the homeland was common. The government had little knowledge of these associations, and no one in the Justice Department could speak or even read Japanese. Therefore, decisions made in Washington, D.C., erred on the side of continued confinement rather than risk letting an ultranationalist go free. Thus, unless there was irrefutable evidence to the contrary, persons were presumed guilty.[37]

In all, 673 Issei were paroled to assembly centers between March 21 and October 30, 1942. This included eighty-eight from Seattle, who took up rudimentary housekeeping at the Puyallup Assembly Center following their release from INS detention.[38]

Those not paroled or released were removed from INS custody and sent to army camps for internment.[39] The transfer began from Fort Missoula on April 10, 1942, when 346 Japanese nationals left by train for Fort Sill, Oklahoma.[40] On August 2, another thinning of ranks took place; 172 Issei boarded a train bound for Camp Livingston, Louisiana.[41] Thereafter, smaller groups went to Camp Livingston and later to Camp Lordsburg, New Mexico, and elsewhere. In all, more than a dozen army internment camps held civilian enemy aliens who earlier had been detained in INS camps.

By fall of 1942, the Fort Missoula Japanese population had dwindled to twenty-eight, including an uncomplaining Matsushita, still awaiting outcome of his February hearing. The handful of people represented differing political circumstances: sixteen individuals had been ordered interned for the duration; four, ordered interned, awaited repatriation on the second sailing of the exchange vessel S.S. *Gripsholm*;[42] six had been paroled and awaited completion of loyalty proceedings; and two, including Matsushita, had received no decision—they were simply detained, and their lives remained in limbo.

Among those ordered interned was Nobuichi Tsutsumoto, whose transfer to army custody was deferred month after month because of his value as a pharmacist in the hospital. Fearing that the Japanese compound was on the brink of closure due to the declining population, which might hasten their transfer to a more unpleasant army environment, Tsutsumoto and twelve others from the group of twenty-eight, who together possessed farming and cooking skills, petitioned the camp supervisor to keep the compound open for them for the duration of the war in exchange for their maintaining a truck garden for the Italian group kitchen. Matsushita had no marketable skills for this proposition but offered his services, if ordered interned, as an office clerk willing to do "any petty work."[43]

The camp superintendent Bert Fraser was sympathetic toward the Japanese. Earlier in the war he had been the officer in charge at the Sharpe Park immigration station outside San Francisco and had arrived at Fort Missoula the previous summer. Wanting to maintain the smooth operation he inherited, he agreed to the group's request, passing it on to his superiors for approval.[44] The Japanese compound remained open.

As the population ebbed, the food improved, and the mingling with the Italians increased, both at the movie theater and on Wednesday afternoon picnics to the riverside. Fort Missoula's Italian population was diminishing too, as inmates were paroled into the community at large; as a result, the two groups switched mess halls in October, providing the Japanese with a welcome change of scenery.

Through January of 1943, 1,025 Japanese nationals passed in and out of Fort Missoula's iron gate, 290 receiving parole or outright release and 735 others being transferred into army custody.[45] As the Montana winter temperatures plummeted, the Japanese compound, now nearly a ghost town with its twenty-eight remaining inhabitants, emitted barely an icy breath.

"Skyline Trail." Hung as an eight-by-ten, black-and-white photograph in at least six salons in North American and Europe during the 1930s.

FOUR

Stone Fever

Since there is no one
To kiss here,
I devour
One raw onion after another.
—Keiho Soga[1]

B Y MID-JANUARY 1942, just a month after their arrival at Fort Missoula, the Issei had created a well-organized and functioning community. A profitable laundry operation under their supervision served the entire camp population, benefiting the Italians and INS personnel as well as the Japanese. A rotating kitchen crew offered Japanese dishes for queasy stomachs unaccustomed to foreign, institutional fare, much as the Italian cooks prepared pasta in the other compound. Religious services addressed the spiritual needs of Christians and Buddhists,[2] all under the guidance of the Geneva accord. Later in the year, a fledgling library grew to house five thousand Japanese- and English-language books, and on Tuesday and Saturday afternoons, Hollywood films were shown to appreciative Japanese and Italian audiences, generating a continuous flow of outgoing fan mail from the Italians.[3] As the weather warmed, the camp supervisor provided sports equipment for softball, tennis, volley ball, horseshoes, golf, swimming, boating, fishing, hiking, Ping-Pong, calisthenics, card games, and craft work.

Unlike others, on whom time weighed heavily, Matsushita, though admitting to a monotonous existence, did not allow boredom to consume his emotional energy or erode his mental health. He threw himself into everyday life, taking advantage of opportunities to volunteer his service to the camp community. Most happy in the classroom where he could

53

draw upon his training as a teacher in Japan, he became head instructor of U.S. history and English classes; the popularity of these classes among the "Missoula University" students was reflected in attendance figures often exceeding one hundred for the one-hour class that met three times a week. Matsushita enjoyed his status as *sensei,* "teacher."

Matsushita subscribed to Seattle newspapers as well as to the New York *Times,* and he read literature during long spells of inactivity. He enjoyed corresponding with a number of friends in other camps, especially Hanaye's uncle, Dr. Koike, with whom he exchanged more than seventy letters throughout his Fort Missoula incarceration.[4] In time his comrades recognized his leadership qualities and elected him mayor, a post he held in 1943 from March to October. These activities succeeded in distracting him, if only partially, from worries associated with being apart from Hanaye.

Elaborate forms of recreational activity evolved out of the creative energies of both Italian and Japanese inmates. More than one hundred musicians and entertainers could be counted among the Italian seamen and former world's fair workers. Accompanied by a twenty-five-man musical ensemble from the seized Italian liner *Conte Biancamano,* the seamen staged several elaborate productions, including the opera *Madama Butterfly,* complete with stage props and costumes for both male and female roles. At least one performance included a number of Japanese. Matsushita, by now well known for his public speaking skills, provided appropriate intro-ductory remarks as spokesman *del gruppo internati Giapponesi.* Productions performed for the entire camp population, as well as for the Missoula community, brought in small admission prices for an evening's festivities on the camp grounds. The Italians' reputation among the townspeople resulted in an eventual complaint by the local musicians union that its members were losing work.[5]

| STONE FEVER

Another innovative wave resulted from an epidemic of "stone fever" that took over the entire Japanese compound during the first spring. Tom Matsuoka retained vivid memories of it after more than fifty years:

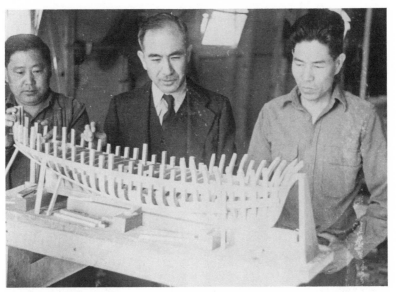

| Matsushita admires a model ship constructed by fellow inmates at Fort Missoula, ca. 1943.

Around March the snows stopped and the thaw began. You could get outside now. All around the camp rocks had worked to the surface. Rocks with really pretty lines and designs. Pretty soon everybody's out digging rocks. They're soft and you could polish 'em up real good, you know. So we'd take the rocks back to our shower room which had a cement floor, and we'd polish 'em up by rubbing them across the floor. Beautiful now. Really beautiful! Then we'd take our government issue blankets and get a really high polish. We made all sorts of things with them; jewelry, ash trays, vases. One guy picked up an empty milk bottle and put cement on the outside. I don't know where he got the cement; maybe where they were building new barracks for the people who arrived later. Anyway he put cement on the outside of the milk bottle then put a rock in the middle. That was something. Two or three times we had exhibitions of peoples' work in the mess hall. Really popular. Someone must have written to his wife at another camp about our "stone fever." Pretty soon a letter comes

55

back from the worried wife wondering about the big epidemic at our camp and if everybody was sick. Ha![6]

Matsushita himself fell victim to the contagion, producing objets d'art from the raw material that had nuzzled to the surface from within the ancient lake bed, thrust upward during the annual cycle of freezing and thaw. He transformed the soft stones into ashtrays, vases, platters, and even a cookie jar. He then posted them as gifts for friends in appreciation for their looking after Hanaye. Moods dictated his progress. However, it was not uncommon for him to spend nine hours a day working at his craft, "giving me a backache, to boot," he mocked to Hanaye. During one two-week stretch he completed fourteen projects. At another time, he spent eight days creating a powder box "masterpiece" in celebration of their silver wedding anniversary, into which he embedded stones of colors symbolizing their relationship.

The "stone pickers" began to enjoy a wide reputation as they shared their work with families and friends at the other camps. Although the inmates were permitted free postage for packages weighing less than four pounds, Matsushita estimated that his colleagues' enthusiasm resulted in a weight excess amounting to five hundred dollars or more in postage surcharges. They presented their work twice in the assembly hall for the benefit of the craftsmen, other appreciative Issei, the Italian community, and the camp administration. The Missoula citizenry showed interest as well. Matsushita entered a monogrammed watch fob for the first exhibition, one of two hundred pieces submitted overall. Chronic low-grade stone fever persisted until the camp's closure in April 1944.

Not all activities orbited around recreation. Opportunities for paid employment also became available. The remote geographical setting of Fort Missoula, coupled with the diminishing supply of unskilled labor that resulted from men being siphoned off to war, provided a chance for inmates to work outside camp in the surrounding communities. Farm labor, railroad maintenance, and work in Northwest forests eventually proved abundant. Requests of sugar beet farmers in the Missoula area, for example, resulted in recruitment of three hundred Fort Missoula Italians to harvest the 1942 crop, at prevailing wages. (A similar program for the Japanese, but of larger magnitude, operated out of the assembly centers

With the spring melt, detainees discovered small, colorful stones littering the camp grounds. They polished them on concrete floors and with government-issue blankets, transforming them into practical gifts. Here, proud craftsmen exhibit the results of their "stone fever" at one of two exhibitions sponsored by the stone artists. Matsushita participated in these shows.

and later the relocation centers.) This program proved so successful that during the next two years more than five hundred Italians, Japanese, and German seamen, some brought in from Fort Lincoln, were placed on farms, on Forest Service projects, and on railroad maintenance gangs in Montana, Idaho, and Washington. Because it offered escape from the daily drudgery while at the same time enabling inmates to earn a living at the prevailing wage, this work remained popular throughout the war.[7]

Despite the availability of outside work, Matsushita avoided the work parties, for he had no interest in physical labor. Instead he continued to read, to compose poetry, to teach, and to craft his stones. In addition, he immersed himself in religious activities with the other Christian inmates, participating in Bible studies, singing in a church trio, and attending Sunday worship, which he often led.

For Easter Sunday 1942, he and his fellow Christians erected and painted white a tall cross in front of their dormitories and then gathered for a 7 a.m. service. He recounted for Hanaye the impressive backdrop of the surrounding snow-tipped mountains and the fresh morning air of the high plateau, which added to the ambiance.

As the weather continued to warm, camp activities moved outdoors. The dwindling population brought a more relaxed atmosphere, allowing camp officials and inmates to come to appreciate one another. Softball and soccer generated considerable interest among the Japanese and Italians. On at least one occasion they met on the diamond, nearly the entire camp population turning out, including an Italian marching band.

As restrictions grew increasingly lax, activities extended beyond the iron gate. Fishing, picnicking, and swimming expeditions to the nearby Bitterroot River diverted the barracks' pent population. Camp guards also joined in the fun. Given his love of the Cascade mountains of western Washington, Matsushita reveled in the pristine setting.

Matsushita and the other men were eventually permitted to enjoy the highland country, and he wrote to Hanaye describing hiking adventures into the mountains with friends. "I was proud of myself that I was able to keep up with the younger men," he boasted following the first hike to Blue Mountain, recalling earlier jaunts to Mount Rainier in a more peaceful time. He frequently included his observations of nature in verse, embellishing his letters to Hanaye and friends with haiku and other poetic forms:

Fort Missoula's internees at a picnic along the shore of the Bitterroot River, posing with the "Minnehaha." The rowboat, built in the craft shop by Issei inmates, was christened on this day. Matsushita, wearing a dark tie, stands behind the boat.

Resting on a rock
beside a stream
on the summer mountain.

Today's snow
glistening
in the morning sun.

Despite these diversions, the guard towers and ubiquitous high fence were constant reminders of lost liberty and the lack of personal autonomy. Incarceration brought not only loss of material comforts and freedom but also monotony and loneliness and, for some, broken human relations, anxieties, and shame. Men of means bore burdens of responsibility as the result of having provided prewar leadership roles in the community. Those with landholdings or businesses worried about their ability to keep them intact during their absence and to pay creditors in the face of reduced personal revenues or no income at all. Businesses lying fallow as a result of internment could not generate income to pay creditors or taxes. For many, the fate of assets hinged on the duration of the owners' incarceration.

Matsushita certainly shared with his comrades the loss of independence and the emptiness without family. But unlike many of the others, he and Hanaye had few economic worries. They had accumulated significant cash assets over the years, which, even though partially blocked by the Treasury Department, were nevertheless secure for the future.[8] They owned no business that required tending or properties with an unyielding tax assessment.

Nevertheless, the couple did face problems. His absence had thrust Hanaye into an unfamiliar role as head of the household. She was hampered by the $100-per-month budget ceiling imposed by the government and now carried the responsibility of paying the monthly bills, handling Iwao's life insurance premiums, filing the 1942 income tax return, and, as the Seattle evacuation approached, selling the car. Like her adopted language, which she never mastered, the tasks were foreign, and her husband's counsel was useful only if both his pen and the wartime mail could convey it.

| EVACUATION OF SEATTLE'S JAPANTOWN

Although individual circumstances varied, most detainees and internees, including Matsushita, worried about their families back home in view of deteriorating attitudes toward the Japanese community as a whole. In the four weeks following Pearl Harbor, feelings toward the ethnic Japanese on the West Coast expressed by private citizens, politicians, various organizations, and the press had been neutral to positive and were characterized by restraint. In January, attitudes started to turn, as stories of fifth column activity in Hawaii and reports of the continuing and unrelenting U.S. defeats in the Pacific mounted. Rumor and innuendo fed latent anti-Japanese sentiment and outrage over Pearl Harbor. As a result, national organizations began calling first for removal of enemy aliens, then citizen Japanese. Farming groups in line to benefit economically from the removal of Japanese farmers joined the howl. By mid-February California congressmen lined up to urge evacuation. Abdicating its watchdog role, the press joined the pack.[9]

Attitudes in the Pacific Northwest changed in February. Most Seattleites appear to have remained apathetic toward the concerns of the

Japanese community during the weeks following Pearl Harbor, or they had been reassured by government confidence in the FBI's handling of potential fifth columnists. Few acts of hostility were recorded in and around the city, and there were no calls for removal of Nikkei (Japanese) public employees. The Seattle *Post-Intelligencer,* however, began to waver in early February. While continuing to acknowledge the unswerving loyalty of many Japanese, it began to publish sinister suggestions:

> A good many arrests have been made by the Federal Bureau of Investigation, but it is idle to argue that a comparative small number of FBI agents, unaided, can do the tremendous job of discovering which Japanese are loyal and which are disloyal. . . . Neither an FBI agent nor anyone else is able to say that any individual Japanese is loyal or disloyal, merely by looking at him.[10]

The *Post-Intelligencer* editorial staff viewed the Japanese problem as a gordian knot that might have to be cut "if it cannot be untied."

Local political attitudes turned negative as well. Mayor Earl Millikin, who weeks earlier had avowed the loyalty of the city's Japanese residents, now in the midst of an uphill reelection campaign stated for the record before a congressional committee:

> I feel that, due to the events of Pearl Harbor and events since that time, the sentiment of the people in Seattle is overwhelmingly in favor of evacuation. . . . There is no doubt about those 8,000 Japanese, that 7,900 probably are above question but the other 100 would burn this town down and let the Japanese planes come in and bring on something that would dwarf Pearl Harbor.[11]

Governor Arthur Langlie and the state attorney, Smith Troy, expressed similar concerns and called for removal of all Japanese, both citizens and aliens. Soon Washington State and Seattle employees of Japanese ancestry, as well as twenty-seven Seattle School District clerks who had all graduated from Seattle area high schools, were terminated or involuntarily resigned their positions because of pressures brought on them by their employers and deteriorating community attitudes.[12]

Silent in the weeks following Pearl Harbor, the voice of the people began to speak. Between January 5 and the end of March, fifty-five letters to the editor appeared in the Seattle *Post-Intelligencer*. The sentiments expressed were divided evenly on both sides of the "Japanese problem," but the even division may have reflected the editors' efforts to balance the discussion rather than the true feelings of Seattle's citizenry. Clearly, the community was agitated.

Matsushita's increasing worries about Hanaye in this climate of growing discord soon proved well founded. On February 19, 1942, President Roosevelt, facing media and political pressures and having little reputation as a civil libertarian, issued Executive Order 9066, transferring to the secretary of war and his military commanders authority to exclude from designated areas anyone they deemed necessary in order to insure national security against sabotage and espionage.[13] Although a reading of the order identifies no specific ethnic or racial group or particular class of individual, it soon became clear that the overwhelming majority of people affected were to be the Japanese. In Seattle, the *Post-Intelligencer's* editors never questioned the order, editorializing two days later: "If the army authorities find it necessary to move all Japanese American citizens or otherwise— out of the defense zones, then they and the public generally should accept it as necessary and cooperate cheerfully and wholeheartedly."[14]

The western defense commander, General John DeWitt, quickly drew up plans for establishing military restriction zones within the states of Washington and Oregon west of the Cascade Range and much of California and Arizona. Seattle's Japanese community found itself in the heart of the exclusion zone. By the end of March 1942, the squeeze on the Puget Sound Japanese tightened further when expanded travel and curfew regulations were applied to all citizen and alien Japanese. That month, following DeWitt's order removing all Japanese on Bainbridge Island, which lies near Seattle's waterfront and close to the Bremerton shipyard, little doubt remained about the imminence of mass evacuation.

Matsushita, as well as the other inmates at Fort Missoula, possessed sketchy knowledge of the impending move. Seattle residents corresponding with their husbands often reported rumor as fact, not knowing the difference themselves. The army deliberately withheld information from the confused Seattle community: although it knew the schedule well in advance, it posted civilian exclusion order notices little more than a week before the planned evacuation.

Matsushita could provide little counsel to Hanaye, who started her evacuation plans as early as April 7. On that day she reassured her husband of smooth progress on the sale of their car and the kindness of their landlord. But two weeks later she reported having to leave their home of fifteen years "because of unavoidable reason" and move in with the couple's friends the Ishibashis. Their Italian-American landlord, who would later write an affidavit supporting Iwao's petition for parole, promised to store the couple's books, furniture, and other belongings in his basement until their return.

PUYALLUP ASSEMBLY CENTER

Posters detailing the first two civilian exclusion orders finally began to appear on Seattle telephone poles and in other public places on April 21.[15] The geographic areas described were located north and south of the heart of Japantown's business district. The orders required residents to prepare for an evacuation on April 30. Because Dr. Koike lived outside these boundaries, he was not affected by the first exclusion orders. Nevertheless, he volunteered to accompany an advance group then being recruited to oversee preparations for the opening of the camp hospital. The other members would set up a temporary kitchen and prepare meals for the hundreds scheduled to arrive in the next wave.

Unlike Koike's residence, the Matsushita house was situated within one of the targeted areas to be evacuated on April 30. Rather than stay behind for two additional days, Hanaye decided to accompany her uncle and join the advance group. She reasoned that this might earn privileges and more favorable housing. On April 28, Hanaye and Koike joined a caravan of buses and private cars carrying 305 volunteer men and women to the Puyallup center, forty miles south of Seattle. Following their arrival, Koike, because of his professional status, was assigned to a relatively comfortable two-person room to share with his niece, a cubicle that would otherwise have housed four people. It was furnished with two army cots and a woodstove. Promised were a table, a broom and bucket, and blankets. Koike then went to work organizing and supplying

63

the rudimentary hospital facility, while Hanaye joined the kitchen crew in the mess hall.

The 7,548 evacuees eventually crowding into the temporary quarters at the Puyallup Assembly Center[16] were greeted with armed sentries and eight-foot-high fences set with guard towers. The center, located on the Western Washington Fairgrounds and surrounding parking lots, had been turned over to the military and converted to a civilian confinement facility in seventeen days, at a cost of $500,000.[17] The physical layout included four rectangular, separately enclosed areas, prisons within a prison. Two of the compounds, Area A and Area D, were each designed to contain as many as three thousand people. The dwelling units were scattered among auto scooters, roller coasters, and a giant ferris wheel.[18]

The inhabitants of the hastily converted facility enjoyed few amenities. Families crowded into slope-roofed barracks two hundred feet long and partitioned off with walls shy of the rafters, which permitted the cries of children and lovemaking of adults to be heard from one end to the other. To many, the barracks resembled chicken coops. Long known for its wet climate, the Pacific Northwest had a rainy spring in 1942. One writer familiar with the poor drainage at Camp Harmony, as it was ironically named,[19] wrote that "residents had to struggle against sinking into apathy on the inside of the barracks and into mud on the outside."[20] In addition, the fairgrounds, a center of recreation in peacetime, was now so crowded with new construction that little room existed for play, causing one inmate, Bill Hosokawa, to advise his Japanese-American Citizens League colleagues in Salt Lake City: "There is not even room for a baseball diamond, and so the problem of recreation is going to be tough, especially during the hot summer months if no work program can be provided."[21]

Within two weeks, Area D, site of the hospital, began to fill. In order for Dr. Koike to be near his work and more readily available for emergency calls, he and Hanaye moved their belongings there from Area A, which was already full. Shortly after the move, she described for her husband the early May Puget Sound season, perhaps conveying her internal landscape in metaphor: "Spring is deep, but the weather is unsettled here. Garden flowers are blooming one by one, but we have seldom chance to see them."

Koike immediately was busy, day and night, having to contend at one point with a measles epidemic caused by the crowded conditions. In addition, because of heightened anxieties related to incarceration, evacuees regularly reported ailments, real or imagined, thereby burdening the four evacuee physicians who served the nearly seventy-five hundred people there. Writing to his friend at Fort Missoula, Koike recalled, in a rare moment of self-indulgence, a recent trip to the Tacoma General Hospital with expectant mothers:

> The other day morning mist was rather deep, but with sunshine. Far to the east, I looked up at Mt. Rainier clearly. Recalling the past to my memory, I was heartily impressed. . . . The nurse asked the driver: "If you take me to the mountain, I will give you anything you want." On the way, I saw an old woman, taking care of a few cows, in her front garden. It was really a pictorial subject. I pitied myself, not having my Kodak for the first time since I turned it to the police court.[22]

Spring passed with no further word from his wife, causing Matsushita to express uneasiness to her about her silence. As rumors surfaced about the next move to a permanent inland location, the strain of incarceration had begun to wear on Hanaye. On July 2 she finally wrote, assuring him unconvincingly about her good health and admonishing him not to worry about her. "I don't know where we are moving. At the same time I feel uneasy about your future. Be [at] ease about me. I am somewhat nervous, but my health is well and sound. . . . I will write you again very soon, but don't wait, as I am not sure myself."

Koike kept Matsushita informed of impending changes: "It is rumored that our next move is very near, but nobody know[s] the reality. Anyway our daily life is like the floating cloud, moving aimlessly in the mercy of various winds."[23] Koike's simile may have reflected his own worsening state of mind. Hanaye reported to Iwao that when not praying or helping with household chores, her uncle "walks around in a daze." She nicknamed him Balloon. Later she complained that he lacked dependability, refusing to help her with her English-language correspondence, refusing to visit the neighbors, and refusing to be helped himself. "Even when I am sick," she complained, "he doesn't take care of me. What is the use of being with him?" Later, Koike, an avid reader, would report to Matsushita, "I have plenty of time, but still I can not read books because of uneasiness of mind."[24]

The rumored move finally became a reality for Hanaye on August 15, when she departed with a group of 493 evacuees on an overnight train, after 110 days of incarceration at Camp Harmony. Koike, who stayed behind to tend to his patients, faithfully reported the news to Matsushita.[25] The group's destination was the lightly populated high desert sagebrush country near Twin Falls, in southwestern Idaho. The War Relocation Authority was then finishing construction of the Minidoka Relocation Center, one of ten permanent camps designed to house more than one hundred thousand people from the West Coast states and Arizona. Hanaye was among the first seven hundred to settle there.[26]

Far to the south of the Minidoka camp rose a low mountain range; to the east and west a flat landscape provided little shelter from frequent windstorms. At four thousand feet elevation, the location meant hot summers and bitter-cold winters. This harsh landscape became home to 6,098 Seattle residents, the majority of the 9,397 inmates.[27] By one evacuee's account, "Minidoka is a vast stretch of sagebrush stubble and

| Inmates of the Puyallup Assembly Center board a train for the Minidoka Relocation Center, August 1942.

shifting, swirling sand—a dreary, forbidden, flat expanse of arid wilderness. Minidoka . . . is the sort of place people would normally traverse only to get through to another destination."[28]

Hanaye may have joined the early party to avoid having to continue sharing a room with Dr. Koike, with whom relations had become strained. Being "single," the "Montana widow" now shared bachelor quarters with an older friend she called Aunt Kaneko. Soon they were joined by another, much younger, roommate, Cora Uno, who before the war had been an officer in the Seattle chapter of the Japanese-American Citizens League. The trio, spanning two generations, resided in Block 2, in one of the endless wood-and-tarpaper barracks where privacy was all but impossible; nevertheless, the arrangement for a time proved agreeable enough. Koike arrived at Minidoka on September 5. He had originally been assigned to room with Hanaye, but moved to quarters nearer the hospital.

| An exhibit of floral arrangements at the Minidoka Relocation Center. A typical, tarpaper/batten residential barracks looms in the background.

The hospital was larger and better equipped than the Camp Harmony facility. Moreover, because there were more physicians in attendance to share the burden of everyday medical problems, Koike's responsibilities were now limited to ear, nose, and throat diseases, all but eliminating night call duty. This left the aging man with more free time for reading, letter writing, spending time with stamp and wild flower collecting, and developing a new hobby that enabled him to craft with his hands. On walks into uncultivated fields beyond the fence, a number of Minidokans discovered greasewood sticks they transformed into walking canes. Soon many people, including Koike, could be seen shaping and polishing the crooked lengths.

Koike continued to advise Matsushita on Hanaye's condition, informing him of her constant worries about his future. And Matsushita's future was anything but certain. He failed to make the list of parolees returning to their families and, as Fort Missoula's population dwindled to a handful by midsummer of 1942, was still awaiting the decision about his political status. The unending wait appears to have weighed on Hanaye, for on July 11, prior to her relocation to Idaho, Koike confessed to his friend: "Your wife is uneasy, being overanxious about your fate, but I don't know how to comfort her."[29]

Matsushita wrote Hanaye reassuringly about his undecided future, but by August 20, shortly after arriving at the Minidoka Relocation Center, she was clearly depressed; she revealed to Iwao her desire to kill herself. Ten days later, however, she wrote again in somewhat improved spirits, perhaps having begun to adjust to her new surroundings. Then in November she wrote about their forced separation for the last time, suspicious that he might be withholding the government's decision from her for fear she would become hysterical. "I am resigned to whatever may happen," she concluded.

During the interminable wait, Matsushita's own spirits ebbed as well. On November 3, now eleven months after his arrest and still with no decision on his case, he confessed in a weak moment to his halfhearted studies and unsettled state of mind. But at the same time he assured Hanaye that he was not hiding anything from her regarding his status.

Finally, on December 7, the first anniversary of his arrest, Matsushita received word of the decision: internment. There was no explanation for the agonizing delay. He stoically told Hanaye that the verdict was "unexpected and regrettable" but admonished her to keep her chin up and please not to cry. Although Francis Holman's Washington State hearing board had recommended parole without bond, the attorney general cast a wary eye on Matsushita's long-term professional association with Mitsui and Company and his short stint with the "subversive" Seattle Japanese Chamber of Commerce. Biddle overruled the board's recommendation and ordered Matsushita interned. The decision, issued on November 16, took three weeks to reach Fort Missoula.

The incriminating findings against Matsushita, summarized in the anonymous Justice Department internal memo justifying his internment, are worth noting in full:[30]

> Brother, a graduate of Vanderbilt University, is Dean of Methodist Theological College in Japan and presently living there. Employee for 20 years, until about 3 or 4 years ago, of Mitsui & Co., at Seattle. At time of leaving the Company he was earning $530 a month. (Mitsui & Co. is an import and export business and subject made surveys of imports and exports for the Company.) Subject left employ of Mitsui with only 6 months' service to put in before being eligible for pension because he did not care to return to Japan. Has deposited over a period of years 50,000 yen ($12,930)[31] in Japan. Alleged by two former employees of Japanese Consulate at Seattle to be "in effect an agent of a foreign principal." This allegation led to consideration of criminal prosecution; Criminal Division came to conclusion that facts did not warrant such prosecution.

Many of these facts might easily have been interpreted as providing support for a decision for parole, especially the allegations of the former consulate employees that proved false. However, the findings pointed to a longstanding attachment to the homeland, while ignoring the fact of his refusal to return to Japan, and, given the better-safe-than-sorry mindset of the Justice Department, that attachment remained compelling as a reason for internment.

Although his being labeled "potentially dangerous to the public safety" was an affront and a personal hardship, Matsushita was not singled out. The attorney general's decisions led to internment orders for the majority

69

of the Japanese detainees. In fact, despite the anxieties it produced, the long delay between his hearing and the decision may have saved him from a much less comfortable existence at an army-run camp. Most internees were transferred to spartan facilities on military reservations run by no-nonsense army personnel. Because the decision on Matsushita came so long after the last transfer order was carried out, and to some degree because of the willingness of the INS to permit the last few Japanese inmates to remain, Matsushita was at least spared an army-regimented confinement.

Matsushita's letter announcing the unfortunate news reached Hanaye while she was recovering in her barracks from a lingering fever that had hospitalized her and would persist well into the first month of the new year. The timing no doubt exacerbated the effects of the debilitating news and delayed her response. Iwao confided his worries about Hanaye's health to his loyal friend Koike, who could provide little consolation and advised Matsushita to "let time dissolve her troubles."[32]

| AWAITING A REHEARING

The Justice Department's decision the previous August to permit rehearings offered Matsushita hope. His objective was not freedom but to share Hanaye's meager existence at Minidoka. The camp superintendent at Fort

70

| Baggage tag with a Fort Missoula censor mark.

Missoula, Bert Fraser, was sure that grounds existed for a review of his case, so Matsushita decided to appeal directly to Biddle. He reasoned that such an approach might improve his chances over a request for rehearing routed through the Justice Department's Alien Enemy Control Unit. A rehearing would require new evidence of loyalty, evidence he could not provide. By appealing informally for reconsideration through a joint petition from himself and Hanaye, and offering affidavits from American (Caucasian) friends, he might be granted parole—and reunion—at a family camp then being organized at Crystal City, Texas.[33] He sought Hanaye's opinion on the matter.

She replied on December 30, making only passing reference to her husband's internment order but making clear her reluctance to transfer to an INS camp because of the potential loss of freedoms she enjoyed at Minidoka. As for the joint appeal, she offered little advice.

On January 2, 1943, Matsushita had not yet received Hanaye's reply and went ahead with the appeal to Biddle. He wrote out instructions for Hanaye to seek affidavits from his University of Washington friend, Professor Eldon Griffin, for whom he had taught the Japanese course in 1927. Griffin had contributed to earlier appeals. Their neighbors, the Benedettis, as well as their former landlord, Mr. Mancini, might also write on his behalf, he suggested. Hanaye was to forward testimonials to the attorney general along with her own appeal, which he outlined for her.

Matsushita then wrote his own heartfelt letter to Biddle:[34]

I was born a Christian in a Methodist minister's family, educated in an American Mission School, came to this country in 1919 from sheer admiration of the American way of life. I have always been living, almost half and best part of my life, in Seattle, Wash., and never went to Japan for the last twenty-four years, despite the fact there were many such opportunities, simply because I liked this country, and the principles on which it stands.

I have never broken any Federal, State, Municipal, or even traffic laws, and paid taxes regularly. I believe myself one of the most upright persons. I have never been, am not, and will never be potentially dangerous to the safety of the United States. There isn't an iota of dangerous elements in me, nor should there be any such evidence against me. . . .

My wife, with whom I have never been separated even for a short time during last twenty-five years, and who has the same loyalty and admiration for this country, is living helplessly and sorrowfully in Idaho Relocation Center. You are the only person who can make us join in happiness and let us continue to enjoy the American life.

Biddle's response three weeks later arrived via the Alien Enemy Control Unit: Matsushita should apply for a rehearing. This was the very thing he had tried to avoid, believing that the key to his reunion with Hanaye lay in the success of other wives who had taken the direct petition route.

A somber Matsushita nevertheless resubmitted documentation to the Washington State hearing board in February. In the meantime the State Department queried him about repatriation. "I've no intention of going to Japan nor have I asked to be repatriated," he wrote to Hanaye. However, he also shared his fear they might be forced to repatriate against their will.

Hanaye, now recovered from her lingering fever, wrote to her husband on January 26, 1943, but without reference to the informal appeal. It would be her last letter for six months. Iwao's worries over his wife's emotional health continued. Her apparent inability to follow through with the tasks needed in petitioning the attorney general led him, on April 19, to confide to Koike:

> As to my wife's condition, all letters from my friends [at your camp] indicate that she must look all right. But as she can't or won't do anything as it should be done, there must be something wrong with her mental condition. I don't think she's normal. Of course, she can't be blamed. This unusual situation made her that way and the only solution is our reunion. But to materialize this reunion, I did my part here and she should do her part over there without too much delay. . . . As she hasn't written to me at all, there's no knowing. That's my greatest worry.[35]

Throughout the weeks following the decision to intern Iwao, Koike had reported to Matsushita on Hanaye's bouts of depression and nervousness, which prevented her from writing to her husband. In January she had complained to her uncle that she needed to get away from her roommates. The next month Koike moved to his quarters at the hospital so that Hanaye could have his space in Block 12. So fatigued was she from moving her few boxes of personal effects that, Koike wrote, "she can't write even a line at present."[36] A month later, he reported that she was settled in, "but she is still nervous,"[37] a condition that persisted into April.

On April 30 Koike wrote his friend that Hanaye had "at last decided to write letters for your sake, under great help of Reverend Joseph Kitagawa," an Episcopal minister.[38] Five days later Matsushita responded with uncharacteristic anger:

> Does this mean that my wife didn't write to Washington in January when I asked her to do? If so, there is no wonder why she didn't receive any answer. By these inconsistencies I can clearly see how my wife is mentally unbalanced. If she is in normal condition, there shouldn't have been such unbelievable delay like this. I can't simply think this is true.[39]

More than two months passed without word from Washington, D.C., on Matsushita's February application for a rehearing. He then turned to Bert Fraser, who agreed to write a letter of recommendation on his behalf to supplement the long-pending application.

Unknown to Matsushita, Hanaye did carry out part of the January instructions. She managed to obtain all three requested affidavits, from Professor Griffin, from their neighbors the Benedettis, and from Mancini, their former landlord. Griffin, who by now had left the university, wrote of his past associations with Matsushita and of Matsushita's admirable qualities—dignity, honesty, directness, and agreeability. He then chastised Biddle: "Mr. Matsushita ought to be engaged right now in preparations for the task of aiding this country in post-war adjustment with Japan, with the active support of our Government or one of its agencies."[40] Hanaye also obtained an affidavit from Dr. Koike summarizing her debilitated mental condition and countersigned by the Public Health Department physician who oversaw the Minidoka camp hospital. It was not until April 29, 1943, however, four months after Iwao's first instructions and a year and a day after her arrival at the Puyallup Assembly Center, that she forwarded the collection of documents, along with her own personal plea, to the U.S. Attorney's Office in Seattle.

In the meantime, Matsushita continued his immersion in camp life, but his discouragement occasionally slipped into his letters to Hanaye. "The spring flowers don't move me as much," he wrote, "since I saw them all last year." However, in late March 1943, his peers elected him their spokesman, to replace the previous mayor who had just been paroled to Minidoka. This gave him new diversions and a new will to go on.

Matsushita's mayoral duties began as the population at Fort Missoula began its second growth surge. The influx of German POWs from the North African campaign was taxing the War Department's ability to house, feed, and guard the growing population of disarmed soldiers. Requiring all the manpower and facilities it could muster, the War Department proposed and the Justice Department agreed that the enemy alien population should return to INS control. Thus, by the end of May, two months after the agreement was finalized, all internees had returned to INS camps, including Fort Missoula.

Intercamp transfers involving Fort Missoula soon followed. For example, on May 27, thirty Issei seeking repatriation on the next sailing of the *Gripsholm* arrived from the army's internment camp at Fort George Meade, Maryland. Another group of 109, also seeking repatriation, entered the Japanese compound on June 5.[41] During the summer, 118 Japanese Peruvians joined their ranks.[42] All the transfers, and the human stresses and strains that necessarily accompany such movements, caused Matsushita to complain to Hanaye that he was at the people's call for all sorts of favors, and he expressed disgust with the unseemly side of human behavior. The job, with its countless requests, complaints, and problems, was thankless: "There are as many varied opinions as there are different places where the people are from."

Matsushita's routine of the past year and a half was turned on its head, and as a result, a whole month passed without writing his wife. He missed the "leisurely feel" of the previous year, observing nature and writing verse. The internees begged him to stay on, and bowing to the need, he agreed to remain at the helm until disposition of his own case. Earlier he had told Hanaye that everyone should do something to contribute to the community's comfort, whether it was barbering, cooking, or some other activity. Eventually, Matsushita adjusted to his increased responsibilities and in a self-congratulatory moment boasted to Hanaye that transferees

| Matsushita with INS camp guards and other government officials during his tenure as Fort Missoula's Japanese "mayor," 1943.

from all over "say this is the most well-run and livable camp they've been to."

In addition to his mayoral duties, Matsushita stepped forward when the new arrivals requested classes in English-language skills. He thus added several hours a week to his already busy schedule. His days and evenings were now full. Foremost in his mind, however, was his rehearing date and receiving word from Hanaye.

On July 23, after six months without a syllable, Hanaye finally wrote to her husband saying she had "undergone various difficulties, but am finally settled." She admitted an inability to sleep and blurry vision due to a "nerves problem." Although hearing from her at last must have heartened Matsushita, he no doubt found the news distressing.

September 1943 arrived with still no response to his January petition and no word on prospects for the couple's reunion. Transferees moved in and out of camp, many returning to their families following favorable rehearings. The persevering Matsushita applied again for his rehearing but this time through his now strong advocate, Fraser, who had come to know him in connection with his work as mayor. More affidavits were collected.[43] The latest effort produced a rapid response and notice of a rehearing, scheduled for November. The further delay in resolution of his case made even one more month of mayoral duties unbearable. He therefore resigned as spokesman for the Japanese on October 15.

Immediately Matsushita resumed his stone craft work, relishing his newly restored peace. He celebrated his new perspective in a poem to Hanaye:

> As I spend late summer
> with my stones
> mountains with their light makeup
> wait winter's coming.

Despite the promised rehearing, in November the hearing board by-passed Fort Missoula altogether. It convened at Kooskia, Idaho, near where 150 Japanese were currently employed for wages by the Public Roads Administration on the Lewis and Clark Highway in the Lolo Pass area. Deeply disappointed, Matsushita turned one final time to the camp superintendent, begging Fraser to remember him when the hearing board next came to the camp in December:

> Many internees who were here with us last year and later transferred to south, had their rehearings over there and [are] now united with their families in Relocation centers, while old timers like me who were destined to stay here seemed to have been left behind in the reunion of families.[44]

With so few remaining internees still seeking rehearings, Matsushita held out little hope that he might successfully plead his case. It was a difficult time of year for the 51-year-old Methodist:

> My third Nativity
> in stockyard ground.

Bert Fraser, an optimist, advised Matsushita to petition the government one more time, this time through the U.S. Attorney's Office in Seattle. With little expectation of success, on December 27, 1943, Iwao Matsushita pleaded for "special permission to live with my wife in Hunt, Idaho Relocation Center":

Many friends of mine who were here with me in 1942 and later transferred south . . . are now enjoying reunion with their families.

My wife, who is ill and under a doctor's care . . . has been patiently waiting for my return for two long years. . . . This was the third Christmas she had to observe so miserably.

I don't like her to be tortured like this on account of my being detained here. I like to help her, nurse her, and cheer her up. . . . As we never lived apart in our married life for 23 years before my apprehension, it is simply unbearable to have to live like this for so long. . . .

I can assure you that there is not an iota of danger to the safety of the American public when I am allowed to live with my wife.[45]

Bert Fraser, superintendent of the Fort Missoula Internment Camp, in June 1943.

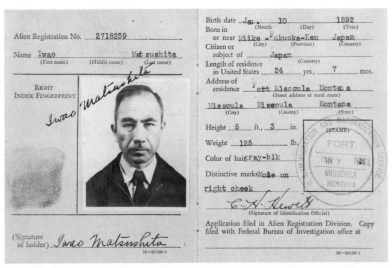

Alien Registration No. 2718233

Name Hanaye — Matsushita
(First name)　(Middle name)　(Last name)

RIGHT INDEX FINGERPRINT

(Signature of holder) Hanaye Matsushita

Birth date March 9th 1898
(Month)　(Day)　(Year)

Born in or near Okayama Okayama Japan
(City)　(Province)　(Country)

Citizen or subject of Japan
(Country)

Length of residence in United States 22 yrs., 4 mos.

Address of residence 905 — 24th Avenue South
(Street address or rural route)

Seattle King Washington
(City)　(County)　(State)

Height 5 ft., in.

Weight 88 lb.

Color of hair Black

Distinctive marks none

(STAMP) SEATTLE WASH. REGISTERED FEB 1942

(Signature of Identification Official)

Application filed in Alien Registration Division. Copy filed with Federal Bureau of Investigation office at

Seattle, Wash.

Alien Registration card, 1942. All aliens living in the United States were required to hold wartime identification.

Alien Registration No. 2718239

Name Iwao Matsushita
(First name)　(Middle name)　(Last name)

RIGHT INDEX FINGERPRINT

Iwao Matsushita

(Signature of holder) Iwao Matsushita

Birth date Jan. 10 1892
(Month)　(Day)　(Year)

Born in or near Miike -Fukuoka-Ken Japan
(City)　(Province)　(Country)

Citizen or subject of Japan
(Country)

Length of residence in United States 24 yrs., 7 mos.

Address of residence Fort Missoula Montana
(Street address or rural route)

Missoula Missoula Montana
(City)　(County)　(State)

Height 5 ft., 3 in.

Weight 125 lb.

Color of hair gray-blk

Distinctive marks Mode on right cheek

(STAMP) IMMIGRATION AND NATURALIZATION SERVICE FORT JAN 7 1944 MISSOULA MONTANA

(Signature of Identification Official)

Application filed in Alien Registration Division. Copy filed with Federal Bureau of Investigation office at

Iwao Matsushita's Alien Registration card was issued January 7, 1944, prior to his parole to the Minidoka Relocation Center.

This final appeal for parole to Minidoka in the end proved unnecessary. The couple's earlier petition, completed after Hanaye's long delay the previous April, had been approved by the attorney general on December 18. The good news from Seattle on January 2, 1944, would bring the long-sought reunion at last.

The facts upon which parole was granted were summarized in an Alien Enemy Control Unit internal memo:

52 years old; educated by American Missionaries—in grade school 5 years and at the Tokyo College of Foreign Languages three years (all in Japan.) Entered the U.S. in 1919; never made any return trips to Japan. Married to Japanese alien who entered the U.S. in 1919; they have no children. Subject's father was a Methodist minister, as is his brother now working in Japan, and he has always attended the Methodist church. After leaving employ of Mitsui & Co. worked as a clerk for the Seattle Japanese Chamber of Commerce. Subject has deposited in various banks in this country about $10,000. He refused repatriation. No evidence of subversive activities or activity in pro-Japanese organizations or of voicing pro-Japanese sentiments. Wife in an unbalanced mental condition due to long separation from subject. Officer-in-Charge at Missoula says subject has been spokesman for the Camp and has been most cooperative and helpful.[46]

After two years and thirty days in captivity apart from her, Matsushita sent his 148th and final communication to Hanaye, a telegram, on January 6, 1944, which read simply: "LEAVING HERE 10TH, MONDAY AFTERNOON. ARRIVING TWIN FALLS, TUESDAY NOON OR AFTERNOON."

"The Mountain That Was God," Mount Rainier. The Cascade peak was a
favorite photographic subject and inspirational source for Matsushita.

FIVE

Fields under Snow

There are the mountains
The fields and the lake clouded,
With a fine spring rain.
—Baigaku Matsumoto[1]

I WAO AND HANAYE MATSUSHITA were reunited at the Minidoka Relocation Center on the afternoon of January 11, 1944, following his overnight train journey south from Missoula to nearby Twin Falls. Their many prayers were finally answered on that day, and the first moments together must have been joyful and tearful. He joined her in her room on Block 2, Barrack 12, where they would spend the next twenty months together until he left for Seattle to help resettle the returning Japanese. Although little within the landscape reminded the couple of happier days in Seattle, they were, nevertheless, among friends, and news of continuing Allied advances found all of them looking toward the end of the war and eventual freedom to return home.

Matsushita was one of 194 former Justice Department internees paroled to Minidoka, and one of 1,735 to enter War Relocation Authority custody overall.[2] The Idaho camp population was nearly fourteen times greater than the Japanese population at its peak at Fort Missoula. The Montana group had included Issei men from throughout the West Coast. In Idaho, Matsushita reacquainted himself with many friends, former neighbors, fellow churchgoers, colleagues, and myriad others he recognized on sight, both men and women. The rich human environment offered him numerous opportunities to serve the former Seattle Nikkei community.

Religious life at Minidoka abounded. Five Protestant denominations had earlier organized themselves into a single Federated Christian Church, staffed by eight Japanese American clergymen and two Caucasian pastors, the Reverends Emory Andrews and Everett Thompson. Both of the latter had served Seattle churches and regularly commuted to the camp from nearby Twin Falls, where they had established temporary residency. The Seattle Maryknoll priest Father Leo Tibesar had also followed his Catholic parishioners to Minidoka and for two and a half years ministered to their spiritual and physical needs. Buddhists had their own groups and clergy.[3] In addition to their work within the Idaho camp, all of these organizations would later play a significant role in postwar resettlement of the Japanese population on the West Coast.

Matsushita soon found a niche in community spiritual life. Calling upon a prewar role as a lay speaker in his Seattle church, he frequently delivered sermons for Sunday morning services. He also wrote numerous articles for the church bulletin, based in part upon his exchange of theological ideas with the Reverend Joseph Kitagawa, the young Episcopal minister who had assisted Hanaye with her petition to free Iwao. The two extended their Christian fellowship outside the camp boundaries as well. In May 1944 they received a travel pass and interim parole from the WRA to attend a week-long religious conference at Spokane, located outside the exclusion zone.

In addition to his religious work, Matsushita took up teaching again. In the fall of 1944, he headed a series of English skills classes, drawing the same enthusiasm from his new students as he had at Fort Missoula. For his services as a teacher, the WRA paid him a professional salary—$19 per month. He later added U.S. history to his curriculum.

| LEAVING CAMP

Almost from the beginning of its existence, the WRA had plans to reduce the populations of its ten centers.[4] First, it released American citizens, Nisei, for agricultural work in the sugar beet fields of nearby states, giving those willing to engage in such backbreaking work a taste of freedom. An indefinite leave policy followed in July 1942, permitting resettlement outside the evacuated coastal area if both a sponsor and an employer could be arranged. Although early efforts were often fraught with bureaucratic red tape and inefficiency, the WRA's Employment Division eventually set up field offices designed to assist resettlers in the geographic locales most likely to receive them.[5]

By the end of 1943, bureaucratic streamlining and improved community relations had led to a reduction of seventeen thousand in the ten camps, not counting the several thousand Nisei students who had by then left for inland colleges[6] and those now serving in the army. Predictably, Nisei between the ages of eighteen and thirty, being more Americanized than most Issei and thus more likely to find employment, chose to leave first. The elders, many of whom were of advancing age and less able to begin life in a new place, and the younger children remained behind, thus altering the demographics in the centers. However, reports from early resettlers revealed both a public hostility toward them and in many areas an acute housing shortage. Thus, departures slowed.

The 1945 new year found the Matsushitas still in camp. Earlier, in a presettlement interview on May 19, 1944, they had discussed their plan to return to Seattle, when permitted, where Iwao would resume "clerking" work. Because they still had $5,000 in Seattle branch banks, they would require no financial assistance from the government upon their ultimate departure. At the time of this interview, return to the exclusion zones was not yet possible. But rather than resettle outside the Pacific Northwest, which Minidokans were being encouraged to do, the couple decided to remain in the center until the West Coast opened up. Hanaye's slow-to-improve health contributed to their decision to stay. By July 1945 they were still "awaiting the right opportunity to return to Seattle."[7]

After January 3, 1945, Nisei could return to the coast as a result of the Supreme Court's decision on the Endo case, in which the justices unanimously agreed that loyal citizens could not be held in detention against their will.[8] In practice, the WRA would allow Issei to return as well. Quickly the WRA's Employment Division established field offices in Los Angeles, San Francisco, Seattle, and other West Coast communities to accommodate many of the eighty thousand people still in camp who were expected to return to their prewar localities. At the same time, the government announced a schedule of camp closures to occur within the next six to twelve months. The Minidoka Relocation Center was scheduled to shut its gates in October 1945.

People with relevant skills were required to staff the new West Coast field offices. The WRA turned to the inmates for help, thus providing an opportunity for Matsushita, who, because of his bilingualism and familiarity with the Seattle business milieu, qualified for the job. As a result of his camp work, he was well known and respected by the Minidoka administration. Thus, his application in July 1945 for a position as special relocation officer in the Seattle field office was quickly approved.[9]

The position provided Matsushita with immediate temporary employment and the chance to seek housing before the swell of returning Minidokans made finding a suitable apartment more difficult. His employment with the WRA would actually continue for nine months, through closure of the field office in 1946. His projected annual salary of $3,640, scheduled to begin on August 7, compared to a college teacher's yearly earnings.[10] The couple agreed that, in consideration of Hanaye's marginal emotional health, she would stay behind until he could secure comfortable accommodations.

Despite the fact that his new employer was the federal government, Matsushita remained a parolee of the Justice Department. The WRA required that the new employee have indefinite leave status, which necessitated clearance from the INS. The Minidoka camp administration applied for clearance on his behalf on July 31, 1945, and approval came five days later. Yet he was still not free: conditions of parole required that he report to the INS station in Seattle within twenty-four hours of his arrival in the city. There arrangements for his indefinite supervision were to be outlined.

Earlier in the year Matsushita had applied for termination of his parole status. On February 13, 1945, the Minidoka attorney forwarded his application to the U.S. Attorney's Office in Seattle, adding that the parolee, having "rendered valuable service in the teaching of English and History in the Adult Education Program," had an excellent reputation. No adverse information had been reported by any internal department within the WRA that might serve to compromise the application.[11] A June 1945 follow-up by H. L. Stafford, director of Minidoka, informed the

U.S. attorney of Matsushita's religious work in camp, further stating that nothing could be found in his record to raise questions about his loyalty. Moreover, he reported, Matsushita

want[s] the United States to win the war with Japan . . . he want[s] . . . to remain in the United States and . . . he would gladly serve in any way possible. . . . he has often visited in the homes of the appointed staff members, and . . . appears entirely at ease and in no way foreign to our customs. No one contacted has spoken detrimentally of his attitude toward the Administration or this Country.[12]

Like his earlier attempts to alter his wartime political status, Matsushita's application to terminate his parole status failed to move the bureaucracy. On September 29, 1945, the Alien Enemy Control Unit informed him, without explanation, that "no change will be made at this time in your present parole status."[13] The nuisance and stigma of parole continued. That the government of his adopted country repeatedly refused to trust him must have been a source of pain and disappointment.[14]

| RETURN TO SEATTLE

His application for termination of parole still pending, Matsushita boarded a westbound overnight train at the Twin Falls depot, on August 7, 1945. Once in Seattle, he was to board temporarily with other WRA field office employees in a house at 1921 Jackson Street, east of the prewar Japantown business district. Upon his arrival, however, the room had not yet been vacated, so he found temporary lodging at the comfortable N.P. Hotel managed by an Issei family before the war.

The next day, August 9, Matsushita fulfilled the first condition of his parole by reporting to the INS station on Airport Way, the very place he spent three weeks behind bars in December 1941.[15] Later that afternoon he sought out his supervisor at the field office in the same Walker Building in downtown Seattle that had housed his old employer, Mitsui and Company.[16]

Matsushita's return to Seattle followed forty-four unbroken months of captivity. Now a government employee working in a former exclusion zone, he and his Japanese American coworkers were hired to interview returning Issei and Nisei to help identify and solve problems relating to housing, employment, discrimination, and other social and medical problems endemic in all West Coast cities still laboring under wartime conditions. The most urgent problem facing returnees was the housing shortage. Seattle had barely managed to accommodate the influx of defense workers who arrived from all parts of the country to work at the Boeing Airplane Company, the shipyards, and other war manufacturing plants in the area. The city's population had increased from 368,302 in 1940 to approximately 530,000 in 1944. Unable to meet the unyielding demand for shelter, many homeowners had rented out rooms or modified space into apartments. Rooming houses doubled or tripled their occupancies. Creatively, some landlords even rented "hot beds" where workers slept in shifts.[17]

The large number of prewar hotel and apartment buildings run by the Issei were slowly being taken over again by the returning operators, who provided Matsushita and his colleagues with referrals. Nevertheless, these multiple-occupancy dwellings could not absorb the growing numbers of returning Japanese. Fortunately, numerous private organizations came forward to assist the WRA field office during this transition period. The Seattle Council of Churches and Christian Education, for example, set up two hostels, which accommodated 526 people between July 1 and October 22, 1945. Residents remained for a period of from one to fourteen nights. People then continued to use the hostels as contact points with friends and for leads to other housing and employment.[18] Some individual churches, such as the Episcopal church, helped with their returning parishioners' financial affairs, as well.

Nonsectarian groups also coordinated efforts with the Seattle field office. One organization, the Seattle Japanese-American Citizens League, forced to close down operations in May 1942, reopened in temporary quarters to offer resettlement assistance and to smooth public relations. In a creative move, the Japanese-language school building on Weller Street, taken over as a military training facility and now recently vacated, was converted once again, this time into temporary housing that enabled twenty-seven families to move meager belongings into the empty classrooms and a shared kitchen facility.[19] There, as elsewhere, families could wait for roomier accommodations. In some cases individuals with financial means leased or purchased multifamily dwellings for personal use and then rented rooms or apartments in the building to other Japanese Americans.

The housing shortage was exacerbated by continuing discrimination. All minorities faced restrictive covenants in upper-middle-class neighborhoods, such as Montlake, Laurelhurst, Mount Baker, Magnolia Bluff, and the more affluent streets and avenues of Capital and Queen Anne hills.[20] Thus, most Japanese Americans found housing in the vicinity of the old Nihonmachi, although dispersal into areas previously unoccupied by the Japanese minority occurred out of necessity.[21]

In addition to providing assistance with housing, Matsushita and his WRA colleagues helped returning Japanese find employment. Directly through their own contacts or indirectly through private organizations like the Council of Churches, they located hotel work and union service work, such as janitorial and porter jobs, for returning Seattleites. Though low-end jobs, they nevertheless eased returnees back into the work force. The Maryknoll Catholics, on the other hand, arranged placements in their own enterprises, such as the area's Catholic hospitals. Some Seattle Japanese found their way, without WRA help, into civil service clerical jobs or into federal employment with such bureaucracies as the Veterans Administration.[22]

While some organized citizens' groups, especially religious groups, openly supported the return of the Japanese to the Pacific Northwest, others, including those made up of people who perceived themselves economically threatened, were equally vocal in opposing it. Outright hostility toward Seattle returnees was relatively uncommon, but it was closely monitored by the WRA field office, nevertheless. Racial epithets were smeared on property, and windows smashed; there were rare shootings and some incidents involving arson.

The federal government, however, stopped the farthest reaching rejections of returning Seattleites, which involved the produce trade. During the early summer of 1945, local florists, out of fear of public sentiment against the returning evacuees, refused to buy from the Japanese growers, despite the overall scarcity of floral products in the area and the superior quality of what was available through Japanese sources. A more widespread form of discrimination involved truck farmers who supplied the whole-salers on Seattle's "produce row." The Northwest Produce Association succeeded in extending the misery of returning Japanese Americans in the spring and summer of 1945 by preventing their fruits, vegetables, and berries from reaching market. The Teamsters Union, headed by Dave Beck, refused to handle their farm produce. The collusion ended only after the Anti-Trust Division of the Department of Justice threatened to intervene on the farmers' behalf.[23]

In the meantime, race-conscious politicians cited the continuing perils of espionage, raised the issue of unknown loyalty, and continued to resist the return. On January 22, 1945, the newly elected Governor Mon C. Wallgren opposed any Japanese returning to coastal states for the duration of the war; he hinted at ongoing underground Japanese American collaboration with Japan, for which he was never able to provide evidence.[24] Washington's freshman senator, Warren G. Magnuson, joined the governor in his opposition.[25]

As summer light weakened on the Pacific Northwest landscape that year, Matsushita's workload increased dramatically. Most individuals leaving WRA camps in early 1945 had settled in regions other than the West Coast. But after June 30, the majority returned to wartime exclusion zones, as early settlers persevered and community resistance wilted. By October, 80 to 90 percent of those leaving camp were returning to the coastal areas; two-thirds of the Minidokans headed northwest, to Seattle.

Even though he enjoyed an apparent advantage by working on the "inside," Matsushita himself had difficulty locating a permanent place to stay. Coming back to Seattle he found that Japantown had changed. Most businesses and residences were now occupied by whites, blacks, and Filipinos who had moved into the area to fill the void created by the exodus to the Puyallup Assembly Center in 1942.[26] Housing in the district was in critically short supply. Thus, despite Matsushita's insider status, he, too, despaired over crowded conditions and warned Hanaye that they might have to relocate outside Seattle or leave the Pacific Northwest altogether.

Matsushita's gloomy forecast brightened when the rental house next door to his WRA lodgings suddenly became available at the end of September 1945. Quickly he signed the lease papers and happily moved his few belongings one door west, to 1919 Jackson Street. He promptly sent for Hanaye. With her departure on a Seattle-bound train, on October 2, 1945, she left behind fewer than 1,000 of the original 9,397 Minidokans. The residence on Jackson Street that greeted her upon her arrival would be Hanaye's last home.[27]

Government employment enabled Matsushita to continue serving his community in the same way he had served both at Fort Missoula and at Minidoka. It demonstrated his loyalty to his adopted country, which he believed could help in his future search for employment in the postwar Seattle job market. His willingness to accept government employment also testified to an absence of bitterness toward the country that turned its back on him during the war. However, it is ironic that Matsushita, a despised enemy alien kept in special confinement from 1941 to 1944, should, as a Justice Department parolee in 1945 and while the war was still in progress, be given an administrative position by the same government that locked him up.

| Reestablishing Contact with Relatives in Japan

The end of hostilities in the Pacific, coming in the wake of the atomic bombs dropped on Hiroshima and Nagasaki, enabled resumption of contact between the Seattle couple and the Matsushita and Tamura families in Japan. Iwao had last received word from his brother, Sekio, a postcard dated August 31, 1943, which had been transported aboard the Red Cross ship *Gripsholm* on the return leg of its second humanitarian exchange voyage to Asia. Sekio had written that the family was still healthy at that point.[28] Now, on November 18, 1945, initial news of the family was sent forth from Fukuoka to the Jackson Street home by Iwao's thirty-three-year-old niece, Teruko Inoue.[29] In this letter and others that followed, Iwao and Hanaye learned of the deaths of his younger sister, Fumi, by starvation in 1944, of one of Teruko's four brothers while defending Leyte Island in the Philippines in 1945, and of Sekio's wife, from radiation sickness following the bombing of Hiroshima. Sekio, himself a medical victim of the bombing, had been subsequently hospitalized for many months.

News of the family's postwar deprivations also reached Iwao and Hanaye. In response, they posted parcels of dresses, towels, candles, soap, toilet paper, sanitary napkins, and simple foods, such as noodle soup, cocoa, and saccharin, to grateful beneficiaries.

Gradually the terrible news from Japan subsided, and within three years, "care packages" were no longer needed. Recovery began. Sekio had regained his health and returned to his duties as dean of the Methodist Women's College (Hiroshima *Jogakuin*). And the niece, Teruko, resumed teaching English at a girl's normal school following restoration of the "enemy language" to the curriculum. At this time she, like her uncle a generation earlier, began to dream of coming to America.

Family losses, however, did not end there. Following his release from the Minidoka Relocation Center, Hanaye's uncle, Dr. Koike, returned to Seattle and reopened his medical office. He again picked up his camera, but now at age sixty-seven, and despite the younger Matsushita's unwavering friendship, he found it impossible to recover his prewar energy and enthusiasm. On March 31, 1947, while picking spring fern shoots in the city that had been his home for thirty years, he collapsed and died of cerebral hemorrhage. Later, Matsushita buried his ashes at the base of a large tree on Mount Rainier.[30]

| RETURN TO THE UNIVERSITY

By May 1946, as his temporary employment with the WRA came to an end, Matsushita, now fifty-four, was considering what to do with the rest of his professional life. After twenty-seven years in the United States, he was bilingually fluent and, through his various American experiences, had embraced the culture of his adopted country. There was no question of ever returning to Japan to live. Seattle was his home. His most marketable skills lay in his fluency in Japanese and English. Thus, with the help of Eldon Griffin, the former professor for whom he had pioneered the Japanese-language course at the University of Washington in 1927, he reestablished his ties to the Department of Oriental Studies. This time the state legislature had appropriated the necessary funds to hire him for a nine-month associate position, which he accepted for the 1946 fall term at a prorated annual salary of $2,016.[31]

90

And finally, two years later, in the summer of 1948, the fifty-six-year-old immigrant entered the baccalaureate degree program in the University of Washington's College of Arts and Sciences, realizing the dream that brought him to America in 1919. His field of study, however, was not to be English, as he had originally planned, but Far Eastern Studies. The university, giving him credits for his three years of studies in Tokyo from 1912 to 1914, waived his first-year requirements, thus enabling him to enter as a second-year student.

Matsushita combined teaching responsibilities with classroom studies and graduated with honors in August 1951. After another year of teaching both credit and noncredit Japanese-language evening classes, he accepted the university's offer of an appointment in the Far Eastern Library as a subject specialist. There he remained until university regulations forced him to retire in 1962, at the age of seventy.[32]

| NATURALIZATION

Although the postwar years brought Matsushita satisfaction in both employment and education, one goal continued to elude him—naturalization. Passage of the Immigration and Nationality (McCarren-Walter) Act on June 25, 1952, however, finally opened the doors to citizenship for him and thousands of other Asian immigrants. This legislation eliminated ethnic and national obstructions to naturalization and struck down the "aliens ineligible to citizenship" bar that had applied directly to the Issei. Moreover, the legislation did away with the basis for the discriminatory anti-alien land acts.[33]

The Issei were now free to apply for citizenship. Matsushita, because of his knowledge of the U.S. and his ability to communicate in the two languages, taught naturalization classes for two years at Seattle's Edison Technical School.[34] The Reverend Jonathan Machida, pastor of the Seattle Japanese Methodist church and formerly of the Federated Christian Church at Minidoka, became the first West Coast Issei to take citizenship papers, on February 10, 1953.[35] Matsushita, one of Machida's parishioners, received his own certificate of naturalization in Seattle on March 22, 1954, thirty-five years after his arrival in America.[36]

With his new citizenship and secure employment, Matsushita turned to his community, once again, to volunteer his time and skills. In 1956, the Seattle Japanese-language school reopened its doors for the first time

| Certificate of naturalization, issued March 22, 1954.

since the beginning of World War II, at its prewar location on Weller Street. On the last Saturday in September, 250 students greeted their new principal, Iwao Matsushita, who, with five other teachers, began language classes for a new generation of schoolchildren attending the weekly two-hour sessions.[37] In prewar days, language school students consisted of Nisei struggling to communicate with their parents, who often spoke little English at home. The reopening of the Seattle school, however, brought a new generation, the Sansei, who possessed little need for the language, since their parents spoke minimal Japanese, and therefore had less incentive to learn. Newsletters sent home by Matsushita and the other teachers to Japanese-speaking parents pleaded for help in conversing with their children in Japanese, for the students' conversational skills were no match for their written skills.

| Hanaye and Iwao on a spring day at Seattle's Seward Park, ca. 1964.

Although most prewar Japanese-language schools in America eventually reopened, they never acquired the influence they manifested prior to the war.[38] Despite frustrations brought on by an often indifferent younger generation, Matsushita remained principal of Seattle's *Nihon Gakuin* for eighteen years, stepping down from his volunteer position in 1974 only after a long-sought replacement had been found.

Meanwhile, Hanaye maintained the Matsushita household as she had prior to the war. Life for her centered again about the home and church and outings with Iwao and friends. Unlike her husband, Hanaye never pursued a formal education in America, possibly because she never achieved fluency in English. Insufficient language skills may also have influenced her decision not to seek naturalization.

Physical and emotional health eluded Hanaye despite the return to Seattle and the comforts of prewar life. In 1954, in a moment of candor with Iwao's niece, Teruko Inoue, she attributed a case of chronic thinning of her hair to her long-standing anxiety condition caused by the war. The onset of cancer years later, perhaps linked in some way to a suppressed immune system brought on by this emotional disorder, proved fatal. She died in a Seattle hospital on February 3, 1965, at the age of sixty-six. Iwao's wife of forty-six years was now gone.

| RETURN TO JAPAN

During their life together in America, Iwao and Hanaye had never returned to their homeland to visit their parents. Nor had they traveled outside North America, journeying only as far as British Columbia during the 1920s and 1930s. Now, after Hanaye's death, and perhaps contemplating his own mortality, Matsushita decided to make the trip to the geography of his youth to visit family burial sites. His plans included seeing his only surviving sister, Tonomi; his one cousin, Aiko; and Teruko, his niece, who was anxious to return the generosity extended her on her previous travels to Seattle. Now freed from the burden of Hanaye's long illness, in the fall of 1966 Matsushita booked passage on a tour that would take him to Europe, the Middle East, and Asia. Its termination in Japan would make possible an extended stay with his family.

Among Iwao's traveling companions was Gin Kunishige, widow of the photographer Frank Kunishige, his friend from the Seattle Camera Club days. During the war Gin and Frank had left Minidoka and resettled in Coeur d'Alene, Idaho. The two couples maintained contact over the years. Following her husband's death in 1960, Gin returned to Seattle, resuming her friendship with Iwao and Hanaye. She stayed on with him during the month-long family visit at the conclusion of the world tour and returned with him to Seattle in November.

In addition to the loneliness of life without Hanaye, the unfamiliar tasks of cooking, washing, and maintaining a residence provided Matsushita a rationale for marrying Gin the next year. The union came as a surprise to his family in Japan, who regarded the couple as a mismatch of temperament and interests and viewed the marriage as one of convenience. Regardless of Matsushita's motivation, the pair stayed together for the remainder of his life. They shared a Christian life. Gin, having been naturalized in 1956, was baptized in the Blaine Memorial Methodist Church on March 27, 1967, by Iwao's friend the Reverend Juhei Kono. Matsushita's association with the Far Eastern Library continued beyond his mandatory retirement in 1962. His reputation as a translator and a teacher to both students and scholars had long since gained him the affectionate moniker "Mr. Far Eastern Library."[39] He continued to provide expertise to grateful knowledge seekers but now as a volunteer. He also shared his scholarly possessions, donating to the library much of his personal collection of books, consisting of more than eight hundred volumes of Japanese-language literature.

During this period he wrote extensively. There were two books on religion and a third, with Hanaye as co-author, just before her death. This 1966 self-published work, entitled *Neko no negoto* ("Sleep Talking of a Cat"), consisted of a series of humorous fictional reminiscences. In addition, he edited a mimeographed religious newsletter, *Nanuka no tabiji* ("A Seven-Day Journey"), which he published from 1954 to 1969.[40]

Rainier *Ginsha*, the haiku society founded by Matsushita's friend Koike in 1934, reorganized after the war. He renewed this affiliation and maintained it for the remainder of his life. For a time he served the organization as its treasurer. He wrote and published haiku in literary magazines in both the U.S. and Japan under the pen name Tadenoha Matsushita.

Religious faith, which had sustained him through the harsh times at Fort Missoula, continued to provide a focus in his life. Among his closest friends was his pastor, Juhei Kono. During periods when Kono was absent, Matsushita served Sunday parishioners as a lay speaker, keeping up the practice so familiar to the Minidoka camp residents. In 1975 he spoke on at least three occasions and, in a similar capacity, served at least one other denomination, the Japanese Presbyterian church. He also maintained affiliations with other Methodist congregations throughout Washington and Idaho.

Matsushita's service to the Japanese American community was recognized twice by the Japanese government. In 1969 he and ten other Japanese Americans received the Sixth Class Order of Sacred Treasure, "for promoting the welfare of Japanese residents in [the United States] and for furthering better relations between Japan and the United States."[41]

| Iwao Matsushita at the University of Washington Far Eastern Library, ca. 1964.

| Iwao Matsushita in 1974 on the day he received the Fifth Class Order of Sacred Treasure from the Japanese government.

Five years later, in 1974, after stepping down as principal of the Japanese-language school, he was awarded the Fifth Class Order of Sacred Treasure.[42]

In the summer of 1972, Iwao and Gin moved out of the Jackson Street residence that had been Hanaye's postwar home and into a house at 2806–17th Avenue South. This location was a short distance from the center of prewar Japantown, in what by now had evolved into the International District.

His energy beginning to ebb, Matsushita gradually let go of his major responsibilities. In 1974 he relinquished his position at the language school; his visits to the University of Washington became less frequent; and his pastoral duties as a speaker gradually came to an end. Nevertheless, he maintained an active correspondence with friends and distant relations, both in the United States and Japan, and his interests in Rainier *Ginsha* and church life did not flag. But as physical health failed, Gin, constantly at his side from the time of their marriage, could not continue to care for him without professional help and, in 1978, moved him to the Keiro Nursing Home in the International District, a facility serving the aged Japanese American population. His stay there lasted a year. Loss of independence, a growing lack of mobility, and a body simply worn out resulted in a quiet end on December 17, 1979.

According to his wishes Matsushita was cremated. Today his simple urn occupies a crypt at a columbarium in Seattle's Evergreen-Washelli Cemetery, a space shared with the urns of Hanaye, Frank Kunishige, and Gin, his late-life companion, who died two years after Iwao, in 1981.

PART TWO

WARTIME

CORRESPONDENCE

"Untitled," ca. 1930.

S I X

Censored

*As the Japanese censor is away
again I write this in English.*
—Iwao Matsushita

T HE ACCOUNT OF Iwao and Hanaye Matsushita presented thus far
has been assembled from family sources and Matsushita's personal
papers. Their contemporaries are either no longer alive or able to share
their knowledge of them. Were it not for the wartime correspondence
left behind by Iwao and Hanaye, there would be no story about their
personal lives during that period. During World War II, family members
knew little about them, their whereabouts and the hardships they endured,
because communications were all but cut off. Cable traffic between North
America and Japan was closed to the public except under the rarest of
circumstances. Written communication, when permitted, was limited
to twenty-five words, enabling only the most basic information to be
communicated, and that was further limited by the inhibiting effects
of censorship.[1] A verbatim Red Cross message in English from Iwao at
Fort Missoula on April 30, 1942, to his brother, Sekio, in Hiroshima
and unaltered by the censors is typical of what little information could
be communicated between civilians in the two countries: "Safe and
sound in camp. Treated kindly. Meals other accommodations good. Wife
moving to new location. Regards to relatives, friends. Take good care,
especially mother." Sekio's reply, in Japanese, similarly terse, only reached
Fort Missoula nineteen months later.[2] Many families did not attempt to
communicate at all, and some addresses in Japan could not be located.

Red Cross message to Matsushita's brother, Sekio, in Japan. Sent April 30, 1942. Censored at Fort Missoula and New York Prisoner of War Unit. Sekio's response was received at Fort Missoula nineteen months later.

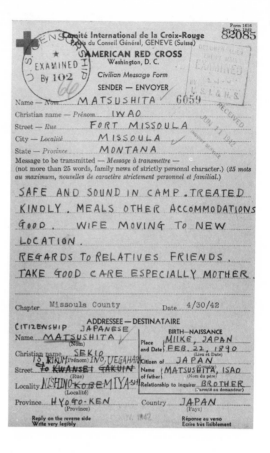

Form 1616

82085

CENS[...] Comité International de la Croix-Rouge
Paris du Conseil Général, GENEVE (Suisse)

★ AMERICAN RED CROSS
EXAMINED I
By 102
Washington, D. C.

Civilian Message Form
SENDER — ENVOYER

Name — Nom... MATSUSHITA   6059

Christian name — Prénom... IWAO

Street — Rue... FORT MISSOULA

City — Localité... MISSOULA

State — Province... MONTANA

Message to be transmitted — Message à transmettre —
(not more than 25 words, family news of strictly personal character.) (25 mots au maximum, nouvelles de caractère strictement personnel et familial.)

SAFE AND SOUND IN CAMP . TREATED
KINDLY . MEALS OTHER ACCOMMODATIONS
GOOD . WIFE MOVING TO NEW
LOCATION .
REGARDS TO RELATIVES FRIENDS .
TAKE GOOD CARE ESPECIALLY MOTHER .

Chapter... Missoula County   Date... 4/30/42

ADDRESSEE — DESTINATAIRE
CITIZENSHIP   JAPANESE
Name... MATSUSHITA   BIRTH—NAISSANCE
(Nom)   Place   MIIKE, JAPAN
Christian name... SEKIO   and Date FEB. 22, 1890
(Prénom) INO, UEGAHARA Citizen of JAPAN   (Lieu et Date)
IS, RIKUM
Street... To KWANSEI GAKUIN   Name   MATSUSHITA, ISAO
(Rue)   of father   (Nom du père)
Locality... NISHINO-KOBE-MIYASHI Relationship to inquirer BROTHER
(Localité)   (L'arenté au demandeur)
Province... HYOGO-KEN   Country... JAPAN
(Province)   (Pays)

Reply on the reverse side   Réponse au verso
Write very legibly   Ecrire très lisiblement

Because of the broken communication with Asia, and because most of Matsushita's contemporaries were in similar circumstances and occupied with their own concerns, the Matsushitas' correspondence with each other is the sole source of details of their everyday lives in captivity and their oscillating moods, worries, and concerns. How typical these lives were under the stresses they bore can be known only by comparing their letters with published and unpublished diaries and letters of those who lived under similar circumstances.[3]

Families in the U.S. whose heads of household were incarcerated in Justice Department camps shared the experience of mail censorship. Any attempt to construct a personal history from such a correspondence, which involved a situation in which daily activities were controlled, must take into account the presence of a censor who necessarily influenced what was or was not communicated. Not only were words, phrases, sentences, and even whole paragraphs excised from both incoming and outgoing letters, but also the mere presence of the censor inhibited letter writers, who practiced self-censorship to avoid the possibility that their correspondence would not be forwarded or that they would lose their letter-writing privileges altogether.

Little has been written about U.S. internee mail censorship during World War II.[4] Although a comprehensive study is beyond the scope of this work, a brief synopsis, nevertheless, may help provide a context for the letters that follow.

| Mail Censorship during World War II

In World War II, postal, cable, radio, and newspaper censorship affected the lives of civilians and military personnel in virtually every nation, belligerent and neutral. The conflict generated the largest censorship operation in the world's history: at its peak in September 1942, each week in the U.S. alone nearly one million pieces of international correspondence passed through the hands of nearly ten thousand censors.

The U.S. Office of Censorship, charged with depriving the enemy of information and collecting intelligence that could be used against the enemy, established a special unit to censor the mail of individuals falling under the protection of the Geneva Convention of 1929. The Geneva accord specifically addressed the individual rights and privileges of prisoners of war with respect to contact with the outside world. Articles 36, 38, and 40 authorized POWs (and, by agreement, civilian detainees and internees) to send and receive letters and postcards in their native language and provided for such communications to be sent free of postal charges with expeditious censorship. The Prisoner of War Censorship Regulations of June 1942 specified that all international and domestic mail of prisoners of war be censored by the Prisoner of War Unit censors; however, for civilian detainees and internees of war, only their international mail was to be examined. In theory, this rule left Matsushita's correspondence with Hanaye free from the censor's eye.

In the meantime, however, the Immigration and Naturalization Service (INS) had been discreetly opening and inspecting, but not censoring, the detained Italian and German seamen's mail since the beginning of July 1941. When the U.S. entered the war in December, this spot-check surveillance immediately expanded to encompass every piece of detainee and internee mail passing in or out of the camps, including that of the Japanese. Thus, while the Prisoner of War Unit of the Office of Censorship censored all international mail of the civilian detainees and internees, the INS censored all incoming and outgoing domestic mail from the outset of the war.

At some district immigration stations, and at Fort Missoula and elsewhere, officers in charge instructed correspondents to write their letters in English until staff proficient in foreign languages could be acquired. This held especially true in the case of Japanese detainees, whose language was largely unknown outside the Japanese and Korean communities.

The language restriction proved a major handicap for some individuals with limited knowledge of English. Thus, the INS looked to the civilian community as a source of censors and interpreters shortly after the U.S. entered the war. Although many people could translate for the German or Italian inmates, Japanese translators were more difficult to find. Ironically, those most qualified, the Issei themselves, were either behind barbed wire or still in their homes fearing arrest and refusing to come forth to volunteer. The vast majority of the Nisei could neither speak nor write Japanese, which the Military Intelligence Service, in frustration, soon discovered while attempting to recruit linguists for the war in the Pacific. In the end, interpreters and censors hired by the INS were either Kibei or alien residents of Korean ancestry. One of the few Japanese Americans eventually hired and who was assigned to the Fort Missoula post was a twenty-nine-year-old Seattle Kibei with fourteen years of schooling in Japan.[5]

On January 7, 1942, Fort Missoula detainees were ordered by camp officials to limit their output to one letter in Japanese per week and two in English, with none exceeding twenty-four lines in length.[6] These restrictions would help control the volume of mail until the Japanese-speaking censor arrived toward the end of the month. Matsushita did not write his first letter in Japanese to Hanaye until March 6, 1942.[7]

The restriction of outgoing letters was modified two months later to conform to Office of Censorship regulations allowing one foreign-language letter, one English-language letter, and four postcards (two if in a foreign language.)[8] Additionally, correspondents could now send one domestic business letter, which would not count against the weekly allotment. Once camp populations stabilized and sufficient numbers of foreign-language censors were on hand, the language restriction was lifted.

There were never limitations imposed on the number or length of letters and postcards that detainees and internees could receive. Moreover, Justice Department inmates were permitted to send and receive parcels.[9]

Correspondence with evacuees, on the other hand, passed freely without any governmental censorship. If plans ever existed to inspect the personal mail of the residents of the Puyallup Assembly Center, the Minidoka Relocation Center, and the other centers, they were never implemented. Thus, camp correspondents enjoyed the same postal privileges as all letter writers in the U.S. for their domestic mail. Their international mail, however, like all other civilian and military correspondence, was subject to censorship.

| OBJECTIONABLE MAIL

Although most INS detainees and internees were incarcerated in remote areas well insulated from troop movements and military installations and had little access to matters of military intelligence, the government nevertheless sought to prevent information deemed objectionable from reaching the outside world.[10] Information relating directly to the camps, for example, was banned: physical layouts, internee arrival and departure dates, population size, location, strength of guards, and transfers from one camp to another. Complaints about mail restrictions or personal treatment, governmental agencies, or the Red Cross were also prohibited. Such information falling into enemy hands could influence how U.S. civilians held by hostile nations might be treated. In an ironic twist, inmates were advised to avoid exaggerating any favorable conditions of detention that might lead the U.S. citizenry to conclude that enemy aliens were being coddled and treated better than American soldiers.[11]

Censorship may help explain the absence of camp details in Matsushita's evocative descriptions of his physical surroundings and of more than passing mention of the people with whom he came into daily contact. Most of what Matsushita wrote was general in nature and accompanied qualitative rather than quantitative information, even during his tenure as camp spokesman.

Because abuse of the censorship regulations might result in the restriction or loss of mail privileges or, in an extreme case, corporal punishment, inmates, hoping to avoid such consequences, rarely violated the rules intentionally. Matsushita's letters to Hanaye and to Dr. Koike approached two hundred in number, and none had excisions of more than a word or phrase. Clearly, he had been made well aware of the regulations. The censor's black obliterator and sharp razor blade removed from his letters mostly the names of other individuals in camp. Later on this restriction was lifted.

If Matsushita had any complaints about his treatment at Fort Missoula, he knew that attempts to communicate them to Hanaye would be futile. The mishandling of detainees by the Border Patrol guards and Korean interpreters that occurred in the spring of 1942 he could never have reported, even though he may have been called upon to provide testimony during the investigation.

| THE MATSUSHITA CORRESPONDENCE

Iwao wrote Hanaye 148 times over the course of their twenty-five months of separation, averaging six letters and postcards per month. Only one-third of the letters were composed in English, the majority of these coming early in his incarceration and under orders from the camp administration. Bilingualism doubtless enabled him to avoid several long delays in mail transmission during his incarceration. On two occasions, after long strings of Japanese letters, he wrote in English, explaining that the censor was away; a delay as long as two weeks could be expected when Japanese-language letters had to be routed to the POW Unit in

New York for censorship,[12] but English-language letters could be read by local INS personnel. Unfortunately, not all of the inmates at Fort Missoula and elsewhere could write English well enough to dance with the censors in this way.

Hanaye also wrote in both English and Japanese. Fifteen of her first seventeen letters were in English, complying with instructions issued by Fort Missoula administrators. In contrast to her husband, however, who was at ease in either language, Hanaye found expression of her thoughts in written English to be difficult. These early letters are short, awkward in syntax, and stilted. They consist primarily of business matters, such as taxes, sale of their car, life insurance payments, and alien property reports.

As evacuation neared, Hanaye's letters reported on the progress of her plans. Her letters were written both on a typewriter and by hand. Several handwriting styles in the original English text reveal that she had help from others, probably Issei women friends, who served as scribes. No doubt her typed letters also involved a third party. Interestingly, the handwriting of her uncle, Dr. Koike, whose English-language correspondence with Matsushita displays considerable competence, is noticeably absent. This absence may support the allegations of inattention that she made about Koike to her husband.

It was not until Hanaye reached the Minidoka Relocation Center that she started to write regularly in Japanese. After that, her prose loosened, and her letters lengthened, becoming more descriptive, at times poetic. In these letters she freely recorded her physical health and emotional state of mind. Throughout her correspondence she wrote that she prayed for Iwao's early return to her and sought God's strength to endure until they were reunited.

The letters in this collection appear in chronological order, by date on the letter.[13] This arrangement provides the reader with a sense of the delays of the mail, especially during the first months of the couple's separation, when letters took from nine to twenty-two days to reach their destination. Later, with improved service and their consistent use of airmail service, delivery time was reduced to two or three days.

The two-way, unbroken sequence of letters between Iwao and Hanaye Matsushita begins with his one-page penciled note dated December 11,

January 5, 1942

Mr. Iwao Matsushita,
Dormitory #24,
Fort Missoula;
Missoula, Montana

My dear husband:

I have received your letters on
January 2nd, Friday morning.
am glad to hear from you and
thankful to the people who are very
kind to you over there. I wish you to
be healthy and to trust in God.
keep calm and be in good spirit,
this coming 10th is your birthday.
Wish you many happy returns from
all my heart, especially this year.

Dear Husband: (Letter #4)   Feb. 11, 1942
    I have received all your letters to date the
last ones #10 and #11 which came together on Feb 9.
Please do not write about, the weather over there
and please send me your signed Income Tax return
as I am afraid it might take some time to reach
me. We have been working on the Alien report of
property and assets for the U.S. Treasury Dept.
I am very well so please do not worry about me
I am not lonely as grandma stays with me
at night.   Your wife Hanaye Matsushita

March 19, 1942.

Dear Husband:

Your letter arrived yesterday morning and feel happy to hear your healthy condition.

According to your request, I forward you the Standard Dictionary and World Almana under separate cover and hope to reach you safely.

We are still waiting for the next evacuation order by army. I do not decide yet where to go, but don't worry. I will manage the matter for myself.

Spring is here and garden flowers are blooming. I will write you again very soon.

Yours,

Mrs. I. Matsushita

Three letters Hanaye sent her husband before her removal from Seattle. Differences in handwriting and her own lack of typing skill suggest that she had help from others when writing in English.

1941, written from his cell at the Seattle Immigration Station. He wrote three letters from there, each in English, and each censored by an INS overseer. He wrote the remaining letters and postcards while at Fort Missoula.

Hanaye, by contrast, posted her first letter to her husband of twenty-two years on January 5, 1942. In all, she wrote fifteen letters from Seattle. She wrote eight letters from Puyallup during her 110-day incarceration there. The remainder of her forty-one-letter correspondence was posted at Hunt, the Minidoka Relocation Center branch post office.

All of the letters written in English appear here exactly as Hanaye (and her unnamed scribes) and Iwao wrote them. Four individuals participated in preparing the Japanese-language letters for publication. Akimichi Kimura, a Hawaiian Nisei, translated Iwao's letters verbatim, consulting the English-language ones in order to maintain a single voice throughout the correspondence. Two students in the Asian Languages and Literature program at the University of Washington and a recent graduate (B.A.) of Japan's Doshisha University prepared Hanaye's letters. Megumi Inoue, a Japanese national, and Christine Marran, a United States native, first made a content summary; later, Takehiko Abe, a native speaker, prepared a verbatim typescript of the original handwritten letters. From this transcript, Marran produced a translation. Hanaye was often repetitive in her letters; her correspondence has been edited to condense or eliminate some passages, where appropriate. The omissions are noted with ellipses.

In the letters appear numerous references to friends and acquaintances whose identities could not be confirmed. Many were no doubt church friends or "mountain" friends who had accompanied the Matsushitas on their many trips to Mount Rainier and elsewhere. The annotations include identifications for them where possible and for Japanese names, mostly foods, and historical events that are not made clear in the text.

It appears that all correspondence written by the couple was ultimately delivered. Matsushita numbered his letters and postcards from Montana with the likely intent to determine whether all were being received. Although Hanaye did not number hers, she dated each letter, and Matsushita refers to most of them by date in his own responses.

Despite the sometimes tortuous path through the wartime mail system and an intervening half century of time, the correspondence remains intact. The letters of Iwao and Hanaye Matsushita represent a complete contemporary account of a husband and wife's two years of captivity apart from one another during World War II.

"Ice Coral," 1933.

SEVEN

The Letters

Dec. 11, 1941
7 a.m.
[Seattle Immigration Station]^a

Dear Wife,

We are <u>very comfortable</u> here at the Immigration station. Thank you for $10—& a package which I was notified last night, but not received yet.[b] I expect to get it today. (P.S. <u>12 noon</u>—received OK)

We have many friends here & not lonesome at all. We are very nicely treated. If possible I want to have some B.V.D.s, socks & the Bible.

We don't know how long we will stay here.

Your husband Iwao Matsushita

Dec. 15, 1941
Monday night

My Dear Wife,

I am well. We are very comfortable. No change at all. Thank you for all you have done for me. If possible please let me have two boxes of Bromo Quinine in case I need it. No hurry. Please take good care of yourself, & don't worry about me.

Best regards to our friends.

Your husband Iwao Matsushita

a. Matsushita's letters from the immigration station were censored by local INS officials.
b. Hanaye hand-carried comfort packages to the INS station.

Dec. 26, 1941
(noon)

My dear wife,

We are leaving Saturday morning for probably Montana. Will write again upon arrival.

Thank you for all you have done for me. Please don't worry about my health. I am 100% well today. We help each other & make ourselves comfortable.

I will take <u>best</u> care of myself, & you keep yourself in best condition & wait for me. Be brave & trust in God.

God be with you till we meet again.

Your husband Iwao Matsushita

P.S. We had a swell turkey dinner on Xmas day.

| LETTER 1[a]

Dec. 28, 1941
Dormitory #24
Fort Missoula
Missoula, Montana[b]

Mrs. H. Matsushita
905 24th Ave. So.
Seattle, Wash.

My dear wife,

After a wonderful trip & nice meals on an N.P. train, we safely arrived here Sunday morning. This place is much more comfortable, every convenience, spacious dining room, & better food.

The ground is covered with patches of snow & surrounding mountains are salt-and-peppery. The temperature is freezing & very dry.

Please don't worry & take good care of yourself.

Your husband Iwao Matsushita

P.S. Mr. Hashino sends his regards.

a. Matsushita began numbering his letters upon his arrival at Fort Missoula.

b. All outgoing and incoming letters were censored by English- or Japanese-speaking censors.

2

Dec. 30, 1941

My dear wife,

It snowed all day Monday & Tuesday & the ground is perfectly covered now. The minimum temperature last Sunday was 6, & Monday 10, but we don't feel so cold. We have icycles from eaves today & much warmer.

Heavy underwears & ski outfits, you were so kindly put in the suitcase & the bag are now very, very useful, for which I can't thank you enough.

The dormitory itself, mattress, blankets, quilt, sheets, & everything is new. Meals are excellent & plentiful. We have rice, too.

We can buy almost anything here, & clothings will be supplied by this place.ª So don't worry about these things.

We have no special work to do now except taking care of our own dormitory.

Wishing you a very Happy New Year,

Your loving husband Iwao Matsushita

P.S. I am in excellent health.

3

Jan. 3, 1942

My dear wife,

We had a famous Montana blizzard on the 30th evening, but the next day, we had spotless blue sky & bright sunshine. The surrounding undulating hills covered with powder snow were really tempting. Toward evening the full moon was high in the eastern mountains, which was made purple by the setting sun. What a magnificent view it was! I wished I could have seen this scenery with you.

The New Year's day was again bright, but the temperature registered 20 below zero, which means 52 below freezing point. But don't lose your heart, because we really don't feel so cold as you might when you hear about this in Seattle.

We are now accustomed to the temperature here, & when it snows it usually is <u>warm</u>—around 10 above zero.

a. Correspondents were forbidden to provide specific details about the camp itself.

Our daily life is so satisfactory that I consider it a sin to expect more. We have a radio set in our dormitory. We even had improvised pickles the other day with our rice.

So please don't worry about my life here, but pray for our happy meeting in the future. Take good care of yourself, & write me sometimes.

Your loving husband Iwao Matsushita

| 4

Jan. 5, 1942

My dear wife,

How do you like 22 below zero, which registered at 9 o'clock this morning? We have more shiny days than cloudy, which means snowy and warmer.

The inside of the window glasses are covered with beautiful fern design of ice, which is almost one inch thick, although we keep the temperature of the room around 60–70.

Our community is called "the Japanese village", electing our own mayor. We have self government & are quite free within the spacious enclosure.

Every shiny afternoon I take a walk twice for half an hour each, enjoying beautiful views.

Some play go or card games, while I compose <u>senryu, waka, hokku,</u> or <u>shintaishi</u> poems.[a]

We have, besides shower, a Japanese-style bath tub, which was made by carpenters in the same dormitory.

The dining room is about 5 minutes' walk from our dormitory & large enough for 1,000 people. Meals are served cafeteria style & it is managed by cooks and helpers chosen from our own group.

I again wish to thank you for ski outfits which prove very, very useful every day.

Write me if you are well, & best regards to all our friends.

Your loving husband Iwao Matsushita

---

a. Poetic forms similar to haiku, with differences in structure, content, or emotion.

Jan. 5, 1942[a]
Seattle

My dear husband:

I have received your letters on January 2nd, Friday morning. Am glad to hear from you and thankful to the people who are very kind to you over there. I wish you to be healthy and to trust in God. Keep calm and be in good spirit. This coming 10th is your birthday. Wish you many happy returns from all my heart, especially this year.

I am living fine and healthy. Since you have left, I gained 3 pounds. I am still taking daily cod liver oil which doctor gave to me. Don't worry about me please. I can manage myself no matter what happens. I am doing things businesslike little by little. I hope peace will come all over the world very soon. Everybody are very kind to me. Pray God day and night. If you want money let me know without hesitate.

Wishing you good health.

Lovingly, Your wife

P.S. I am sending you Reader's Digest January number under separate cover. Wish you will like it.

| 5

Jan. 10, 1942

My Dear Wife,

As I don't receive your letter at all, I worry a little bit, but wish everything O.K. We had heavy snowfall & ski boots are now very useful. You may be worrying about my ankle in this cold climate, but no pain at all.

Today is my 50th birthday, so I composed a poem like this:

OMOIKIYA MISSOULA DE IWOO TANIYOBI

(Translation—Unexpected to celebrate my birthday in Missoula)[a]

If possible, won't you send me a couple of English novels?
Take good care of yourself.

Your husband Iwao Matsushita

117

a. Hanaye's English-language letters were written with help from various scribes.

a. Matsushita's translation.

My Dear Wife,   (NO. 5)   Jan. 10, 1942 .
As I don't receive your letter at all, I worry a
little bit, but wish everything O.K. We had heavy
snow fall + ski boots are now very useful. You
may be worrying about my ankle in this cold climate,
but no pain at all.
Today is my 50th birthday, so I composed a poem
like this :– OMOIKIYA MISSOULA DE IWOO TANJYOBI
(Translation – Unexpected to celebrate my birthday
in Missoula)
If possible, won't you send me a couple of
English novels? Take good care of yourself.
            Your husband,
                Iwao Matsushita

Jan. 10, 1942

Dear Husband:

I received your two letters marked #3 and #4 for which I thank you very much.

I am glad to know that you are comfortable and well. I am very well, too.

I have received Income Tax forms from the Treasury Dept., but as I do not know what your income was last year, I am enclosing two forms for you to fill out. Please fill out one form whichever you think is best. I think Form 1040A is simpler.

Please fill in the space for salary and sign your name on one of the lines. I shall examine the bank books to see what interest we have received during 1941. If you return one signed form to me I shall fill in the rest and take it down to be filed.

If there is anything you wish just let me know and I shall send you whatever I can.

Please be assured that I am very well.

Yours sincerely Hanaye Matsushita

P.S. Kizo Kawasaki sends her regards.

6

Jan. 14, 1942

My dear wife,

On the 10th evening all members of our dormitory held a birthday party for me, having small <u>mochi,</u> or rice cakes, & tangerine oranges. They came from Seattle & were used in celebration for me. Many performances of our friends[a] brightened up the party. It was the first time in my life that my birthday was celebrated by so many warm-hearted friends, & I was very much impressed.

I found a lonesome cat in our compound & it is a funny or rather sad sight to see it busy itself deep in powder snow when it tries to jump across the ground.

Last Sunday I saw a few children ski on the golf course just outside the inclosure & that night I dreamed that I skied on Mt. Rainier. I heard that there is a very good ski ground not far from here.

For a couple of days we had fog & bare branches, wire fences, & everything was covered with frozen fog & it needed artists & poets to portray this beautiful scene. Yesterday we had wonderfully warm sunny days—over 50 degrees.

I worked as a waiter in the dining room & also in the laundry plant one day each as a duty in our self-governing community and found the work interesting.

As I received no letter from you, I wonder if you are well. Take good care of yourself.

Your husband Iwao Matsushita

7

Jan. 17, 1942

My dear wife,

On 15th I received your first letter of 5th (no Reader's Digest yet) & was glad to know that everything is OK with you. We are now accustomed to cold climate. I still have enough money & can buy almost everything here, so you needn't send anything without my request. We

---

a. Correspondents were forbidden by the censor to identify other inmates by name.

don't know how soon we will have hearing.[a] In our dormitory we arise at 7, official roll calls at 8 & 4. We had real <u>udon</u> [macaroni], & <u>takuan</u> [pickles] I'm now in perfect health.

God bless you.

Your husband Iwao Matsushita

| 8

Jan. 20, 1942

My dear wife,

Received Reader's Digest today with many thanks. Enjoying many sunny days—beautiful snow scene. Heard about Hiroshi's illness—best regards. Met Hide's father. Last Sunday we had services by Christian & 2 other religions in the same hall.

I am in perfect health. Take good care of yourself & don't be disturbed by rumors & fakers. I trust everything to your best judgment and management.

Your husband Iwao Matsushita

Jan. 22, 1942

Dear Husband:

Under separate cover, registered, I am sending you your passport and registration card. You say nothing yet about them, but you may need them any time, I suppose.

I will write you again very soon.

Wishing your health earnestly,

Lovingly yours Hanaye Matsushita

P.S. I have just received your post card dated January 10. I have already send out my letters twice. Maybe they will reach you some time soon.

Also, I will forward you an English novel as soon as possible.

a. Loyalty hearings to determine whether detainees should be released, paroled, or interned.

| 9

Jan. 24, 1942

My dear wife,

Your letter #2 dated 10th arrived on 22nd. Income Tax return will be studied & sent back later as March 15th is the last day. Please thank Wataru for the birthday card which also came on 22nd. We have the North American Times[a] and other Seattle papers. Best regards to neighbors, friends, & Kiyo-san.

Take good care of yourself.

Your husband Iwao Matsushita

| 10

Jan. 28, 1942

My Dear Wife,

My passport, & registration card which you sent 22nd arrived today, for which I thank you. Hearing for Seattle detainees are being held here now, but it may take a long time before the decision is reached. Don't be disturbed by rumors & wait patiently. We are having rainy & above freezing weather now. Your book arrived yesterday, but it may take some days before I actually get it, because it must be censored. Don't send anything unless I request it. Take good care of yourself.

Your husband I. Matsushita

| 11

Feb. 2, 1942

My dear wife,

Your letter (typewritten) of 22nd was received on 30th. It takes a considerable time for letters to come & go, but letters are the only things I really appreciate & wait for. For Sunday service yesterday Mr. Smith[a] of Methodist church from California preached in Japanese. Japanese hymn #538 was sung by Michio Ito[b] & I was very much impressed.

a. This was the *Hokubei Jiji*, a Seattle Japanese-language newspaper with an English section. It ceased publication on March 12, 1942, because of the evacuation.

a. Dr. Frank H. Smith was superintendent of the Japanese Methodist churches and former missionary in Japan.

b. Note inconsistency of censor's application of the censorship rules.

Let us try to make the best of this unfortunate circumstances & pray that peace will come soon.

Take good care of yourself.

Your husband I. Matsushita

Feb. 6, 1942

Dear Husband:

Your letters, Nos. 6 and 7, arrived this morning and I am glad to hear your healthy condition. Don't worry about me as I am all right, too.

As you know we must leave our places at least to the east of Columbia River not before long.[a] Sumner and vicinity are prohibited area next to Evacuation area and are not suitable to stay longer. Because of many reasons, there are numerous rumors from time to time. They spread quicker than field fire ear to ear and vanish sooner than spring snow. We are waiting impatiently for the next order by army when and where to go, but don't trouble yourself over the matter. I will manage myself with the aid of friends of mine.

Now I remember that the teller of the Bank of California once advised me to let you know that you can issue the checks there as before you did, so I am sending you a copy of check book for your convenience. The amount is $118.30 for your own use and I will never touch the check for myself. If it is not practical, let me know that. Then I will send you money as much as you want. Anyway I wish to finish the matter before we go away and perhaps out of touch at least for awhile.

Our property and income tax reports are completed already. Be easy over the matter.

Under separate cover, I sent you the copy of The Methodist Hymnal for your daily use. Your summer clothes will follow very soon.

Yours, Hanaye Matsushita

a. Voluntary relocation beyond the exclusion zone, east of the Columbia River, was permitted by the army until March 27, 1942.

Feb. 7, 1942

My dear wife,

Reader's Digest (Feb) was received on 4th. Hide sent me cookies & candies. I sent her a card of thanks. As to "Property Report" which should be filed by Feb. 15th is being referred to Washington D.C. by Mr. N. D. Collaer, the supervisor of this place, how to do. It is impossible for detainees to make correct report without looking at our records at home. But it may be safer for you to notify the authorities in Seattle & explain the situation.

Take good care of yourself & write often.

Your husband I. Matsushita

My Passport #436394. Registration #2718239.

Feb. 11, 1942

Dear Husband:

I have received all your letters to date the last one was #10 and #11 which came together on Feb 9. Please do not write about the weather over there and please send me your signed Income Tax return as I am afraid it might take some time to reach me. We have been working on the alien report of property and assets for the U.S. Treasury Dept.

I am very well so please do not worry about me. I am not lonely as grandma[a] stays with me at night.

Your wife, Hanaye Matsushita

Feb. 16, 1942

Dear Husband:

Please sign the enclosed alien property report all five copies and have it notorized. You may keep one copy but return four copies as soon as possible as the deadline is Feb. 28.

Hanaye Matsushita

a. An elderly friend of the couple.

Feb. 16, 1942

My dear wife,

I am returning herewith by registered mail 1941 Income Tax Return with my signature (Form 1040A). The income I received should be (1) salary etc.—7 months—$1,375.00 (2) interest from 4 banks—$? (3) Amount received from Mitsui & Co. $73 or $75? Total ——? The Bank of California gives no interest. You can find (3) in the Bank of Cal. pass book which was with the check book. I think it was the last entry. This represents the co's partial help for income tax, which should have been received in 1940, but actually received in Nov. or Dec. 1941. If the total does not amount to $1,500—it is not necessary to file a report. If you think you are not very sure what to do, you'd better consult Mr. Iwao Hara, who is a public accountant & a notary public. The return should be notarized. I wish to <u>warn</u> you to read newspapers carefully and observe <u>regulations</u> regarding <u>enemy aliens.</u>

Convey my heartfelt thanks, if possible, to Grace Read,[a] Eldon Griffin,[b] Bushee, who so kindly wrote to the authorities regarding my character & personality for my hearing which was concluded a week ago.

A week ago more Japanese joined us & we expected to see Seattle friends but they went elsewhere.[c] I think of you specially dearly when I wash my woolen underwear, socks, etc by hand instead of sending out to our laundry shop.

Will write again.

Your loving husband Iwao Matsushita

14

Feb. 19, 1942

My dear wife,

It snows during the night, it melts by beautiful & warm sunshine next day—a sea of slush & mud in the afternoon. It freezes again toward

a. A former missionary in Japan, Read joined the army during the war and later served in the Civil Censorship Detachment with the occupation forces in Japan.

b. Matsushita's former colleague at the University of Washington.

c. Probably to Fort Lincoln, North Dakota.

evening—fresh snow next morning. This was our situation ten days ago, but weather changed again with thermometer registering way, way below zero. Frozen fog makes branches beautiful with snow flowers against the azure sky. The sun shines bright—my heart flies into the glittering snowslope which can be seen without obstructions thru the [CENSORED][a]—miles & miles of waving hills with dotted groves here & there. What a scene to look at!

Daily exercise in the early morning, two half-an-hour walks, early retiring made my health perfect.

A book of English novels which arrived on Jan 27th was handed to me on Feb 14th & I am enjoying it now with thanks. We have daily lectures on English, U.S. history, etc. and Sunday service by missionaries in perfect Japanese.

As to "Property Report" we are informed that we should file it, but wait until we are notified how to do it. You may probably have received the form. Read it carefully & make preparation. Take good care of yourself & write _often._

Your loving husband Iwao Matsushita

| 15

Feb. 21, 1942

My dear wife,

I am returning herewith by registered mail 4 copies of "Property Report," signed by me & notarized. If you received these too late, you may explain to the authorities that "Reports" sent from Seattle on 16th was received by Missoula post office on 17th and handed to me on 20th. I noticed a few typographical mistakes which I corrected and added a note which I thought was necessary.

Be careful about _fakers_ who might visit and ask you to do something. Don't act unless you are very sure or until you hear from me. However I

a. Words, phrases, and sentences censored out of Matsushita's letters were either obliterated with indelible black ink after the paper was roughened or cut out with a sharp blade.

trust in you for everything. Use your best judgement. How about your health? I'm 100% healthy.

Your loving husband Iwao Matsushita

P.S. As these reports were notarized late Saturday afternoon, this letter may not go out until Monday or Tuesday. I will send this by <u>special delivery</u>. One copy is being held by me for my file. The hymn book which I picked up Sunday (22nd) had Toku Shimomura's name on the back. Best regards to her.

| 16

Feb. 26, 1942

My dear wife,

I trust you received my registered & special delivery letter, enclosing 4 copies of "Property Report". I heard that Hide called on you & her father even suggested that you may come to Hide's house for summer to kill time by picking peas, etc. if you may stay around Seattle.

More and more are coming here. We still have snow on the ground & everywhere. Beautiful sunshine but cold.

Best regards to our friends.

Your loving husband I. Matsushita

Feb. 26, 1942

My dear Husband:

I have received your letters #12, 13, and 14 and your signed income tax forms for which I thank you very much. I am glad to know that you are well. I, too, have been very well so please do not worry about me. I would like to write you oftener but must rely on others, as you know, I cannot write as often as I like.

You must have received the alien property report which I made out and sent you by registered mail. Mine has been filed already so it does not matter if yours is a little late in coming.

Please take good care of yourself.

Yours affectionately, Hanaye Matsushita

Feb. 27, 1942

My dear Husband:

I received the alien property report which you signed last night by registered mail. Thank you. I shall file it as soon as possible although the deadline has been extended till Mar 14.

Please take good care of yourself.

I am well, so please rest assured.

Yours, Mrs. Hanaye Matsushita

| 17

Feb. 28, 1942

My dear wife,

The other night we were entertained by string quartet of the Italian detainees & we were really entranced by their excellent operatic music, including Madam Butterfly. We know something about Seattle men who were recently picked up. I hope everything will be settled as soon as possible & wish to see old days. I wish to know how you are getting along. Won't you write me sometime & let me know about you & home?

Your loving husband Iwao Matsushita

| 18

March 5, 1942

My dear wife,

I'm worrying about you, for I haven't heard from you for a long time. I'm always very healthy—not a single day have I been in sick bed. It's a pity that I have to let you burden yourself alone with hard problems like evacuation, tax return, property report, etc. Let's be brave & take everything as God's trial to make ourselves worthy of God's children.

If you can send me without much trouble my copy of the world almanac & my medium sized "Standard Dictionary"—black cover with my name printed on it—I'll appreciate your kindness very much, for I am one of the teachers for the English class for the whole detainees. To my surprise I found my former pupil in Takuyama & he gave me a dozen fresh eggs, which came from California.

127

I believe March 9th is your birthday & I regret that I can't celebrate with you, but please remember that my heart is always with you. I like to dedicate the following poem which I composed for your birthday:

> [line in Japanese characters]
> (Translation—700 miles away amidst snow in Missoula,
> I alone celebrate beautiful flower's day of birth)

It is allowed now to write letters in Japanese, so you may do so, if it is more convenient for you. Take good care of yourself and write, <u>please</u>.
Your loving husband Iwao Matsushita

| 19

March 6, 1942
[Translated from Japanese]

Dear Hanaye,

Yesterday, after I mailed you my letter in English, I received your card that was postmarked on February 11. For some reason it took 22 days to reach here. We're permitted to write in Japanese now, so I'm trying it here. Please do the same. I believe March 9th is your birthday. I really regret that I'm not able to share the occasion with you. I've written this verse for you:

> Midst the snows of Missoula 700 miles away
> I celebrate alone my Hana's[a] day of birth.

I ate two sushi and sashimi the other day. Of course, they weren't mess hall fare but something my friend shared with me. I happily relished the morsel as a taste of freedom.

I'm very sorry that you have to cope with all the problems of relocation, taxes, estate reports, etc., by yourself, but I leave them in your good hands.

128

a. Hanaye. Compare the translator's rendition of this poem with Matsushita's own English version in the previous letter.

Please take good care of yourself. I'm extremely well and haven't spent a day in sick bay.

I mentioned this previously in my English letter, but if it's not too much trouble, I'd appreciate it if you can send me my English dictionary (it's the medium-sized one with the black cover with my name inscribed on it), and a two- or three-year-old world almanac. I'm conducting an English class in camp, but I'm in a quandary without texts.

Kiyo-chan must be lonesome. Please give her my regards, and to Grandma, too.

Goodbye, Iwao

| 20

March 9, 1942

[Translated from Japanese]

Dear Hanaye,

Just when I was feeling edgy about not receiving any letter for some time, I rejoiced when your postcards arrived on three consecutive days, on the 5th, 6th, and 7th. I'm relieved that all of your mail is apparently reaching me, even though it takes a long time.

Spring has arrived in Missoula. The snow has melted from the flatlands; the green grasses have begun to show their shoots, and the wild flowers have begun to bloom. Even the birds are chirping. Perhaps this is a site of an ancient river or sea,[a] for polished pebbles are strewn all over and everyone is immersed in collecting these stones, like children.

For your amusement, here's a typical week's menu:

Sun.	Breakfast:	bacon, eggs, creamed potato, raisins
	(no lunch on Sunday)	
	Dinner:	stuffed beef, beans, lettuce, rice, pickled cabbage, pudding
Mon.	Breakfast:	creamed potato, jam
	Lunch:	sandwich, lettuce, rice, applesauce
	Dinner:	pork and beans, radish, salad, raisins

a. Actually, Fort Missoula stood on the 10,000-year-old lake bed of Lake Missoula, which at various times was the size of present-day Lake Ontario and more than 1,000 feet deep.

Tues:	Breakfast:	mush, apricot
	Lunch:	meatballs, rice, lettuce, pickle
	Dinner:	bologna, spaghetti, pickles, peas, pudding
Wed:	Breakfast:	bran flakes, jam
	Lunch:	boiled beef, rice, lettuce, *takuan*
	Dinner:	salted mackerel, pickles, rice, peas, jello
Thu:	Breakfast:	cornmeal, prunes
	Lunch:	salted pork and cabbage, beans, lettuce
	Dinner:	meatballs, rice, pickles, prunes
Fri:	Breakfast:	bran flakes, jam
	Lunch:	cod fish, lettuce, rice
	Dinner:	liver, onion, lettuce, pudding
Sat:	Breakfast:	mush, raisins
	Lunch:	curry-rice, salad, peach
	Dinner:	wiener, sauerkraut, rice, figs

Naturally, in addition, there is bread at each meal, coffee in the morning, and tea with the other meals. Sugar has been rationed since February 19th. For a light eater like myself, my ration is more than ample.

I believe today is your birthday. I can't send you anything but my sincere best wishes as I gaze to the west. Please give my regards to our friends. Won't you please try writing in Japanese, too? You must have lots of things to worry about. Please take care.

Goodbye, Iwao

| 21

March 13, 1942

My Dear Wife,

"The Methodist Hymnal" which arrived a few days ago was handed to me today & I thank you very much. Spring is here now, & we hear meadow larks singing. It is said that more Japanese are coming here soon. Everybody here is worrying about evacuation problem, but I think you should act according to the government instructions. Health comes first, so take good care of yourself.

Your loving husband, Iwao Matsushita

22

March 17, 1942

My dear wife,

Your letter dated 6th with check book was received today. I still have enough money,[a] so please don't bother about it. If you have not sent summer clothes yet, please do not send <u>too much</u>, but I will appreciate if you will send a pair of suspenders with metal clasps (x),[b] a leather belt (old one), a few packages of razor blades, <u>or</u> a blade holder (▲)[b] both I kept in the bath room cabinet, so that I can sharpen old blades.

It pains me very much when I think that you have to do everything for evacuation without my help. But I leave everything to your best judgment. Consult your best friends & go with them if you will be allowed to do so. Take good care of yourself & best regards to our dear friends.

Your loving husband Iwao Matsushita

March 19, 1942

Dear Husband:

Your letter arrived yesterday morning and feel happy to hear your healthy condition.

According to your request, I forward you the Standard Dictionary and World Almanac under separate cover and hope to reach you safely.

We are still waiting for the next evacuation order by army. I do not decide yet where to go, but don't worry. I will manage the matter for myself.

Spring is here and garden flowers are blooming. I will write you again very soon.

Yours, Hanaye

23

March 20, 1942

My dear wife,

I am sending back to you under separate cover today by registered mail a power of attorney and auto title, duly signed & notarized. I

---

a. Detainees could purchase comfort items from a canteen.
b. Matsushita here inserted parenthetical marks keyed to small sketches he made below.

received these from Hide yesterday and appreciate her sincere kindness very, very much.

According to Mr. S. Watanabe,[a] a Seattle lawyer in the same dormitory, it will be very convenient for you in the future if you will register this power of attorney at the King County Auditor's office (charge may be 25¢) before you use this original. Then you can get copies of this power of attorney whenever you require same for other purposes. This power of attorney gives you all my power & you can act anything instead of me.

As to my auto, you may sell it or whatever you may think advisable to dispose of.

Please give my very best regards to Hide & Kiyo & those real friends who render you such help that you need most now.

Take good care of yourself. I'm in A1 condition.

Your loving husband, Iwao Matsushita

March 23, 1942

[Translated from Japanese]

To my husband: . . .

I received your letters marked 18, 19, and 20. I received your letter #20 this morning. All have arrived safely. I saw your poems in the newspaper.[a] Thank you very much for the birthday poem.

Depending on the situation, I may want to sell the car. I'm sure you are worried about me, but I continue to live in the house without incident, and everyone is being most helpful.

I may be evacuated soon, but please, please don't worry. Things will work out somehow. Everyone seems to be making visits, and I'll try to visit somehow (provided I receive permission) if you're feeling up to it. Let me know right away. Are you in need of money? . . .

God and Christ will protect you, so put everything in their hands. I'll continue to write regularly. Things are extremely busy here now, but don't worry about a thing. I pray for your safety.

Hanaye

a. This name, according to censorship regulations, should have been excised, but inconsistencies in what was removed by censors throughout the war abound.

a. Probably the *Great Northern Daily News* (Seattle, Wash.).

Mrs. Hanaye Matsushita   March 26th, 1942
905 - 24th ave So.   Yo Dormitory #24
Seattle, Wash.   Fort Missoula,
                                     Missoula, Montana

My dear wife,

     Spring is here, + birds are singing, but the
air is still chilly in the morning. It is very
invigorating to have walks early morning.

     Thank you for an abdomen belt which I
received from Mr. Okawa, + I am glad to hear
from Mr. Nimura that you are physically well
now. As I told you before, I am 100 %
healthy + my teaching occupies my mind and
keep me interested all the time. The Standard
Dictionary + the World Almanac arrived already
but still they are being held for censor, + I expect
to have them in a few days. I am now the
most popular teacher, having classes 3 times a
week, + more than ▮ students. We call this
school "the Missoula University."

     Take good care of yourself + best regards
to our friends.
                     Your loving husband,

                     Iwao Matsushita

(Letter #24)

24

March 26, 1942

My dear wife,

Spring is here, & birds are singing, but the air is still chilly in the morning. It is very invigorating to have walks early morning.

Thank you for an abdomen belt which I received from Mr. Okawa, & I am glad to hear from Mr. Mimbu that you are physically well now. As I told you before, I am 100% healthy & my teaching occupies my mind and keeps me interested all the time. The Standard Dictionary & the World Almanac arrived already but still they are being held for censor, & I expect to have them in a few days. I am now the most popular teacher, having classes 3 times a week, & more than [CENSORED] students. We call this school "the Missoula University."

Take good care of yourself & best regards to our friends.

Your loving husband Iwao Matsushita

25

March 31, 1942

My dear wife,

Thank you for a pair of new hiking boots, and another pair of old golf shoes. They will be very convenient for my daily walks. I received a letter from Sumi yesterday & Hide's father told me that according to her letter you are ready. I'm sorry that I couldn't help you. Take care of yourself.

Your husband Iwao Matsushita

March 31, 1942

My dear wife,

Thank you for April number of Reader's Digest & Federal Citizenship Textbook. I heard Hide's going to Colorado from father & received some nuts from Hide through Mr. Kashio's hands. All my friends here are well. We have real spring now.

Hope you & your friends are healthy.

Your husband Iwao Matsushita

[Translated from Japanese]

To my husband:

I received your letters marked 21, 22, and 23. They all arrived safely. And I received the car and assets trust letters. Thank you. Last week by train I sent one box of oranges, a suitcase, and shoes packed in a shoe box along with a dictionary and the Reader's Digest (the April issue). Sueko [?] left for Denver (alone) on the 29th (Sunday). She said that she may see you. Wouldn't it be great if you were able to see each other?

I'm sure you're worried about my evacuation, but with the help of everyone here I'll be able to take care of things, although at this point I don't even know when the evacuation may occur. I'm trying to plan what to do with our belongings and will let you know once I've decided. The landlord has been kind enough to let us pay the rent at a later date, and we can leave our belongings behind if we get permission from the government office. I've also decided to sell the car once I get permission. I'll put the money in the bank immediately. The person who will be moving in here can probably take care of the cat. . . .

Have you seen Mr. Tsutakawa? His wife has been most helpful. Please give him my thanks. Everyone you know is fine. Summy's mother has also been a great help. . . .

Continue to pray to God. Adieu.

Hana

| 27

April 2, 1942

My dear wife,

Yesterday I received your letter dated 19th of March, and am glad to know that you are well. We know about the evacuation by the newspapers & thru radio & worry very much, because we can't help our dear folks at home.

Please accept my sincerest thanks for a crate of oranges & a suitcase of summer clothings & various articles. Oranges were distributed in the same dormitory & to Okawa, Izui, Mimbu, Sato, etc. Oranges were specially appreciated by everybody, because we have never seen such beautiful & large ones before in this place.

When I thought that every article in the suitcase was handled by you with the fondest love and thoughtfulness, I was deeply moved. When I think that you will have to go some place without me, I can't feel but very sad. But this is God's will, & God will never forsake us. So be brave & take best care of yourself. We will meet again sometime somewhere. God bless all of us!

Your loving husband Iwao Matsushita

| 28

April 5, 1942

My dear wife,

Today is Easter Sunday. We have erected a huge cross in front of our dormitory & painted it white. We got up at 6 o'clock & had a service at 7 o'clock in front of this cross. We even had Easter lilies. Many small birds, puppies, and even distant chanticleers joined us in singing.

I never had such impressive Easter service before in my life, perhaps because the surrounding snow-tipped mountains & fresh, brisk morning air of the high plateau added to the atmosphere.

Tears rolled down when we say hymn No. [CENSORED]. Three brothers were baptized by an American pastor. Let us have renewed faith in Christ & trust in God who will never fail us.

Today I changed all my clothes to the new ones which you so kindly sent to me. Wearing a new pair of hiking boots, I had a usual daily walk, & composed many poems on Easter.

Take good care of youself; as for me, I am 100% healthy.

Your loving husband Iwao Matsushita

April 7, 1942

Dear Husband:

Please sign on the included notes and send them back to me at your earliest convenience. I will take care of the payment for you promptly.

We don't hear yet about the date and destination of our evacuation, but it will be very soon, we suppose.

Our house owner is very kind to me and everything is progressing smoothly. I am going to sell our auto and the negotiation is almost completed. Don't worry over the matters.

Lovingly yours, Hanaye Matsushita

P.S. I will write you again very soon.

| 29

April 8, 1942

My dear wife,

Your Japanese letter dated March 23rd was received today via air mail, & I am very glad to know that you are mentally & physically well. Kiyo-chan wrote me yesterday & I wrote her back.

Please do not come to see me & don't bother about money. A part of the detainees here is being moved somewhere else,[a] but I still stay here. However, we can't tell the future, we only follow the government's order just like you will.

The snow on the mountains is almost gone. We see green on the slope which was covered with snow a month ago. Meadow larks are singing & we see golfers outside the camp ground.

We were surprised & sorry when we learned from the newspaper Mrs. Okamura's death.

Please take good care of yourself & be strong in body & mind, & leave everything to our Heavenly Father. Best regards to our friends.

Your loving husband Iwao Matsushita

| 30

April 11, 1942

My dear wife,

Your 2nd Japanese letter with list of goods in the suitcase (4/1) & Easter card were received on 9th & I'm glad to know that you are all well. Please tell Kiyo-chan that Kato-san was moved from here. How about my insurance payment in May? Ask West Coast Ins. Co. & do whatever should be done. Now you have all power to act for me by

137

---

a. To the army's internment compound at Camp Livingston, Louisiana.

that power of attorney I sent to you the other day. Take good care of yourself.

Your husband Iwao Matsushita

April 11, 1942

Dear Husband:

We are still in Seattle, waiting for the Army's next order which will be very soon.

Under separate cover, I am sending you the following articles for your future use:

1. Summer hat	1
2. Razor blades	6 packages
3. Blade holder	1
4. Shaving cream	1 tube
5. Cotton kimono (after bath)	1
6. Cotton belt (the same use)	1
7. Belts (new and old)	2
8. Suspenders	1
9. Mosquito cream	2 tubes
10. Chocolate	2 boxes

Somebody need dictionaries in your fort, I was told. So I send you a few copies, though they are very old. If they are out of use, just throw them away please.

Lovingly yours, Hanaye Matsushita

| 31

April 15, 1942

My dear wife,

Yesterday I received a package from you & it contained a hat, suspenders, a blade holder, kisses, a night gown, belts, etc., for which kindly accept my sincere thanks. The dictionary was held for inspection; if it has no writings or underlinings[a] I will get it later.

138

a. Censors suspected that such markings might contain hidden messages.

Today's radio broadcasts that the evacuation order has been issued for some part of Seattle[b] & I think you will be moved sooner or later. Go together with your best friends if it is permitted to do so. Keep yourself mentally & physically fit, trusting in God all the time.

There is no change since I wrote you on 11th. My health is 100% perfect. I trust that you told Kiyo that Mr. Kato was moved somewhere else.[c] All Seattle friends are all right. So much for today.

Your loving husband Iwao Matsushita

| 32

April 17, 1942

My dear wife,

Yesterday I received your letter of 7th, enclosing insurance premium and dividend notices. I signed the dividend notice & return herewith. I think by the power of attorney I have sent, you have the full power to act for me, & it is not necessary for you to send everything for me to sign. However you may ask some lawyer about this matter.

I received a small Webster's dictionary, and four other are being held as they are marked inside. I received a copy of the New York Times (Sunday Edition) direct from the publisher[a] & it seems as if you have subscribed for me for one year. I appreciate your kindness very much.

I suppose you are very busy & uneasy as the evacuation draws near. Please do not overburden yourself & be careful about your health. Best regards to Wataru & others.

Your loving husband Iwao Matsushita

P.S. When you evacuate, don't forget to advise the insurance co. & all other places the change of address.

---

b. He refers to a general announcement. Details of specific areas to be evacuated were not made public for another week.

c. Kato went to Camp Livingston. Censorship regulations prohibited disclosure of camp destinations.

a. Inmates could receive both Japanese- and English-language publications, but only if sent directly from the publisher, thus avoiding possible alterations and secret messages from being inserted.

April 20, 1942

Dear Husband:

Your letter No. 31 just arrived this morning and thank you very much. Our evacuation seems to be very soon, but I was obliged to move to Summy's[a] residence because of unavoidable reason. Our house owner promised to take care of the books and furniture. Be ease over the matter. Later I will write you the details.

Kiyo's husband came back the other day and yesterday I met him for the first time.

Uncle Doc[a] is with me. We will move together with Summy's family, someday somewhere.

Yours, Hanaye

| 33

April 21, 1942

My dear wife,

We have glorious days, but high peaks are still snow capped. Received a notice from Reader's Digest that you have subscribed for me. Notice from Insurance Co. says that my <u>accident</u> insurance was cancelled which I think can't be helped. Take good care of yourself.

Your husband Iwao Matsushita

| 34

April 24, 1942

My dear wife,

Your post card of 20th arrived yesterday. I hope this will reach you before the 28th, your evacuation day. Please remember me to Summy's family and Doc, who must have helped you a lot & will help you in the future. May God bless you and all your friends, very dear to you.

Health must be your first consideration.

Your husband Iwao Matsushita

a. Ishibashi

a. Doctor Kyo Koike

April 26, 1942

Dear Husband:

Your letter No. 33 arrived to me safely and I am glad to hear your healthy condition.

The time of our evacuation had come at last. I am moving, with Dr. Koike, to Camp Harmony, Puyallup, the coming Tuesday, April 28. He is one of advanced party and expect to take his part at the Camp Hospital. Please be ease about me as he will live with me and watch me all the time.

I paid already to the West Coast Life Insurance Co. for you.

Now I am extremely busy for the preparation to move. When I am settled there, I am sure to let you know the details. Dr. Ishibashis are in the second or third party, leaving Seattle next Friday.

Lovingly yours, Hanaye Matsushita

| 35

April 28, 1942

Mrs. Hanaye Matsushita
A-3-112
Camp Harmony
Puyallup, Wash.

My dear wife,

Your air mail of 26th arrived today, and I am very glad to find out the improved mail service nowadays. My letter #34 addressed to Ishibashi's[a] might have arrived after you left. I'm very glad to know that you are with Dr. Koike.

As we can write a short letter to Japan thru the kindness of American Red Cross & thru Geneva, Switzerland, I'm going to write to my brother. I don't know how long it will take, but I will try it anyway.[b]

a. When the evacuation was announced, Hanaye and Dr. Koike moved in with their friends, the Ishibashis. Their teenage son, Wataru, corresponded with Matsushita and provided Hanaye with many kindnesses throughout her period of internment.

b. His twenty-five-word message, sent April 30, reached Sekio six months later. The reply arrived at Fort Missoula in December 1943; total elapsed time to complete the circuit, nineteen months.

141

This morning I started to make a small pendant out of a chocolate colored oval stone for your necklace, but you have to wait until the time we meet again to get it.

Take good care of yourself, & give my best regards to Dr. Koike & other friends.

Your loving husband, Iwao Matsushita

P.S. The date of my arrival here & that of your evacuation is same,ᶜ this is quite a coincidence.

April 29, 1942

Puyallup Assembly Center

Dear Husband:

We came here to Puyallup about 11 am yesterday, April 28, as one of advanced party. We were very much fortunate and treated differently from the others. Our baggages were carried out by the Army, directly from our home. Others were obliged to handle their belongings themselves to the gathering places. We were allowed to travel freely, separate from the group, in the private car driven by a white woman and welcomed by Rev. Norton at the camp.

Our new quarters are located at the end of a wooden building, on Allen Street, Camp Harmony. The room is wide enough supposedly for four persons, but we will live here just two alone until you should come back some day. We are expecting Mr. & Mrs. Kashima, our mountain friends, to be the nearest neighbor, but they does not arrive yet. We don't know yet where Ishibashis will live. They will arrive here within a few days.

I am a little too much tired, but I am sure I can live here all right. Just imagine a mountain camp. When the sky is clear, we will see our holy Mt. Rainier, I suppose.

We don't settled yet and our belongs are in confusion all over in the room. Perhaps it takes a week or ten days to arrange everything.

Here in our room, there are two Army cots and a stove for wood. Today we are expecting to get a table, a broom and bucket, and blankets may follow very soon.

c. December 28, April 28.

Our house owner was very kind to me. He allowed to keep our things in the basement safely. The new tenants are just married young couple and promised to take care of Blacky.[a]

I will write you again very soon.

Lovingly yours, Hanaye Matsushita

| 36

May 1, 1942

My dear wife,

Your airmail of April 29th arrived today, & I'm very glad you have safely arrived there. I can picture your camp in that familiar Fair Ground. We read so much about your camp in newspapers & saw pictures of evacuation. I can feel how tired you are after so many days of preparations and how you felt when you left that house where we lived together so long. I'm glad to know that the house owner will take care of our things in the basement & Blacky will be taken care of by a new tenant.

It seems that your camp is similar to ours. We have [CENSORED] army cots in one dormitory & have a coal stove beside modern heating system, the latter was installed a couple of months ago.

The other day we had an evening of entertainment by fellow detainees in a recreation hall, which is large enough for over 1,000 people. [CENSORED] did a comic dance, wearing a gorgeous costume painted by Mr. [CENSORED]. He is enjoying himself & others by painting pictures.

We have dandelions, buttercups, shooting stars, spring beauties, & a couple more wild flowers, but they are all pygmy kind, presumably because of the high elevation. [CENSORED] So much for today.

Take good care of yourself & best regards to Dr. Koike & other friends who are dear to us.

Your husband Iwao Matsushita

a. The couple's cat.

May 6, 1942

Dear Husband:

We live in A District which is the parking ground for Puyallup Fair. There are eleven avenues and the main street between the camps and mess halls is called Burma Road.

Dandelions on the ground are still blooming. Boys are playing baseball or football on the back ground of our room.[a]

About our food, fresh vegetables will served very soon, it is said. My appetite is very good, rather better than usual.

We govern ourselves in the camp and more Seattle Japanese are coming very soon. The conditions are improving by and by.

Our nearest neighbor is Mr. & Mrs. Kashima, living in the next room. Dr. & Mrs. Ishibashi also live in the same district, but five avenues away.

After severe rain, the sky became clear and we saw Mt. Rainier over the hill yesterday for the first time. Camp in name is just the same, but our feeling absolutely differ from the mountain's.

Your letter No. 36 arrived today and I am very glad to hear you are healthy. Never mind about me. I am sure I can stand in the present conditions. There is no canteen yet in the ground, but we can buy almost everything from the outside, even a soda or ice cream.[b]

I am waiting for the pendant you promised.

Now the sun is down, sky is cloudy and breeze is coming through the window.

The room is becoming dark and I will put light soon. Good sleep, dear.

Lovingly yours, Hanaye Matsushita

| 37

May 7, 1942

My dear wife,

The spring is here, but the leaves are just coming out of trees. It is rather warm in the afternoon, but we have frost in the morning. The high peaks are still covered with snow.

144

a. The assembly center consisted of four separate and enclosed areas. Only Area A appears to have had sufficient space available for such team sports.

b. Purchases were made from outside vendors through holes in the fence.

By your thoughtfulness I am receiving N.Y. Times Sunday Edition & Reader's Digest & am enjoying them very much. I sincerely appreciate your kindness.

The other day we enjoyed another evening of musical entertainment by Italian detainees & this time ten musicians participated.

I'm glad to learn from friends here that you have good neighbors in your camp.

I have made several pendants & paper weights already. The English school is still going on, and the students are very much interested in my teaching. I was given a dollar watch the other day for the trouble of teaching.[a] My health is A1. Please take good care of yourself & your room mate.

Your husband Iwao Matsushita

| 38

May 13, 1942

[Translated from Japanese]

Dear Hanaye,

A few days ago we had a typical Montana electrical storm. It reminded me of the fearsome thunderstorm we encountered on the highway on the way to Glacier Park in 1940. Do you remember it?

It's been mostly cloudy and rainy for several days, and occasionally I can see snow on the mountains.

I received your letter on the 9th, which you mailed on the 6th from Puyallup [Assembly Center]. I'm glad that you're well. I'm in very good health, too. Recently I've been singing in a trio at Sunday service with Mr. Kanazawa and Mr. Sato.

To the west of this camp is a mountain called the Lolo Mountain, soaring to a height of perhaps eight or nine thousand feet. It is still cloaked in snow that glitters when it's bathed in the rays of the morning sun. To the north is a Mount Fuji–like spire called Squaw Peak. This peak appears to be quite high because I can see it glisten white. I frequently recall beloved Mount Rainier. Though the mountains here are different in that they are gently undulating, there's no

145

---

a. Matsushita received no pay for teaching while at Fort Missoula.

question that we're blessed by the beauty of the scenery which soothes my soul.

Puyallup must be bustling with the influx of people. You'll probably undergo some physical adjustment and feel unsettled in your new surroundings, but I'm sure you'll become used to it in time. You needn't be too concerned since a doctor will always be available. When it is all said and done, one's health is of the prime importance.

Please give my regards to all.

Sayonara, Iwao

| 39

May 20, 1942
[Translated from Japanese]

Dear Hanaye,

I haven't heard from you in awhile, but I trust that you are fine. I'll ask Mr. Fukano in detail about you. I'm healthy as usual.

The lilacs in the camp are displaying their purple blossoms, and the white flowers that Mr. Ito planted are also in bloom. The sweet peas should be blossoming soon as well. Time passes so swiftly that soon it'll be summer. A few days ago as the snow melted and the ground could be seen, stone picking began in earnest. People have polished or shaped the stones, and there have been some remarkable specimens produced. So avid is this stone picking that it is said that anyone not involved in this hobby is not human. They have even come to organize a stone exhibition for which about 200 specimens have been entered for display. I submitted a monogrammed watch fob that I painstakingly made from a round piece of river stone.

I composed a "Stone-Picker's Song," which has become quite popular. I wrote it to the tune of the *Kusatsu Bushi*:

> Long, long ago where water stood in Missoula
> The captive tenants, oh what carefree stone-pickers they were,
> Squatting on the roadside on way to each meal, picking stones I saw.
> From morn 'tis day, can in hand, the ebb tide gatherers dig with glee.
> Dig they do, and small, colored and round ones endlessly they appear.

Rolling stones from ages past, shiny ones tho oft I see, wish I could a diamond find.

Up in the morn, chores done, I sit on my bed to polish my stones,
Gritty dust gathers all over as Spring goes past.

Goodbye, Iwao Matsushita

May 21, 1942

Dear Husband:

The other day we moved from Area A to Area D—Hospital Center—though the hospital is not opened yet. Area D is located in the Western Fair Ground.[a]

Almost all Seattle Japanese are moved in Camp Harmony here, it seems,[b] but we don't know how long to stay.

Spring is deep, but the weather is unsettled here. Garden flowers are blooming one by one, but we have seldom chance to see them.

This is only to let you know our change address. Later I will tell the details.

I heard from Mrs. Izui[c] that you are very popular for teaching English and I am heartily delighted.

Lovingly yours, Hanaye Matsushita

| 40

May 23, 1942

My dear wife,

I sent to you today a parcel containing stones as follows:

   1—semi-circle red—polished
   1—natural stone—mountain painted
   1—oblong green—polished
   1—small white—like a bird's egg
   1—small green—wave-like design
   1—string of necklace pendants

a. Areas A, B, and C were located on adjacent parking lots.
b. On May 21 the camp population stood at 7,374, 16 short of its peak population, reached four days later.
c. Mrs. Izui's husband was detained with Matsushita at Fort Missoula.

a.—white   b.—green striped   c.—tiny chocolate color
flower painted   d.—blue—cross embossed (took me half a
day to make this cross)

I didn't send the pendant mentioned before because I like to hand this
direct from my own hand. Be careful about the holes of the pendants,
because if you force something thru them you might chip them. You
may see other stones sent by our friends here to your neighbors.

Take good care of yourself and Doc, & best regards to your neighbors
& friends.

Your husband Iwao Matsushita

May 25, 1942
[Translated from Japanese]

Dear Hanaye,

I received your airmail of the 22nd on the 23rd. Lately the mail
service has improved greatly. Did you get my message about the change
of address[a] and the stones I sent you? We've been having occasional
heavy thunderstorms that turn the landscape into a veritable lake. We're
happy when that happens because the stones are washed to the surface
and we can find them easily.

For your amusement herewith is the recent menu:

Sun.	Breakfast:	boiled eggs, bacon, cornmeal, jam
	Dinner:	roast beef, rice, cake, jello
Mon.	Breakfast:	cornflakes, jam
	Lunch:	stew, corn, rice, pickled scallions
	Dinner:	pork and beans, beets, prunes
Tue.	Breakfast:	cream of wheat, apple sauce
	Lunch:	halibut, beans, rice, *takuan*
	Dinner:	liver and bacon, potato, apple pie
Wed.	Breakfast:	mush, jam
	Lunch:	hamburger, lettuce, rice, sauerkraut
	Dinner:	cold cuts, orange, pickles, corn, macaroni

a. Matsushita moved to a different barrack after the camp population declined.

Thu.	Breakfast:	cornflakes, raisins
	Lunch:	boiled meat, rice, beets
	Dinner:	meatballs, rice, pickles, prunes
Fri.	Breakfast:	cornmeal, jam
	Lunch:	salmon, spinach, rice, pickled cabbage
	Dinner:	stew, lettuce, rice, figs
Sat.	Breakfast:	mush, raisins
	Lunch:	stew, tomato juice, pickled cabbage
	Dinner:	*somen* [thin wheat noodles], beans, orange

There'll be people transferring to other camps,[a] and I don't know what the future holds. But let us be steadfast in our faith, and no matter where we may be, trust in the Lord and pray for peace and the day we can be together again.

Your health is of the utmost importance. Please give my regards to all. Goodbye, Iwao

| 42

June 2, 1942
[Translated from Japanese]

Dear Hanaye,

I've been waiting anxiously to hear from you, but I haven't received any word, not even an acknowledgement that you received my "song" or the stones I sent you. Mr. Fukano and others have received their letters a week ago. According to a letter from your camp, my stones apparently have reached you, but since I don't have direct word from you I'm worried.

I hear that many in your camp have become ill, and I'm concerned that you are busy at the hospital or that you yourself have gotten sick.[a]

Letters are the sole comfort and assurance when we are far apart like we are. I realize that you aren't an ardent letter writer, but please write at least once a week.

a. Army internment camps.

a. Intestinal upsets resulting from improper food handling in the central kitchen were common.

It's OK to write in Japanese.

I'm pretty well informed about the situation in your camp. You're not certain how long you'll be there, are you?

We are having excellent weather to complement the greenery of this place. Up ahead on the hillside pasture I can see animals (can they be sheep?) grazing, and to the rear I can still see the glimmer of snow on the mountain peaks.

I don't know what tomorrow will bring, but that has to be left up to fate. I don't know when it will be, but I know for certain we'll be united again.

So until then let's keep healthy, live our faith, and persevere. I pray that the Lord's blessing will be upon you.

Please give my regards to Doc and others.

Goodbye, Iwao

| 43

June 6, 1942
Mrs. Hanaye Matsushita
D-4-97
Camp Harmony
Puyallup, Wash.

My dear wife,

This week is passing again without hearing from you, & I feel very uneasy. There must be some reason why you don't write. According to letters from your camp to our friends here, I have no doubt that you received my stones, because they request their husbands to send stones like I sent to you.

Last night we had another evening of entertainment & my song of "Picking Stones" was sung by many friends and the whole audience joined & made a big hit because that song describes everybody's present camp life.

Mr. Okawa again was a master performer by his skilful dance with five fans & his famous "Hundred Faces." A few days ago I received two crates of celery from Spokane, ordered by you, & I distributed them not only in our own dormitory, but also among Seattle people, & they appreciated the vegetable very much, as they were so crisp & tender. I was advised by Spokane shipper that they sent one crate each of celery & lettuce, but both were celery, & it was better that way, for we have lettuce on our menu very often.

Mr. Kawasaki wrote me & I will answer him soon.

Take good care of yourself & Doc, & best regards to all.

Your husband Iwao Matsushita

| 44

My dear wife,

Well, I'm still here safe & sound, and I hope you are still there safe & sound, too. I hear much about conditions in your camp & sympathize with you for hardships you have to endure.

Last Sunday we had another exhibition of stones & other things made with scanty tools here, but it was a wonderful affair & everybody enjoyed it. I composed another song called "Stone Digging Song."

Last night I made a lecture on "How to enjoy mountains" & some persons asked me to talk more about mountains. The World Almanac you so kindly sent to me is a great help now for my English teaching & lectures. I am enjoying Readers Digest & also the New York Times. They help me a lot.

We still have snow on high peaks, but green covers everything. We have some flowers, too. Meadow larks are singing, and sparrows are prettier than those in Seattle. So long for today.

Yours ever, Iwao Matsushita

| 45

My dear wife,

Yesterday I received a very interesting letter from Shigeko for the first time & was very glad to know that she saw you many times in Seattle. Her sister, Chiyoko might have seen you in your camp, too. All reports that you are all right, so I think the fact that you don't write is the sign of your normal life of old days when you never wrote even to your parents. Don't feel that you are obliged to write, but do as you please. Take it easy, thinking of your health first. That is most important.

We are permitted again to write a longer letter to Japan through another channel,[a] and I will write again. The other day a N.Y.K.[b] man left for New York to sail on to Japan,[c] & I asked him to see Tsuyoshi-san.

Many more wild flowers are coming up in the camp ground, the sky is blue with white clouds, birds and crickets are chirping, & all is well with the world.

Will you please thank Doc. again for his interesting letter & his care for you?

Yours ever Iwao Matsushita

| 46

My dear wife,

I saw a copy of "News-Letter"[a] published in your camp & found it very interesting, as it announced funerals, weddings, etc. I learned from letters received by my friends here from their families that you have been molested by rainy weather & accordingly the sea of mud. We had that in March when the snow on the ground began to melt.

Our kittens are growing rapidly & they are so cute and innocent that we wish to be like them. The ladies in your camp who don't receive stones from their husbands here write "Why don't you send some like the others?" A nisei boy whose father wrote him "we have stone fever here" asked the doctor seriously what kind of fever that was, & the doctor, not knowing what it meant, said, "I never heard of that before, but it must be some kind of epidemic."

I'm writing this now, looking at Lolo Mountain, white with snow & glistening in the morning sunshine. The following is one of my recent hokku poems:

---

a. Inmates in Justice Department camps were permitted to write letters up to twenty-four lines in length to family members. Inmates in assembly centers and WRA centers, however, could send only occasional, twenty-five-word messages, through Red Cross channels.

b. *Nippon Yusen Kaisha* Steamship Company

c. The first voyage of the exchange ship, S.S. *Gripsholm* to Asia left New York harbor in June 1942, with nearly 1,500 repatriates aboard.

a. Camp Harmony *News Letter*

LOLO ZAN NO YUKI WO UTSUSU YA KUMO-NO MINE.
(Translation) Mountain of clouds reflect the snow of Lolo Mtn.[a]

So much for today.
Your loving husband Iwao Matsushita

| 47
                                    July 2, 1942
My dear wife,
    Until the end of last week, we had quite a long spell of rainy days,
reported to be unusual around here but this week has brought real
summer weather, having warmer days. However it is cool in the morning
& after sundown. Even in the afternoon, we have breezes, so it isn't so
bad, if we keep ourselves outside.
    Poppies, bachelor buttons, sweet-peas, & other plants which grew out
of seeds are now beginning to bloom around barracks. Trees have thick
foliage & it is real summer in every sense. We see many Italians basking
in the sun, stripped everything but shorts—sometimes short of shorts.
We see white cumulus clouds tumbling over dark blue mountain tops
against the azure sky. Now you can picture this glorious scenery in your
mind, can't you?
    The following poems are for Doc to criticize:

    MONTANA YA UCHIWA NO HOSHIKI KINO KYO
    (Translation) Montana needs fans yesterday & today.

    TSUMA OKURISHI UCHIWA YAKUTATSU YUGEDOKI
    (Translation) Fan sent by wife became useful at dinner time.

Please take good care of yourself & Doc.
Yours ever, Iwao Matsushita

153

a. Matsushita's translation

July 2, 1942

Dear Husband:

Summer came here at last. For three days the temperature in my room reached 102 degrees. It is rather unusual, I guess.

I neglected to write you for a long while, but please do not scold me. You know what I am thinking in my mind.

Enclosed find the Claim, for which your sign, notarized, is needed. Please forward the claim with your passport to <u>the Sumitomo Bank of Seattle</u>, directly. The passport of mine is in their hand at present.

I don't know where we are moving. At the same time I feel uneasy about your future. Be ease about me. I am somewhat nervous, but my health is well and sound.

Your letter about stones was delayed, but received the stones already. I like them very much and will keep them safely. I heard about stones which other people have send to their families, but I have no chance to see them yet.

I wish your place is not too hot for your health. I will write you again very soon, but don't wait, as I am not sure myself.

Lovingly yours, Hanaye Matsushita

| 48

July 10, 1942

My dear wife,

Thank you very much for your letter with a copy of "Proof of Claim", which, after being signed by me & notarized, will be forwarded direct to the Sumimoto Bank, with my passport.[a]

Well, we have a spell of hot weather now, but we have a large electric fan which keeps the air in the room moving, and ice-cold water is always ready at the faucet, thanks, maybe, to the snow fields and glaciers of the Glacier Park.

Yesterday a bunch of us were taken to the Missoula river[b] which runs near our camp as a special reward for some work done for the place, and

154

a. This paper work was evidently an attempt to reclaim deposits impounded by the government in the Japanese bank.

b. Bitterroot River.

[CENSORED] & I took off shoes & waded thru the water. A few small trouts flitted around my bare feet. Tall trees like cottonwood decorated both banks & reminded me the days we enjoyed together at the Cedar River. This was the first time I ever went out & touched the raw nature in my life here.

I receive many letters now from friends in your camp and also from those who were here before, but now moved elsewhere. Take good care of yourself & best regards to Doc. and Wataru's family if you ever see them.

Yours ever Iwao Matsushita

July 15, 6 a.m.
[Translated from Japanese]

To my husband:

Monday I received your letter. Thank you so much. I'm glad that your letters of late seem to be arriving quickly and safely. I'm glad to hear that your health is good. I'm doing well. I want to write more often but my eyesight seems to be going. It's probably my age. My nerves are also on edge, and when I take up a pen my heart leaps into my throat and I can't write. Forgive me. I've really gotten old and embarrassingly weak-spirited. Every day keeps me busy, with little free time to do what I want.

Uncle is as you left him although he has experienced some difficulties as well.

Please know that I'm working as hard as I can. I continue to pray to God that we will see each other as soon as possible. I'm overwhelmed with thoughts of how you spend each day. While I realize that I need to stay level-headed, it's depressing to feel as though I have to take care of everything myself. I've come to know the people next door and that helps, but I still spent the last two weeks in tears.

My neighbors on both sides are doctors. Do you know Dr. Kato from Tacoma? He lives next door. Lillian married Jack and moved in with him. Their quarters are in Area C, so we don't see much of each other. Wataru's place is in Area A, so I hardly ever see him either.[a]

a. Movement from one area to another required passes, and numerous restrictions applied. Passes were issued rarely, if ever, for personal visitations.

Since I didn't know a soul when I arrived after Uncle, I was constantly on the verge of tears and lost weight until I was nothing but skin and bones, but recently I've been trying to get over my loneliness and have gained some weight. . . . I'm not ill so don't worry. I have so many stories to tell you that although I may risk death, I won't die until we see each other and you've heard them in person.

Take heart. Whatever happens, pray to God and live on. No matter how sad I may feel, I'll keep going. I keep myself busy every day with this and that. With so many visitors coming and going, I don't have much time for reading. People I don't even know have been extremely charitable, while those I had counted on don't even give me a second glance. I now understand human nature. I sometimes think about how wonderful it will be when peace prevails and we can go back home to Seattle.

Doctors have to get up in the middle of the night to treat patients and are even busier in the afternoons, though things have gotten much easier for them with the completion of the hospital.

Shigeko's younger sister Chiyoko lives in the same flophouse.[b] She's a nice girl.

I eat well every day, so don't worry. I imagine the move was hard on everyone over there. I'd like to send you something but am unable to reach anyone outside. Forgive me. If it's something insignificant I can buy it at the canteen. Let me know and I'll send it right away. Don't hesitate to request anything you might need.

Thank you so much for the stone talisman. Everyone enjoyed looking at it. I'll keep it with me forever. It will protect me I'm sure.

Sunday we were shown a movie and I was finally able to forget about everything for once. As long as I'm here, I'm safe, fed, and can buy things at the canteen.

From here on out, I plan to write you once a week. Stay in good spirits.

Hana

b. Barrack, resembling a chicken coop to some inmates.

| 49

July 16, 1942

Dear Wife,

Toward evening yesterday we had a hailstorm which we never experienced before. Hailstones literally as big as marbles visited us with terrific noise on the roof. We heard about this kind of storm before, but this was the first time we ever witnessed such big hailstones. Hence this poem:

> MONTANA NO HYO NI ODOROKU DETAINEE.
> (Translation—Detainees were flabbergasted by Montana hailstones.)

Tell Doc I received mimeographed song sheet.
Yours ever Iwao Matsushita

| 50

July 18, 1942
[Translated from Japanese]

Dear Hanaye,

Thank you very much for your long-awaited letter. I've been living quite a carefree and enjoyable life in this all-male world, enjoying the beauty of nature, doing what I like best . . . teaching English and writing letters in English for people. Mr. Kanazawa and I are always saying how wonderful it would be if only our families could be with us now.

Most of the original Seattleites interned with me have been transferred, although there are folks from Seattle among the new arrivals.

My future has not been decided, but even if it turns out to be unfavorable you mustn't lose faith, and you must remain strong. Just as the Bible says, "All things work for the best," one's choice in a situation will decide a favorable or unfavorable outcome. You must take advantage of the present circumstances to cultivate your spiritual growth. It's important that you are prepared in your heart to accept gladly whatever is in store for you as God's divine will. Please don't be concerned with rumors or criticisms. As long as your heart is right with God, that is all that matters.

157

I'm in an excellent state of health both physically and mentally, so please don't be concerned about me. I'm sorry that you have so much to bear alone, knowing you tend to fatigue easily. However, you must know of others in similar straits who were left alone with many children and husbands sent to internment camps. When I see the aged and decrepit being shunted about, I'm thankful that I'm still young.

You needn't send me anything since we're able to buy whatever we need from the canteen. There are sodas and ice cream, too.

Nothing makes me happier than to hear from you, but please don't worry too much about it, and write when you're in the mood.

Please give my regards to the Takayamas and Tamaki-san. We'll be able to see movies beginning next week.

Yours ever Iwao Matsushita

| 51

July 20, 1942

Dear wife,

Yesterday afternoon we had a baseball match between Japanese & Italian seamen's teams. As it was the first Italo-Japanese game we ever had, almost everybody turned out to see the contest. All players marched into the ground headed by the Italian band, & it was a real fun as Italians did not know the rules & made many errors. Our team made an easy 27-7 victory over Italians. There wasn't a speck of cloud in the sky, but it wasn't too hot. All of us had a real gala day.

Yours ever Iwao Matsushita

July 20, 10 a.m.
[Translated from Japanese]

To my husband:

I just received your postcard dated the 16th and am glad to hear you're doing well. Recently I've also begun to settle in more and finally feel comfortable writing, although I must apologize that my left eye, going bad with age, often delays my replies. I spend each day happily under the watchful eye of God.

Uncle and I see each other only in the mornings when we wake up and in the evenings when we go to bed. When he isn't busy with work, he wanders around in a daze. I've given him the nickname Balloon. When I ask a favor of him, he suddenly takes off mumbling that it's too much trouble, but I've gotten used to it so that it doesn't discourage me as much as it used to. . . .

I bought vitamins through Ed. They cost $18.19. I increase my strength while waiting for our return day. Isn't there anything you need? Please let me know.

I take care of everything myself. Uncle won't help out with anything, but pretending that I live alone keeps me from getting upset. I happily remind myself that God is protecting us. I've gained weight so don't worry. I look forward to seeing you as soon as possible.

Take care of your health. I have been enjoying meals much more, recently. We may move again, but until then I quietly await God's orders.

I'll write soon. I pray for those suffering.

Hana

July 21, 2:00 p.m.

[Translated from Japanese]

My dear husband:

I am settling in more each day. Happiness comes only with gaining control of oneself by oneself. I quietly await God's orders. . . . Let's try to focus on comforting others. . . . There's no need to be anxious about anything. . . .

As usual I have no idea where Uncle is or what he is up to, but at least his health is not a concern. His incompetence at visiting with the neighbors creates a bigger strain than anything else. He doesn't like to be helped or be asked for help by others. I think he was paid a small salary yesterday,[a] but I've heard nothing of it from him. He's a strange bird. Sometimes he seems senile. When we go to our next place, I'd like to live alone. I can't rely on him when I am ill, but don't worry, I can handle things. Take care of yourself.

Hana

159

a. Doctors were paid $16 per month.

Mrs. Hanaye Matsushita
D-4-97 Camp Harmony
Puyallup, Wash.,

Co Dormitory #24
Fort Missoula, Mont.
July 22, 1942

My dear wife,

The summer seems to be at its zenith. The sun is sizzling hot, the sky is crystal clear, + large electric fans are whizzing at full speed in the room.

Happy-go-luckies are taking naps on beds almost stripped. Occasional stone grinding sounds in the bath room disturb the stillness of the air.

We take bath every evening in the Nippon-buro, cool off in the twilight + go to bed at 11 o'clock. Morning freshness is beyond description.

A recent poem follows :—

　　　甘人なき キャンプの 庭や 裸群れ

(Translation) — Camp grounds void of women, hence stripped groups.

A couple of wild flowers from the camp grounds.

Yours ever,

Iwao Matsushita

(Letter #52)

52

July 22, 1942

My dear wife,

The summer seems to be at its zenith. The sun is sizzling hot, the
sky is crystal clear, & large electric fans are whizzing at full speed in the
room.

Happy-go-luckies are taking naps on beds almost stripped. Occasional
stone grinding sounds in the bath room disturb the stillness of the air.

We take bath every evening in the <u>Nippon-buro</u>,[a] cool off in the
twilight & go to bed at 11 o'clock. Morning freshness is beyond
description.

A recent poem follows:

[line in Japanese characters]
(Translation)—Camp grounds void of women, hence stripped groups.

A couple of wild flowers from the camp grounds [enclosed].
Yours ever, Iwao Matsushita

53

July 25, 1942
[Translated from Japanese]

Dear Hanaye,

I'm very glad that you were able to write the letters dated the 20th
and 21st. Our health is of the prime importance. Be sure to take vitamins
to build up your strength. To this day I'm able to read and write without
glasses. I do believe, though, I have more white hair. I've lost my pot
belly and feel much better. Last night for the first time in eight months
we were able to see a movie. It was a tasteful show, one with a musical
theme like the "Blue Danube" and music of Victor Herbert. Although
the movie hall was very hot, we enjoyed the show immensely.

The items from the Sumimoto Bank arrived. This evening
we're playing softball against the Italians. Teams of white-haired
over-fifty-year-olds will be playing like youngsters. As I was writing this

161

a. A Japanese-style bath constructed by detainee carpenters.

letter, I could still see some snow left on Mount Lolo, but how long will my view last? There's a possibility that we may be seeing new sights before not too long.

Across my desk, in the vase that my friend made from a Missoula stone, are poppy, sweet peas, wild morning glory, and other pretty flowers.

I enjoyed reading Nogiku-san's letter. I'll hear the songs of Puyallup at Mr. Kanazawa's poetry lecture. Why don't you take this opportunity to study haiku or *waka*? I believe it's important for one to achieve an inner peace, and leaving everything to God, strive to nurture one's self.

I sing in a trio with Mr. Sato and Mr. Kanazawa every Sunday.

> The colors are changing on the plateaus,
> Autumn must be near.
> Upon my prisoner's tray
> Red sit the tomatoes.

Show it to Doc. My regards to everyone.
Yours ever, Iwao

| 54

July 27, 1942

Dear Wife,

I wish to show you a part of this city—our camp is in the suburb.[a] I have not seen this town yet. It's rather cold this morning. God bless you.
Your husband Iwao Matsushita

| 55

July 30, 1942
[Translated from Japanese]

Dear Hanaye,

I get up at 6 a.m., and at 7 a.m. I pocket my ration of sugar[a] and head for the mess hall for breakfast. The setting moon is hung in the deep

162

a. The message is on the back of a black-and-white aerial photograph postcard.

a. Sugar had been rationed in camp since February 1942.

blue sky, and the morning air of the highlands is extremely clear. It's so pleasant it's as if this is a summering place.

American morning glories, sweet peas, gladioli, and other flowers are prettily in bloom around our compound. The snow atop Mount Lolo still hasn't melted. When the war is over I'd like to climb that mountain.

There are now fewer than eighteen people in our forty-man barracks, so it's very quiet. It's an ideal situation to do my studies. Aside from being assigned to occasional chores like waiting on people at the mess hall, laundry, and night work, we've no steady job to do. On Mondays, Wednesdays, and Fridays I spend about an hour teaching English. The enrollment is not as large as before, but the few students I have are studying very hard.

Normally it gets really hot around this time, but I haven't been with only my underwear on yet. In fact, when the cool breeze blows around 9 p.m., while I'm at my desk after bath and in my robe watching the beautiful sky, it gets to be cold. There aren't any mosquitos to speak of, so I rarely use the repellent that you sent me.

Our lot has improved a great deal recently. We've been issued tobacco (I don't smoke at all), toothbrush and paste, and we've even been told there will be movies on Fridays and Saturdays. Although we won't be in this camp for too much longer, meals are very good, which include genuine Japanese fare such as miso soup and salmon basted with miso. For a light eater like myself, the servings are more than I can handle.

I'm spending each day with thankfulness and good spirit. Please give my regards to Doc.

Sayonara, Iwao

| 56

Aug. 1, 1942

My dear wife,

No change so far. Saburo wrote me from Baker, Oregon[a] saying he would be back to Spokane soon. Haven't heard from Shigeko yet from Washington. Mr. Miya is making a suiban [flower basin]

163

a. Outside the exclusion zones.

of stones for you, but unless I will be allowed to join you, I don't think I will send it to you, because it is rather heavy & will be in your way when you move soon. However if you want it now, let me know. May God bless you all! Best regards to Mrs. Izui, Mr. Izumi & others.

Yours ever Iwao Matsushita

| 57

Aug. 5, 1942
[Translated from Japanese]

My dear wife,

Mr. Ihashi wrote me that he saw you and you were very healthy and in good spirit. I am very glad to hear of that. Yesterday afternoon it was extraordinarily stuffy and dark clouds began to gather over Mount Lolo, which always proved to be the cradle of storms. About 9:30 p.m. sitting on a bench outside the barrack, we watched over an hour a beautiful display of atmospheric electricity followed by roaring thunder. It zigged this way and zagged that way across the dark sky accompanied by incessant sheet lightnings. Around bedtime strong gusts of wind blew in dust and fine sand from outside, and the room lights were literally darkened in the dust fog, and it was hard for us to breathe freely. It was during the small hours this morning that I was awakened by the noisy patter of raindrops on the roof and I remember even though I was in a semidormant state that it was a real downpour. Many pools appeared on the camp grounds this morning. But what a refreshing dawn we had today! When I think I am given a healthy mind & body as well as daily bread, I sincerely thank God for His blessing on me. Don't you think so?

Your loving husband, Iwao Matsushita

Aug. 6, morning
[Translated from Japanese]

164 My dear husband:

Yesterday I received your letter of the first. Thank you. I'm glad to hear that you are doing well. I've enjoyed the dry pressed flowers enclosed in the last letter and cried with nostalgia remembering the fun days we've had. . . .

Every day has been busy. I just finished cleaning the bathroom and now hastily pick up my pen to write. I'm behind in responding to you because my left eye has worsened and makes it hard to write. It's probably just age, so don't worry. I told Uncle about it, but he ignores my complaints, so I cling to God. Most days we don't see each other all day long. I look forward to living by myself after the move.

Until now I've used Uncle's family number, but I'll get my own soon. He continues to demonstrate the usual disregard for anything and everything. I've finally gotten it through my head that he's a completely unreliable person, but don't worry, I live with God.

Those from whom I wouldn't have expected anything have been very generous, while I've grown apart from friends with whom I used to be in contact. Now I only see them once in a while. It's comforting having Aunt Kaneko[a] living nearby.

Two days ago I received a $2.50 coupon book[b] for the second time, and I'm thankful for the money since I am too weak to work. Uncle apparently received $15 or $16.[c]

The morning of the 7th: Yesterday was so busy that I couldn't finish the letter so will continue writing today. The day of our move to Idaho approaches. We'll probably move around the 16th. I'm too busy to relax. I'm in charge of packing the bags. Uncle is always at the hospital. I 'd prefer that he return home earlier in the evenings, but there's nothing I can do about it.

Writing a letter in English is difficult and it frustrates me that Uncle won't help me. Every morning I go to church to pray that you are well and that you'll return as soon as possible. . . .

My heart is racing; I'll put down my pen here.

Hana

---

a. An older friend.

b. Single evacuees over sixteen years of age received a monthly allowance of $2.50, in scrip, to pay for personal items. Families received $7.50.

c. Unskilled workers received $8 per month; skilled workers, $12; and professionals, $16.

Aug. 8, 1942

[Translated from Japanese]

Dear Hanaye,

I've begun to feel the chill in the mornings and nights of the Missoula highlands. Autumn must be just around the corner. The chilly morning makes me want to bask in the morning sunshine, but it gets quite warm in the afternoons. Yesterday as I was teaching my class, I could feel the perspiration running down my back.

I see from my friends' letters that the time is getting near for those of you at Puyallup to be moving out to another camp. Even though it's been only three months in your temporary quarters, it must have been like being settled, and I know it must be hard for you to make a move again.

The population of this camp has diminished a lot, and it has become very quiet. Food has improved, and there's a movie every Tuesday and Saturday afternoon. They say we'll be allowed to go down to the Missoula River on Wednesdays starting next week. I have a feeling, though, that this won't last for long.

To give you an idea of the kind of meals we are getting, here's what we had recently: *gomoku*,[a] veal cutlet, French fried potatoes, and jello. Quite a fancy meal. Occasionally our trays are adorned with lettuce and tomato, too. It's great. We cook our own *somen* and fish cakes.

> The room is cold
> my stroll outdoors.
>
> Buzzing wind cools
> an electric fan.
>
> I call, "come on"
> kitten scoots.
>
> Kittens two
> in the barrack loitering.

a. Seasoned rice with vegetable slivers.

Health's first. Please give my regards to Doc. Also to your doctor neighbor. I'm sure you'll be in his care, too. Give them my thanks and regards.

Iwao

| 59

Aug. 11, 1942
[Translated from Japanese]

Dear Hanaye,

I was greatly relieved after seeing your letter with the enclosed pressed flower. If, as you say, your vision is due to age, I wouldn't be concerned. But shouldn't you see the doctor in case there's something wrong?

You must be in the midst of packing and looking after other matters readying for the move to Idaho. I apologize for the helpless situation I'm in and not being able to help you through this. Don't be overly concerned, be calm and collected, and make an effort to relax. I know this may be asking too much of you because you're such a hard worker, but it's for your health.

No matter what the circumstances, let us have faith in the Lord that He will protect us, and live our daily lives with gratitude. Although it's unnatural and painful to be separated for so long, there are others who are in similar straits. There are many in much more trying situations. I'd like to think that God is testing our faith and polishing our lives.

Kumasaka-san has asked me to thank you for looking after his family. Please relay my many thanks and regards to Kondo-san. Health comes first.

Iwao

Aug. 20, morning
Minidoka Relocation Center
[Translated from Japanese]

My dear husband:

On the 15th we left Puyallup and arrived here around four in the afternoon on the 16th.[a] The doctors will stay in Puyallup until the 28th   167

---

a. In a party of 493, joining 213 others who had arrived on August 10.

or 29th of next month.[b] Or, at the worst, they'll be sent somewhere else. I'm resigned to try living a bachelor's life. Aunt Kaneko and I are doing well living together. I owe a lot to her. Two or three single women will move in nearby since there are not enough living quarters to go around. . . .

It's unendurably hot and dusty, though eventually I'll get used to it. My body is weak and can only stand so much. I pray to God for strength and tolerance. At times like this I wish day and night for your quick return. . . .

I have many things to tell you, but in the afternoons I am worthless because of the horrible heat. When I dwell on this situation, I have suicidal feelings, but I've got to keep myself together until your return. I imagine you're also experiencing rough times. I have come to understand what it's like to live alone in this world. People tease me, calling me the Montana widow. . . .

I can hear the violent winds blowing across the wide plains. In the distance I hear the sound of the sagebrush blowing in the wind, rattlesnakes, and the howling of coyotes.

I'm thankful to this country that we can live here in safety. The soldiers stand guard day and night. I shed tears of sympathy for them standing in the scorching afternoon heat and the evenings that are so cold as to require lighting a fire, for each soldier is someone's son. At night a crescent moon shines brightly, the grandiosity of nature brings tears to my eyes. I need to focus my mind on something. I'll ponder God's benevolence.

The house we are living in now is built for winter and equipped with a new coal stove so we won't die of the cold. We eat at the cafeteria.

Our boxes have yet to arrive, so we have no tables or chairs. I am writing this letter on my lap. We should be settled in a few days. I anxiously await your next letter and pray that your day of return comes soon. Take care of your health. I'll write again.

Hana

b. The last Puyallup evacuee left the center on September 12. Dr. Koike left on September 4.

Aug. 25, 1942
To Mrs. Hanaye Matsushita
1-2-C, Minidoka WRA
Eden, Idaho
[Translated from Japanese]

Dear Hanaye,

I was happy to receive word of your safe move. I studied the map the other day and learned that you were located far south of us. I imagine it's very hot there. Once you've become used to it, it shouldn't be too bad. Take care of your health, that's of the primary importance.

The number in this camp is gradually diminishing as people are transferred or released to the "outside." It probably won't be long now. My fate is entirely unknown. Be prepared for the worst, should that happen. [CENSORED] is being transferred, too.

As I have said many times, if you remember that there are many others who are worse off, we'll be able to give thanks no matter what may befall us. If we trust in the Lord, even if we are left alone in the wilderness, we'll not feel any loneliness.

With the lessening population, my chore days come almost daily. However, meals continue to get better. For example, for breakfast we have hot cakes, corn flakes, bologna, and pears, and for dinner miso salmon, cucumber pickles, miso pork, and mixed rice. It's sumptuous. We have movies twice a week. I was reminded of the old days when I saw *Sun Valley Serenade* and *Charley's Aunt*.

Reports from other camps indicate that apparently there aren't places that are as good as Missoula. No word can describe the air of the highlands. Snow is still left on Mount Lolo. To be sure, they say there are lots of fireflies in the forest of Louisiana.

My regards to Aunt Kaneko. I'll write again. Please take care.

Iwao

Aug. 28, 1942

My dear wife,

It seems that summer is gone. We had rain the day before yesterday & Mount Lolo has new snow now. No change. Fewer people, better meals. A few days ago we had a mountain fire just in front of us—we saw it burn uphill. In the evening we saw the red glow in the sky & also the moon eclipse at the same time. Best wishes to Mrs. Kaneko and Kumasakas. Take good care of yourself in a strange land.

Yours ever Iwao Matsushita

| 62

Sept. 1, 1942

My dear wife—

How do you like your new location now? I suppose you are more or less accustomed to your new home. There is no change for me here, it is getting so cooler every day that basking in the sun is rather comfortable. Our food is getting better—good for a king! We had chawan-mushi,[a] maze-zushi,[b] to say nothing of ocassional ice cream, oranges, [illegible] etc. Best regards to Kaneko-obasan & others who are kind to you.

Yours ever Iwao Matsushita

Sept. 1, noon
[Translated from Japanese]

My dear husband:

I received your letter and postcard and am happy to hear that you're doing well. We've finally settled in. It's been cold enough in the mornings and evenings to use the stove. . . .

Aunt has been of great help.

The place where we currently stay has a good view. At night I can hear the rush of the Snake River.[a] It flows rapidly and is apparently quite

a. Egg dish in soup stock, meat, shellfish, and other ingredients.
b. A type of sushi.

a. Actually, she heard an irrigation canal that wound through the camp, bringing surplus water from the American Falls dam.

dangerous. I can see the green grasses on the riverbank. The mornings are especially tranquil.

Uncle should arrive around Friday together with patients. . . .

I feel safe and assured that you'll return soon. Whatever happens, I'll remain calm, so please don't worry. Everyone moving here from Puyallup should be here by Friday. This is going to be a big place. They're constructing a large hospital and building houses throughout the day in preparation for the winter. The well water is drinkable though it's a bit hard. Since last week I've been able to boil water for laundry.

It seems like only yesterday when we went picking *matsutake* mushrooms at the end of August last year. It all seems like a dream.

Bruno[a] came to visit me once in Puyallup, though unfortunately all I could do was cry. I couldn't utter a word. Kuro-chan, who is doing well, says that Bruno's mother takes good care of her.

Hiroshi Tada has been sent to a Tacoma hospital with a head-related illness that may be a result of depression. It's really too bad. I am praying for his quick revival. When I feel hopeless and that all is lost, I think of your homecoming to boost my spirits.

Sorry to be using a pencil but I gave Uncle my ink. I hear that snow has fallen in the mountains. I reminisce and wait expectantly for the day when we can sit together in peace and quiet. Peaceful days will return. I pray for everyone's happiness. Take care of yourself. I pray for your safety until the day we can see each other again.

Hana

| 63

Sept. 5, 1942
[Translated from Japanese]

Dear Hanaye,

I was happy to receive your second letter from Minidoka. You seem to have settled somewhat, and I hear the water is good. I think that's wonderful. When I heard about Bruno, Hiroshi, and Sato-chan, it brought back memories of nine months ago. It seemed like a long time

a. Bruno Benedetti was a former neighbor who later submitted an affidavit supporting Matsushita's parole appeals.

ago, but actually it hasn't been so. Anyway, I'm thankful that I'm able to live without concern for my well-being.

When I got up this morning at seven for my morning walk, I saw the flowers we planted in the spring . . . dahlia, sweet peas, zinnia, morning glory, cosmos, and others, in wild bloom. There were only four horses last February, and now we have nine that are used in place of cars. They've been let out from the stable and they are happily drinking water from the trough.

I hear the barking of the dog the Italians are keeping. The Italians are also raising tomatoes, cucumbers, and other vegetables.

The sun is about to appear from the shadow of the mountains to the east. The air of the meadows shaded by the 4,000-foot hills is indescribably soothing. I'm glad we were able to experience a break in the monotony by having the Italians with us, though it's hard to communicate because many of them don't know English. In the evening we have a softball match between the Italians and us (I don't play).

A few days ago I played tennis for the first time in thirty years.

Because the population has decreased, I've been working as a scribe and typist for various offices and people. At the request of the few remaining students, I'm still teaching English.

I pray daily for your health and spiritual well-being.

Goodbye, Iwao

Sept. 7, 1942
[Translated from Japanese]

My dear husband:

It's been ten months now since we separated in December, and I'm amazed at how well we've survived thus far thanks to God. Thank you for the postcards of the 21st and 22nd. I cried with joy to hear that you were able to eat your favorite *neginuta* [scallion salad]. I'm finally able to eat again. I try not to forget to take my medicine. On the 4th, Uncle came to visit. Since yesterday he's been sleeping over at the hospital. I'm glad it's is not too far from here. He's aged suddenly from working so much, though his health is good.

A beautiful moonlit night. After finishing all of the responsibilities of the day, I gaze upon the quiet sunset wanting to cry and cry until I have no more tears left to shed. Listening to the quiet rush of the river in the morning, I feel as though you are calling to me. Even the coyote's howl is nostalgic.

On the 8th at four in the afternoon: Yesterday after getting this far, surprise visitors interrupted my writing. Everyday I keep busy with something or another. . . . Cora Uno[a] began living with us three days ago (I think you remember her). With the three of us including Aunt, it's become pretty lively around here.

The two of them have been in bed with stomach pains since last night, so now I'm finally getting down to writing you this letter. Thank you for the beautiful pressed flowers. I'll cherish them as an important memento of you. The weather is a little cooler today at 82 degrees, but it's so dry that we place buckets of water in our rooms to increase the moisture in the air.

I'm doing much better than when we first arrived on the sixteenth of last month. . . . Uncle visited this morning so I asked him to write a short letter and a change of address for me. I'm watching out for black widows and ticks. I haven't seen any rattlesnakes yet. People who go out to work bring them back, but only one person has been bitten so far. Coyotes sometimes howl at the dawn. Surprisingly, rain hasn't fallen once since arriving.

Breakfast is from 7 to 8 and we keep busy with cleaning and laundry from 12 to 5, leaving little time for reading. And we still don't have a real bathtub. Visitors help me forget about my loneliness. I don't get to Ishibashi's place much since he lives so far away, although I did visit him once. We can travel by bus now, so I'll be able to visit every so often. Unfortunately, everyone I want to see lives far away. Construction continues daily. We'll soon have a comfortable place to live. It's a help that the quality of the well water is better than I imagined it would be.

The stars here are beautiful, as Montana's must be. When I imagine that you're looking at the same moon and the same stars, I begin crying and praying to Jesus Christ. I pray that I can accomplish all that needs to be done and that you'll be returned to me soon. Last year we spent

a. A younger, adult friend.

pleasant days thinking about nothing. I look forward to the day when we'll all be happy. Return to me in good health.

Hana

| 64

Sept. 11, 1942

[Translated from Japanese]

Dear Hanaye,

Early yesterday morning I was awakened by the sound of large raindrops that fell without stopping and formed numerous lakes that forced us to make long detours to get to the mess hall. Since there are so few of us left, there's only one mess call at eight, for breakfast. "We're short two people but they're on their way by boat!" someone would joke, and we'd all be in a gay mood and join in the fun.

They say, a delicious meal is a few diners, and I ate with gusto. Veal cutlet, tomato, lettuce, pineapple . . . we're assaulted with good food. Right now we're gathered around a stove talking. Frost should be arriving soon. The morning glory doesn't appear to have strength to blossom because of the cold.

We have a pretty good idea about your camp from the correspondence that our people have received. I can only be thankful that you've been assigned to a safe and permanent site where your daily needs are being met.

According to a card from Mr. Nakamura, he'd gone to visit you and Mrs. Suzuki, whom you're staying with. I don't know which Mrs. Suzuki she is, but please give my regards to her for I know she must be of great help to you. I heard that Doc also came by. I'll write again.

Iwao

P.S. As I was about to mail this letter I received your third letter. Regards to Cora Uno.

65

Sept. 16, 1942

[Translated from Japanese]

Dear Hanaye,

It's exactly a month since you've relocated to Minidoka. I have yet
to receive any word about my situation. As usual, we are occupying
ourselves with stone craft, playing ball, and enjoying the meals.

Several cats that were born in the spring have grown up and are
cavorting around the barracks. They even sleep on our beds. There are
times I wish I could be carefree like them.

It must already be autumn at your camp. They say home is where
your heart is, so once you've become used to anything, it's not too bad.
As I mentioned before, your health is most important, so please take
care. I can only be thankful that I'm all right despite everything. I think
that making the best of the present circumstances is the smartest thing to
do. Why don't you consider studying the subjects you wanted to take at
the university?

Last night I saw the movie, *If I Were A King*, starring Ronald Colman.
We had *Popeye*, too. There are so few Japanese now that we mingle with
the Italians at the movies or picnic down at the riverside.

At seven I listen to the radio in bed, go to the mess hall at eight, and
clean my barrack after I return. After reading the Bible, doing some
outdoor calisthenics, reading the newspaper, and taking care of the mail,
I'm still not hungry for lunch at noon. In the afternoon I spend the time
polishing rocks, read and write, teach and listen to the radio. But at
mealtime at seven p.m., I'm still not hungry.

Please give my regards to Aunt Kaneko, Uno-san, Koike-san, and the
others.

Iwao

66

Sept. 19, 1942

My dear Wife:

Two days ago we had a miserable rainy day, and had to turn on the
heating pipe besides burning coal in a stove. Nobody went outside, but
stayed around the stove, chatting on various subjects.

Yesterday Lolo Mountain glistened with new snow in the morning sun. The same white mountain welcomed us this morning. When we had the first snowfall a few weeks ago on Lolo, it didn't stay long, but this time it seems to stay, because the air is pretty chilly even on this camp ground. To this Lolo Mountain, which proved to be our shrine, we may be taken tomorrow carrying picnic lunch with us. Some hope to find mushrooms, remembering last autumn in the forest near Mt. Rainier.

> The year's at the autumn
> And the day's at the morn,
> Morning's at eight,
> The sky's blue,
> Lolo shines white,
> God's in His heaven—
> All's right with the world.
>   —With apology to Robert Browning

Please take good care of yourself, and best regards to Oba-san, Uno-san, Doc., Wataru, and others.

Yours ever Iwao Matsushita

Sept. 19, 1942, morning
[Translated from Japanese]

My dear husband:

Your letter of the 16th arrived yesterday. . . . Thank you for the stone vase. Did you make it? I used it for arranging flowers that I received yesterday, and they look beautiful. Many thanks. I don't know a Mrs. Suzuki. It must be someone else. Aunt Kaneko, Cora, and I are living together. Aunt is a good person. My eyes fill with tears of nostalgia when she talks about cats. With everybody gone I wonder who is feeding the cats. Yesterday was a lovely Indian summer day. The weather has been a paradise—neither too hot nor too cold. There was no wind and we had no sand devil "treats." Today looks like good weather too.

Daily cleaning keeps me from becoming bored. I'm happy to sleep well, exhausted from a hard day's work. Everyone's being very considerate.

I think of your return day and night and pray once a day at the riverside that God will return you to me soon. How will I survive the cold, cold winter alone? I pray that you'll come to me. When I think about this while eating, suddenly I can no longer get food down. I may sound like a coward, but weak me needs faith and strength, for which I pray to God, to get through the day. I feel certain that you'll be released soon.

I enjoy watching children fish along the river. As I look out at the river, the passing days float before me like *nishiki* [wood block] prints. I read psalms from the Bible everyday. I believe that God will certainly return a good person like you to me.

Snow should fall within a week or two. People started using their stoves a couple of days ago.

The bank will send cash upon receipt of a letter, so don't worry. A canteen has been built, but hot water isn't available for bathing.

Uncle lives in a room in the hospital. Once in a while he visits me. He's aged but healthy. Ishibashi lives quite far away in the direction of Block 41, but will move to Block 4 or 5 this week to be closer to the hospital.[a]

The river is beautiful. I look forward to seeing you. Morinaga, who I see once in a while, has not changed a bit. Sawaji lives in the same block as I do so we see each other frequently. Believing that you'll be released, I can bear this situation. . . .

Hana

| 66[a]

Sept. 20, 1942
(Chronicle of a mountain hike)
[Translated from Japanese]

Dear Hanaye,

At 10 a.m. on September 20, a number of us Japanese were loaded on one of two military trucks. We traveled along the familiar Missoula River and wound our way westward past apple orchards and white-barked

177

a. Ishibashi was a dentist.

a. Matsushita misnumbered this letter and never caught his error.

aspen forests. The trucks had to shift gears frequently as the road became steeper. A peaceful vista of a vast pasture with grazing cows came into view. Soon, hills carpeted with yellow flowers appeared on both sides of the road. I imagined the hills would make ideal skiing slopes. The trucks continued to climb the road lined with white pines, coming to a stop about thirty minutes after we'd left the camp. We then hiked for more than a mile over an abandoned road, and arrived at a plateau. There we saw a pitched tent and two large picnic tables and a stream trickling nearby. We quickly began to look for stones. The water was so cold we couldn't keep our hands in it for long. Monkey flowers were in bloom.

We brewed tea and feasted on rice balls, *umani*,[b] pie, cake, and boiled eggs. We offered the two guards sandwiches.

We organized a party of fifteen or sixteen climbers and started up the trail around twelve o'clock. We slid along as we climbed with our spikeless GI shoes and resorted to applying sidesteps used by skiers. Fallen leaves, moss covered old trees, deer and bear droppings reminded me of my long ago climb of Mount Rainier. Some hikers dropped out along the way, and when we finally reached the 8,000-foot elevation, there were only eight of us left. It was many long hours of tough climbing, but I can't begin to describe the feeling as we surveyed the town of Missoula, our nostalgic camp, and the winding Missoula River from the summit. We were blessed with perfect mountain climbing weather, and some were moved to say, "I've added ten years to my life!" After viewing the snows of Glacier Park, we began our descent. Since our time was limited, we had to hurry down, but I was bothered by my feet swimming in the shoes. I was proud of myself that I was able to keep up with the younger men.

Someone even caught 4 trout from the stream. We didn't find *matsutake* [mushrooms], but were able to gather quite a bit of champignon.

We left at 1:30 p.m. and returned to the camp past three o'clock. I am filled with gratitude that we were accorded such treatment, even as prisoners.

178   (The End)

b. Bamboo shoots, fish cake and potato.

67

Sept. 23, 1942

My dear wife,

Last night I saw a movie of ski thrills—the picture included glimpses of Alta Vista & Tatoosh Range of Mt. Rainier. On our way back from the Recreation Hall to our barrack, I saw the moon of the 13th night shining bright. I thought you were looking at the same moon, probably a solitary coyote howling at the moon, hence this poem:

MINIDOKA YA COYOTE MO HOETE TSUKI MAROSHI
(Translation) At Minidoka
The moon is round
A cayote's howling.

From Your Husband

68

Sept. 25, 1942
[Translated from Japanese]

Dear Hanaye,

Last night, we moved our cots and benches outside the barracks, and with plenty of food, cake, pie, cocoa, and noodles, we spent a memorable, once-in-a-lifetime evening viewing the full moon as we sang the song I composed:

Tsukimi Ondo (The Moon-viewing Ditty)
1. So, autumn's come to Missoula's Camp,
   what glorious feeling morn and eve'n.
2. When the ball game's over with the Eye-talians,
   the moon reveals herself over Mt. Mitton.
3. Missoula's sky's the place to view the moon,
   don't you see its beaming smile?
4. Tho many nights the moon we see,
   'tis the eve'n for the moon of moons.
5. Dance in Missoula if dancing you want,
   the moon herself will dance with you.

6. What pity for such a beautiful moon,
   dancing here are only we men.

7. Don't weep, my love, e'en tho we're afar,
   the moon we view is also yours.

8. O, Goddess Moon, can you this eve'n at least,
   my wife's vision reflect?

I was happy to receive your letter posted on the 19th.
Iwao

Sept. 27, 1942
[Translated from Japanese]

My dear husband:

I received your letter and postcard and am glad to see that you had a good time hiking. How envious I am of the box lunch they made for you. Everyone here is fine. Ishibashi has moved to Block 4 and is much closer now. Doctors and dentists now live nearer to the hospital.

Every morning and evening the color of the sky is too lovely for words. I've had no luck in seeing a rattlesnake. Sometimes I take walks along the river with Uncle where small birds chirp in their nests, and it feels as though I'm back in Seattle and have just taken a trip out to the countryside.

I was relieved to find that the Bank of California immediately sent the cash upon receipt of my letter . Let me know if you're in need of money. I worry that you may need something.

I read Uncle's Seattle newspapers, which arrive a few days late, but I just want to read the funnies so it doesn't matter. Various items are for sale at the canteen, and Yamagata is great about picking up things for me there.

It's really an Indian summer. The autumn days are refreshing. The young people are saying that after it snows this winter they'll be able to ski.

I am writing this letter alone while Aunt is out doing laundry. Some people on this block have been getting food poisoning, but we're OK.

All I think about is you. Whatever I'm doing, whether it's eating or even laughing, I just can't seem to get away from the situation and am constantly on the verge of tears. In the evenings I look at the moon and pray for your homecoming. When the wind blows I pray to the wind. Seeing the small birds flying free brings tears to my eyes, and I appeal the airborne birds for your return. I haven't heard any coyotes recently, though once in a while I see a scorpion. I saw a porcupine in the distance and caused everyone to break into laughter when I mentioned seeing a skunk.

Thanks to America, the camp is daily becoming an easier place to live. There will actually be a day when you'll be released and we'll be able to rest peacefully. Once in a while I dream around running around the base of Mount Rainier. Remember the times we hiked through the mountains together? It all seems like a dream. . . .

Hana

| 69

Sept. 28, 1942

My dear wife,

Last Saturday we saw a movie—western story—kind you like—wild nature, wild cattle, horses chasing horses, cowboys, BANG, BANG, BANG!

Every Tuesday and Saturday we see motion pictures and Wednesday we go out to the Missoula River—a 10 minuites' walk from the camp. Some boys enjoy fishing. I was lucky last week to be given a fried trout. The trout caught in the mountain stream a week ago is still living in a bucket in the bath room.

Last week we kept a snipe in our mess hall for several days. She was a little hurt when she appeared in the dining room. We fed her with water, bread crums, and grasshoppers. She became so accustomed to us that she came at our call, but we finally let her go away when she became strong enough to fly.

We have about ten dogs and half a dozen cats. These dogs are sometimes scratched by cats when they go near out of curiosity and scamper away whining painfully.

Well, I think I have told you enough today.

Best regards to Oba-san, Uno-san, Doc., Wataru, etc.,

Your husband, Iwao Matsushita

Sept. 29, 1942, Monday
[Translated from Japanese]

My dear husband:

Last night I walked to the river bank with Kumasaka where there was a profusion of waterfowl, and we experienced the beauty of the sky at sunset. The clouds reflected in the water were beautiful, and the sagebrush on the plain was red with the sun. I cried and prayed to God while gazing at the setting sun. My feelings have become intense from living alone for so long.

I can see people fishing and am envious of those with families. I'd be much happier looking at the scene of cattails with you.

The days go by. I put willow branches in vases. Thistle is more pleasing to the eye, but it has disappeared with the fall. Some have been eating thistle saying it tastes like *gobo*.[a] There are no eels in the river, though there are carp and whitefish.

The weather is good again today. I pray for your health and await your homecoming.

Hana

| 70

Oct. 2, 1942
[Translated from Japanese]

Dear Hanaye,

I'm very glad that lately I'm hearing from you about once a week. I see you're enjoying the sunrise and sunset of the great plains. I think that's wonderful. I pray that we'll be able to enjoy them together soon.

It's already October. We had all speculated that by mid-August there would be a decision on our status, but it ended up being just a speculation. We're into a pleasant time of the year and food is plentiful. The guards treat us decently, and we're like friends and living a life of Riley.

Thanks for the offer for any money, but it won't be necessary, since there hasn't been any need to spend the check I've gotten before.

a. A Japanese root.

I've been reading the funnies a lot. I don't care to read "Superman" or "Tarzan" and the like, but "Jiggs" and "Timid Soul" are funny, aren't they?

I took a walk along the perimeter of a large fenced-in pasture that was off-limits until recently. It took me exactly thirty minutes, so it was over a mile, a good exercise.

The following are my compositions:

> Bathed with October rays
> I walk the green meadow through dew.

> As I near the Italians' garden plot
> a harmless mutt comes barking at me. (ha! ha!)

Give my best to aunt, Cora, Koike-san, Kumasaka-san, and the others.
Iwao

| 71

Oct. 5, 1942

My Dear Wife,

Saturday's movies were consisted of Father Hubbard's adventure of glaciers and icebergs of Alaska, and "Tin Pan Alley". The former, a short subject, was really a grand picture for a nature lover like me. Do you remember "Tin Pan Alley", which we saw at the 5th Avenue Theater[a] last year? It was a hilarious picture, full of peppy and comic songs, with Alice Faye and Jack Oakie starring.

On account of the [CENSORED] here, we swapped dining rooms with them. From Sunday we are eating in a small refectory in the Italian quarter in a real concrete building. The kitchen is all tile-walled, the dining room is large enough for 100 persons. The wall is ivory-colored. It's really ritzy, but we have to walk a few minutes longer from our barracks.

The following is my poor imitation of the popular song, "Idaho".

> Away beyond those hills in Idaho
> Where beautiful Snake greets the sun

183

a. An ornate downtown Seattle movie theater.

As it peeps over the prairies in Idaho
To say another night is done,

Away, away at Minidoka, Idaho
Where yapping coyotes look up the moon
As it smiles on the sagebrush in Idaho
To bathe the plateau bright as noon,

There my heart is turning ever
There my dreams are roaming ever
Let me go and see the Snake
That's the trip I'd like to make.

Please take good care of yourself, and convey my best regards to
Oba-san, Uno-san, Doc., Wataru-san & his family.
Yours ever, Iwao Matsushita

Oct. 6, 1942, morning
[Translated from Japanese]

My dear husband:
Yesterday I received your letter dated the 2nd. . . .
Intrigued by the song you sent the other day and feeling happy, Aunt
and I burst into song. Itoi read it, and eventually the four of us including
Kumasaka began dancing and laughing hysterically while crying at the
same time. It was an unimaginably bizarre scene.
Three of us have had been in bed with a slight fever for the last three
or four days, but with sleep have improved considerably since yesterday.
Everyone has a touch of the flu, and the worst off can get fevers of 103
degrees, although I've not been affected that much. Wataru, who has
been spending a lot of time, with us says that his mother is confined to
bed again, but I'm not quite up to paying a visit yet.
We haven't had any water since yesterday while they put in a hot
water pipe. For the next three or four days we'll have to fetch water from
Block 2. We'll be happy to have hot water.
I saw a baby snake. I don't know if it was a rattlesnake, but it had a
pretty design. Maybe it was a baby that hasn't grown its rattle yet. It was
adorable.

First page of a letter from Hanaye at Minidoka Relocation Center to Iwao, October 6, 1942. Censored at Fort Missoula.

A black dog that drinks our water and busily cleans itself at night was sleeping under Aunt's bed. The three of us burst out laughing at Cora's surprise to find it there. In trying to figure out what was going on, she thought Kaneko was having trouble sleeping and had started to mop the floor on her hands and knees, or that Matsushima was cleaning her dentures. She was trying really hard to figure out what was going on when the big black dog sneezed. The humor was too much for the three of them, and I began to laugh until the tears came. The dog, on the other hand, was totally calm. He slept until Aunt put him out the following morning, sauntering out unconcerned. Animals are adorable little angels totally unaware of this horrific war.

Although he pretends disinterest, Uncle always reads your letters. He offers no greeting and then starts looking over your letters with no expression or comment and then moves on to some unrelated topic. He's so insensitive that he only talks about what he wants to talk about. He has no reaction to haiku or poems, as if he doesn't know whether he has read them or not. That man is like an Immortal. He brings in willows with bugs all over them, which are a bother to deal with because they may be infested with black widows. I have to wash and cut them until they are cleaned off. He doesn't say a word of thanks and leaves, it's ridiculous.

Mr. Yamagata brought a bright red *hoozuki*.[a] I put them in the vase you gave to me. If I had a few more it would look better. I had him buy me a chest of drawers to have a place to put clothing and small objects. It's a joy to have. Jerome, next door, is the owner of a store where I can get most necessities, but that may not be the case in the future. . . . Nothing has changed, but I do pray that you will return soon. For weak me, winter is a big worry. It's better to die than be ill among strangers. . . .

Hana

a. This is a summer plant with small red fruit resembling cherry tomatoes, and closely associated with native summer festivals, particularly *obon*.

Oct. 9, 1942
[Translated from Japanese]

Dear Hanaye,

I had my hair cut today in the vacant lot between the barracks as I basked in the ten o'clock sun on this springlike morning. It felt really good. I'm writing this after returning to my quarters.

The clear autumn days continue every day. Wild asparagus with their red berries are growing prettily along the banks of the Missoula River. The foliage in the camp is gradually turning color too. It's autumn wherever we turn.

It's bustling with [CENSORED] Italians. There are lots of Italian gardens even in the Japanese area, and it's interesting to see the many signs posted in Italian. Since my interest is in language, I've learned quite a bit from the signs that I've seen on my walk around the camp. For example,

Proibito entrare. . . . . keep out
Gardino Roma. . . . . Roman Garden
Ospedale Zona Silenzio. . . . . Quiet, Hospital Zone
Servizio Posta. . . . . Postoffice

For anyone who knows some English, it's not hard to understand Italian of the above difficulty.

Tomorrow, Saturday, is supposed to be a mountain hike again. This time we'll probably use spiked shoes.

Give my best regards to aunt, Cora, Doc, and others.

Suddenly I turn to spot the solitary cat in camp.
(I just saw it now.)

Iwao

My dear wife,

To Blue Mountain Lookout
(10 miles' hiking)

Leaving our barracks at 9 Saturday morning, we arrived at the same base camp, as we went before, at 10:30, after walking around one mile on an old, abandoned auto road.

Experienced by limited hours of last climbing, our husky gang left at once, a young man carried lunch in my rucksack. We decided to take a trail this time along a telephone wire which we noticed last time. I told the boys that it should lead to a fire lookout station on the top of a lofty peak.

A short way up, we found, much to my satisfaction and expectation, a familiar arrow-shaped, antiquated sign with these words; BLUE MOUNTAIN LOOKOUT 3.6/10 MILES. Horses' droppings further convinced me that the trail must be fairly good, so we pushed on and on. Occasionally we encountered steep climbings of 45 degrees, but sometimes were rewarded by quite a long stretch of level goings. As I had spiked shoes on, it was much easier for me than the last ascent.

We found white rhododendron trees, larch, bear grass, thistles in bloom, and grouse. The higher we climbed, the grander the scenery became. Mt. Mitten, Mt. Jumbo, and other mountains were seen tamely nestled below our feet across the spacious, yellow plateau.

When we spied a lookout station, towering above the pine trees, and against the sky, everybody began to whip his shanks' mare. Two hours' laborious climbing took us to the rounded ridge of Blue Mountain. The top was almost devoid of trees, and the tower was twice as high as that of Mt. Rainier.

Three long flights of steps carried me onto the highest veranda around the watch-house. Looking straight down from there, even an experienced mountaineer like me felt my knees knocking, like Mr. Kashio on Gobblers Knob,[b] not only by the stupendous height of the

a. Matsushita again misnumbered, and the error went undetected.
b. At Mount Rainier.

skeleton-like support on which the house stood, but by swaying of the whole structure in the strong and rather cold wind. Nobody could stand there long for the same reason.

On terra firma we enjoyed lunch, consisting of rice-balls sprinkled with sesame-seeds, boiled bamboo shoots and carrots, chicken, eggs, oranges, etc. When my friend offered me a cup of hot coffee from his thermos bottle it was, boy! oh boy! a cup worth $1,000.

The scenery all around us was really beyond human description. Fourteen fellow alpinists shouted "*Banzai!*" three times, loud enough to move heaven and earth, facing our beloved, majestic Mt. Lolo, which stood before us like a giant, with patches of snow in its cirque.

On the other side the Missoula River snaked its way through the crazy-quilt fields into the city, which snugly sat in a far corner of the wide basin, surrounded by a conglomeration of mountains.

Nothing on earth could surpass this grand and glorious feeling we had on this lofty top of Blue Mountain.

On our way down, Mr. Humpty Dumpty, like Doc. (excuse please) got hellish cramps, and I had to convoy him with another man. It took us two hours again to get to the base camp, as we were compelled to walk at funeral pace.

Yours ever, Iwao Matsushita

The 12th, afternoon
[Translated from Japanese]

My dear husband:

I received your letter of the ninth and am glad to hear that you continue to be doing well. The three of us were having stomach trouble but are fine now. . . .

Yesterday we were blessed with rain, settling the dust storms that carry contagious illnesses. I read the newspaper in peace all day long because the road was so muddy that no one could visit. Occasionally I like to just sit and think about things but haven't had a free moment for over two months. The rain was truly a blessing. Aunt rattled on with irrelevant stories while I read, but I'm getting used to it. Uncle did some shopping for me while he was out on an errand. He leaves the camp with an American doctor. I had him buy me eggs and honey since I've been feeling so weak from illness.

It sounds like you hiked into the mountains yesterday. I'm glad to hear you enjoyed it so much. . . . On the 16th exactly two months will have passed since my arriving here. Thinking about what a long, painful road it's been makes me depressed. There's nothing to do but rely on God. I pray for a swift peace so that many lives may be saved.

The rain has cleaned the sagebrush and revived everything, inviting thoughts of God's blessings. He will return those without sin to me. . . .

There are many American soldiers putting their lives on the line. Pray for them and everyone suffering in the world. Thank God we live in a place where there is no life-threatening danger. Let us pray for those who far worse off than we.

You mentioned that there is a field Italians use at your place, and I nostalgically recalled our neighbors in Seattle. Our only home is Seattle, our house. I'll never forget it. We've lived there in times of pain and joy—I'll never forget it. I even see it in my dreams. . . .

Everything seems like a dream, as if you are just away at the office. It's been almost a year since we were separated. Almost a year has wasted away since we parted. . . . I plan on turning to ashes, happily fertilize this country that has let us live here for over twenty years. I happily await peace. Take care of your health.

Aunt and Cora send their regards.

Hana

The 13th

[Translated from Japanese]

My dear husband:

Another quiet night. . . . Last night on Block 4, a film was shown, but since it began at nine I didn't go. Adults pay ten cents and children five cents. Uncle and Sawaji came by and we talked until ten. It's rather chilly since coal is so hard to come by. I want to go to the river but I'm just too exhausted. . . .

190   Hana

73

Oct. 17, 1942

My dear wife,

Your letter of 6th via air arrived on 9th. Don't use air, because there is no difference in time. I received letters from Wataru and Doc. I always reply immediately to all mail I receive.

Fog, yesterday and this morning, reminds me of mushroom hunting in the Cascades. Last night I saw a half moon; next Thursday, the 23rd, will bring us another full moon. We saw a movie, entitled "Mighty Treve," a story of a very nice dog. Do you remember this pathetic picture we saw several years ago? We couldn't see this picture without having lumps in our throats. Please take good care of yourself, and give my kindest regards to Obasan, Unosan, Kumasaka-san, Takase-san and others.

Yours ever, Iwao Matsushita

74

Oct. 20, 1942

[Translated from Japanese]

Dear Hanaye,

I received your longed-for letters dated the 12th and 13th. I trust you've received my piece on the mountain hike. A couple or three days ago, we had a heavy frost that left the wild flowers drooping.

Frost drooping the wild flowers
spells the end of dropping maple leaves.

There was a letter from the trustees of the Methodist church that needed my counter signature, so I took care of that.

There's still no word about what's going to be done with us. Perhaps this is God's way of teaching us to be patient. I'm sorry that you're having some difficulty because of the lack of facilities in comparison to ours. It goes without saying that I wish you could be transferred here. Lately our government supplies have increased so that we have been issued shoes, socks, shirts, and trousers, handkerchiefs, bandannas, tooth paste and brush, razor blades, towels, etc. We've had such an excess of mattresses, blankets, and quilts that we're using two mattresses to sleep on.

191

My fellow boarders call me *sensei* ["teacher"] and treat me very kindly.
Of course, I do my share by writing English letters, typing, and helping
in the galley, etc. The other day a talented fellow gave me a superbly
made desk. I hope to use it as a memento for the rest of my life.

There's an old saying, "Sickness comes from the mind," but modern
science has also announced that one's attitude can greatly sway the
gravity of the person's illness. Please don't overextend yourself and, like
someone you know, try and learn to take it easy, even if it's being a little
like a dullard. You needn't be concerned about me at all for I haven't
been sick even a half a day since I got here.

We've been told that we could write to Japan, so I wrote to father
Tamura,[a] among others. Give my best wishes to aunt, Cora, Doc,
Tsune-san, and the others.

Iwao

Oct. 20, morning

[Translated from Japanese]

My dear husband:

I was happy to receive your postcard this morning. . . . Last night
I was invited by Wataru to see the film *Citizen Kane*. You probably
remember it. The projector wasn't working too well so a few parts were
confusing, but it reminded me of Seattle. I walked home by the light
of the moon feeling terribly lonely. No matter how much money one
has, without God's blessings, there will be no happiness. The greatest
happiness is to be together as a couple. . . .

Your hiking travel diary was a joy to read. It sounds as though you
had a wonderful time. I burst into tears wishing we could have gone
hiking together. Last Sunday, Wataru and I went for a walk along the
riverbank where quite a few people were fishing. The Indian summer is
beautiful, but I don't feel satisfied somehow, and am always on the verge
of tears. I thought I had been settling in recently, but the loneliness of
autumn gets to me. . . .

Do you know Mr. Yamamoto? He gave me a pile of kindling, and
I was so grateful I started crying again. Every time someone is even

a. Hanaye's father.

slightly kind to me tears well up in my eyes. I can't help wondering why I'm so weak, and I pray for God to give me strength. . . . I tried to write on the 17th, but the arrival of guests kept me too busy to write a response. Sorry I'm so late in replying to your letter. . . .

I heard the hopeful rumor that we may be able to live with the families of guards, but it may just be a rumor as usual. . . .

Everyone's talking about gathering *matsutake* mushrooms in the winter. . . .

I am going to take a bath now. Give everyone my regards.

Hana

| 75

Oct. 23, 1942
[Translated from Japanese]

Dear Hanaye,

> With gathered collard this morning
> I stroll in sight of fallen leaves.

(This was yesterday morning.)

Last night's rain turned to snow in the mountains and is glittering in the morning rays. The peak that just had a fire lookout built yesterday is also shining in the snow. It goes without saying that Mount Lolo is snow covered too. Though what a pity that the rays from this beautiful sun should melt the snow.

The following is a short verse by an anonymous person and called "Space":

> Here is a fairy world,
> Small creatures scurry here there,
> Empires rise and fall.
> Ladybugs climb dizzily
> Upon a lily stalk.
> And I disturb a [illegible]
> Upon my morning walk.

193

Iwao

76

Oct. 29, 1942

[Translated from Japanese]

Dear Hanaye,

The mountains all around us are still powdery white due to the cold.

Several hundred Italians in black shirts gathered yesterday and had a twentieth anniversary celebration of the Fascist party. A Catholic priest wearing a beautiful robe conducted the service. Later there was a speech and singing accompanied by a band.

Yesterday I was supposed to go down to the river but decided not to because it was too cold. An angler caught an eighteen-inch trout. On my outing last week, I picked a cactus, and I have it displayed on my desk.

Since the decision is taking so long, we've decided to make an inquiry. I know it's hard to be separated so long, but there's nothing humanly possible to do. I believe the wisest thing for us to do is to take advantage of the opportunity to study something. It'll be useful in the long run. We should forget the past and be prepared to live in the future. I'm sure the cloudy days won't continue forever, and someday it'll be clear again. They say there's a silver lining even among the dark clouds. I think it's very essential that we try to see the bright side of life and live accordingly.

It must be getting colder at your camp. I heard there's not enough firewood to go around. I'm a bit worried, but this being America, I'm sure something will be done. When we first arrived here, we were taken aback by the subzero weather, but once we got used to it, it wasn't that bad. And if we stayed indoors with the stove burning, we couldn't feel the cold at all. However, when we go outdoors we're careful to dress heavily so we won't catch a cold. Your health is most important, so please don't overdo things.

Please pass my very best regards and thanks to Aunt, Uno-san, and Yamamoto-san who brought firewood for you (which Yamamoto?).

Iwao

[Translated from Japanese]

My dear husband:

I received your postcard, thank you. I'm thankful that we are both able to live in safety. Winter is just around the corner. A cold wind began blowing this morning. It sounds as if snow has fallen in your area. We don't have snow yet, just wind. . . . I'm thinking about going to collect willows at the riverside to use as kindling, but I'm hesitating because it's become a bit late. Sagebrush also works as kindling, but we try not to burn it because apparently it damages the stove.[a] Recently we've started receiving coal, which is a great help. The distance we go in fetching it with buckets is rather far, but if we don't go once a day the nights are unbearably cold. Thankfully we've had hot water since last week and I can now take a bath in the bathhouse. To everyone's irritation it is a small shed that, on days when the wind blows, is just like the one where we went skiing. And there's no electricity at night so I bought a flashlight.

Aunt has been sleeping since getting her teeth pulled last Saturday, so I've been busy with little time to write. Because she had all of her top teeth pulled and only the front teeth put in, she can't eat much. Since yesterday she's been able to get some food down. Her age keeps her from going out much anyway, so I take care of all outdoor chores. As long as my body can keep up, going out helps me take my mind off of things.

Last night I went alone to a . . . get-together at the Fifth cafeteria.[b] The place was humming with dancing, a raconteur, and comedy skits. I returned home around ten, surprised at the cold.

I've borrowed Cora's book to read. Apparently the pocket edition of *My Sister Eileen* was for sale at the canteen for twenty-five cents. It was pretty interesting. From Summy I borrowed William Davenport Hulbert's *Forest Neighbors*. I'm now reading about the beaver. The trout, lynx, porcupine, loon, deer, and buck stories were interesting.

I hope you continue to do well. I can't seem to relax here although I'm trying my best to remain in good spirits. I haven't gained any

a. Inmates were eventually forbidden to use it.
b. Mess hall.

weight either, while Uncle on the other hand no longer fits into his pants and continues to gain weight. He won't have anything to wear if Kashima doesn't take his pants out for him. I envy those who lead such hallowed lives. Still, he brings me newspapers and flowers. When I show your letters to Uncle, he doesn't utter a word. What a strange bird.

I don't even see autumn leaves in my dreams here and contemplated that beautiful leaf [you sent] with nostalgia. Those who work are always going getting out, but there's absolutely no chance for weak-bodied person like me to leave. Yesterday Cora came back with a beautiful flower and pot for Aunt and me. It's a paper begonia with beautiful thick leaves like the unforgettable one I had in Seattle. With so little greenery here, it's nice having plants around. We've had three goldfish since yesterday. They're Cora's. Seeing them swimming around so happily reminded me of our tropical fish and I burst into tears. Whatever I see reminds me tearfully of the past. I'd be comforted if we were together. Living alone is unbearably trying. Three women in the same quarters anxious about the others all day long allows for no rest.

I just got back from lunch. Aunt is finally up and made it to the cafeteria. On the way home we noticed that someone had been growing three different varieties of pine trees at their place. Feeling nostalgic, I recalled the green of the Cascades and Mount Rainier and the adorable animals.

A yellow bus has been running since last week, though I have yet to ride it. For ten cents you get three tokens, which amounts to three cents a ride. I want to try it on a good day when the weather's good. Right now it's cloudy with signs of snow. I need to gather kindling before snow falls. We receive coal, but since there's a lot of wood around, kindling is not provided.

When we get up in time to eat breakfast at seven, it's still so dark we have to turn on the lights. We eat lunch at twelve and dinner at five. We have three meals on Sunday too. When I heard that at Missoula there are only two meals on Sunday, three meals seems sacrilegious. . . .

Hana

77

Oct. 30, 1942
[Translated from Japanese]

Dear Hanaye,

In virgin snow
a kitten runs.

This is what I actually felt this morning as I was on my way to the
mess hall. Snow has finally reached us here below, although it's still
sparse.

How white the roof
where no soul resides.

The barrack next door is vacant, so it's without heat and the roof is
white with unmelted snow.

Someone's mending his shirt, another writing a letter, and still another
gazing at his polished stone. There are five or six of us in the quarters,
and there's not even a sound. The heater fan is quietly purring as it sends
the warm air around. My best to everybody.

Iwao

78

Nov. 3, 1942
[Translated from Japanese]

Dear Hanaye,

There was heavy rain last night just like Noah's great flood, and this
morning there were small lakes formed here and there. I received your
letter of the 29th. I'm really glad that your letters are arriving more
frequently and in such detail that I'm able to know how you are getting
along. I see you are reading English books. Please continue to do it
regularly.

While you're at it, why don't you take up penmanship and spelling
since they won't take too much of your time. Even if you do a little
every day, you'll be surprised how much you can progress.

My studies are halfhearted because I feel unsettled due to the indecision about our situation. But I am studying English through newspapers, magazines, and the radio. I've been doing art a little each day since the beginning of October.

Mr. Hayasaka told me that his wife mentioned in her letter that she knows you quite well, and when she saw you the other day she thought you were quite plump for a frail person.

Wakasugi-san and State Drugs'[a] Sasamoto-san share quarters with me. Their families are at your camp.

I wish they would allocate firewood to you folks quickly. We've no problem with fuel for we have plenty. And since we have central heating, the stove is used just for supplemental purpose. The restroom and bath are conveniently located under our same roof, so it's very handy even when we get up at midnight. I can only sympathize with your situation there. Recently, we are given three meals on Sunday also, though the noon fare is light stuff like rice and tea with pickled vegetables, pie and cake.

My turn at doing chores comes every five days because there are so few of us now. When I was in my apron and cleaning up after meal, several of the men told me to please leave because the young ones would take care of the rest.

My very best wishes to aunt, Cora, Yamaoka, Doc, and the others who're been so kind to us. I pray that God's rich blessings be upon you. Please be careful not to catch a cold.

Sayonara, Iwao

Nov. 4, 1942
[Translated from Japanese]

My dear husband:

Rain. The water freezes, but it doesn't seem cold because the air is so dry. We are receiving coal.

There was a community inaugural ceremony at the church last Sunday. My hope is that everyone will amicably join in prayer to God. I'm not taken with the idea of small groups forming various different congregations.

a. A prewar drugstore in Japantown.

Last night Iwai, Kumusaka, Aunt, I, and two others went to the riverbank to gather kindling. A cold wind blew, but the sunset was gorgeous. We sang hymns in prayer. Standing perfectly still listening to the small birds chirping and the pure river gurgling in the quiet of the night is worth more than any riches the world has to offer. Living with you is all I could ever want. . . .

Last night Summy and his mother brought over a partition they constructed to serve as a screen for me. I sleep in the middle of the room, which makes it hard to rest. Having a screen at the head of the bed makes it seem warmer, more like my own bed. I slept really well last night. The screen helps block the noise of young people coming home with their boyfriends after twelve which makes me feel really uncomfortable even if I'm already in bed. I'll sleep much better now. . . .

Remember that the November edition of the Reader's Digest ran stories about skunks and wolves? The skunks are so adorable they brought tears to my eyes. The book I borrowed from Summy was enjoyable enough that I wouldn't mind reading it over and over. You should read it when we are together again.

At her age Aunt has good periods and occasional bad periods. It's sometimes hard to tell how she is doing so. Occasionally I take meals to her. I hope she gets well soon. I don't go out much, in order to keep her company. . . .

How is the cat at your place? Probably suffering from the cold, poor thing. Someone is raising one or two cats that I imagine are comforting to have around. And I don't know whose they are but there are quite a few dogs around here. If you need something let me know. . . .

Write to Summy to thank him for the screen. A postcard is fine. Stay well.

Hana

| 79

Nov. 6, 1942

[Translated from Japanese]

Dear Hanaye,

For the past few days we've been having an overcast of snow clouds with occasional light falling flakes. The day before yesterday and this morning, there was enough snowfall to whiten the landscape. The snow on the mountains no longer melts away, but here on the ground it's not so cold that the snow wouldn't disappear. To be sure, there was real ice falling yesterday.

> Ice crunches on every step,
> my morning walk.

> Jacket collar gathered high as I stroll,
> Mount Lolo's snow comes falling.

It has been eleven months since we've been apart. But those eleven months have been times of such uncertainty. No one can guess what heartaches there have been for both of us, although we must be deeply grateful to God for keeping us healthy and guiding us through the hard times.

There's a saying: "Think about the misfortunes of others that you may be satisfied with your own lot."

If we think of those in snow-bound plains or those in the desert and the south without food and shelter, we can only count our blessings that our physical needs are provided for. There's even a case where the father is here in this camp and three children without a mother are being cared for in a relocation camp by strangers.

They say everything comes to him who waits, so I guess there's nothing else to do but wait. After all's said and done, without life there's nothing, so let's maintain our health, pray to God that we can meet again very soon, and live courageously.

Someone turns on the radio at 7 a.m. (your 6 a.m.), so I listen in bed for half an hour, and as I'm having breakfast at 8 o'clock, we have roll call. After returning to quarters I mop the barrack, read the Scriptures, and by 11:30 a.m. I gather the mail and take it to headquarters. I try not to miss my morning and afternoon walks. I think that I should do more walking when it gets colder. I read the Bible again and by about 10 p.m. I go to bed.

It'll be getting colder in your area, too, so take care not to catch any cold. My best regards to Aunt, Cora, and the others who are being so good to us.

Iwao

P.S. Yesterday I had a vinegar-and-miso-flavored sashimi of whitefish caught from the Missoula River.

| 80

Nov. 7, 1942

My dear wife,

Today I'm sending you a parcel in which you will find an ash tray, 6 stones, & a Durham sackful[a] of pebbles. This ash tray was made by a friend of mine using stones of my own careful collection. The pattern in the bottom was made by putting real elm leaves, which were found around barracks. This tray can be used without the glass top if you found it broken. Inside this ash tray you will find a stone with fine grass pattern, this is not really glass, but said to be chromium crystalized when this rock was formed, say 100,000 (?) years ago. The bottom is flattened so that you can stand it upright. An oval green stone with wavy pattern is very common here. You will see crazy pattern on the other side. This & a red stone with wavy pattern will shine more by polishing with cloth. A stone with Japanese picture was painted by Mr. Izui. You may laugh at a red stone which looks like worm-eaten. Straight, diagonal red lines on a smooth oval stone will show better if you will put a little oil on it. Pebbles in the sack should be seen in water, you may put them in a goldfish basin. Each pebble, however small, was carefully picked by me, so please do not make light of them.

You may give away these if you wish, except the ash tray & a painted rock, the latter being given to me by one of my students as a keepsake. If you want more stones to be given away, please let me know.

Yesterday Doc. wrote me that you folks over there were crazy about oil trees,[b] just as we have been crazy about stones here. Even now when

201

a. Sack for Bull Durham tobacco.
b. Greasewood branches that were transformed into walking canes.

I take a walk, I can't help but stop & pick up a couple of stones with beautiful design.

I wanted to include "cactus" in the package, but it can't be done without the permit from the Dept. of Agriculture. I'm afraid I wrote too much today. Give my best regards to your room mates & others.

Yours ever Iwao Matsushita

| 81

Nov. 9, 1942

[Translated from Japanese]

Dear Hanaye,

I received your letter dated the 4th on the 7th. I wrote Wataru a long letter of appreciation right away. I sent you some stones and ashtray on the 7th. For details please refer to my letter in English dated the 7th.

Why don't you give one of the stones to Wataru-san since I have a lot more. I made a box for our cat, and when I placed the box over a steam vent, he was as happy as he could be going in and out of it.

The other day a minister from Hong Kong visited us and said he was a prisoner too.[a] When he saw the Bible on my desk he was very pleased.

Let me know what kind of food you are eating. Are you folks making getas,[b] too? I'm not too fond of them so don't send any. The skunk [illegible] is very cute, isn't it?

Give my regards to everybody, and take care not to catch a cold. I'll send a haiku next time.

Sayonara, Iwao

| 82

Nov. 14, 1942

[Translated from Japanese]

Dear Hanaye,

For a few days we had cold, subzero, but clear weather. It has turned to rain now. You've probably received the stones I sent the other day. Do

a. He was probably interned at the Stanley Internment Camp in Hong Kong and later repatriated aboard the exchange ship *Gripsholm*, on its return voyage to the U.S. in July 1942.

b. Wooden footware, similar to sandals.

you know the status on the premium for the Westwood Life Insurance that I asked Koike-san to enroll me in? Another thing, I received stamps from Koike-san, so please thank him for me.

Here are some of my recent crude verses:

A she-cat given a red ribbon round her neck.

North mount armored in white,
bathed by western rays.

As I stroll this November morning,
I feel I could touch Lolo's snow.

There are some folks down at the river, so I suppose we'll have whitefish miso soup and trout.

Please give my best wishes to Aunt, Cora, Itoi-san, Yamaoka-san, Yamamoto-san, and those that we're indebted to for their care. Remember health comes first.

Sayonara, Iwao

Nov. 16, 1942, morning
[Translated from Japanese]

My dear husband:

A beautiful sunrise and snow. The frost is deep. From early morning on the 14th a strong wind blew, giving me enough of a shock that I got up, dressed, and then returned to bed. The houses shook as if an earthquake had hit, but everyone greeted the sun unharmed.

I received the beautiful stone, and the ashtray arrived in perfect condition. But more than the stone I'd like to be given you.

High school has started. Breakfast is at seven when it's pitch black, but the stars glitter. . . . There will be an art exhibit that I plan on going to see at noon. They say some interesting works are on display.

Last week Aunt and I worked ourselves into a tizzy carrying lumber scraps home from quite some distance. Poor Wataru helped us tremendously. We borrowed the neighbor's wheelbarrow, although pushing it was quite a chore for me. Wataru was much better at it and carried two days' worth of lumber in one day. I cried out of sheer gratefulness. Putting eight pieces of lumber in a seabag made it heavier than I am. In getting it home, I carried the bag on my back, hanging heavier pieces from my front to balance out the weight. By the time we finished I was more exhausted than when we took that twenty-mile hike. We continued the work for three or four days. It was hard on the three of us, but if we don't gather lumber we won't make it through the winter. . . .

Last Sunday, to celebrate the birthday of Aunt's nephew (a three-year-old boy) from breakfast they had *sekihan* [red rice], *norimaki* [rice rolled in seaweed], and fried chicken. Last night Wataru and his mother, Aunt, and I had a wonderful meal. Tonight there will be a cowboy movie which I'll go ahead and pay the ten cents to see.

I've been wanting to record the menu of recent meals. Yesterday morning we had coffee with cream and a teaspoon of sugar, two pancakes with butter, one boiled egg, and an orange (half). For lunch we had spaghetti, potatoes, and salad. The evening meal was a pork chop (which was big), rice, carrots, rice soup with vegetables, and cake with applesauce. This morning we had two slices of toast, scrambled eggs, and coffee. I ate a lot. The cook is getting used to the work, and recently the meals are quite good. The cafeteria in the morning is sunny and warm.

More snow has fallen. Construction of the barbed-wire fence around the camp has just been completed. I'm glad that we can now go down to the riverbank during the day. Wataru and I often talk about what a shame it would be if we weren't able to go there when you come. What a relief that we will be able to do that. A dog has been visiting me a lot recently, but we don't want its dirty paws in the house and we don't let him in. One night the nuisance slept on my bed, though it was actually comforting to have it there.

I'm impatient to see you.

I'm tired of having single men make fun of me, calling me the Montana widow.

Recently hot water has been available every night, and I've been able to take a bath, which really saves a cold-blooded person like me.

Uncle hasn't changed a bit, although last time he was in town he bought me two boxes of Kools, I think with the money I've been putting away. He also brings me cigarettes that others give him. I'm trying to give up smoking, but with my nerves it's hard to stop. I'm still taking medicine.

I am helped by those from whom I least expect it. It's very strange that I haven't seen the Horiuchis at all. They've become complete strangers. Recently I'm beginning to understand peoples' hearts as if they're being reflected in a mirror. I don't see the people from the church very often. Iwai, who I met through Hiroshi, often consoles me. I don't know how Hiroshi is doing. . . .

I received your letter of the 14th. It sounds like your weather has been miserable, but it's been nothing but rain here either. We have to puddle-jump to get anywhere. The weather should clear soon, though I certainly don't mind the lack of dust. . . .

I haven't anything from West Coast [insurance company]. I paid that long before leaving Seattle. I had Sueko [?] pay it. I did hear that the bond will reach its maturity date next year. That needs to be paid once a year right? I also have the certificate with me.

I haven't seen Uncle since last week. He's probably been busy at the hospital.

My trunk sent under the name of Koike should have arrived with the others, but appears to have gotten held up in Twin Falls. . . .

Hana

| 83

Nov. 17, 1942
[Translated from Japanese]

Dear Hanaye,

Your letters are overdue. Nor have I heard that you got my stones, so I'm a bit worried that you might have caught a cold. I'm fit as usual and do my exercise and daily walks. The snow has started to fall in earnest now and [illegible]. It's snowing like mad at this moment (nine o'clock), and the whole world is covered in white. I think it's going to be hard to take my walk without snowshoes. I'm really lost for words when I hear about the firewood situation at your camp. There's so much firewood here, if I could, I'd like to mail some to you! However, after going through all these hardships, I've learned to appreciate my past freedom.

Until we meet again, I pray that God's abundant blessings be upon you. Please give my best to everyone.

> My stroll, lightly clad
> I return for more.

Sayonara, Iwao

| 84

[Translated from Japanese]

Dear Hanaye,

Your long-awaited and lengthy letter dated the 16th arrived on the 19th. I was relieved that you weren't sick but were busy with gathering firewood. I see you also received my stones. I sent them to relieve you of your monotony, so please look at them in that light. I wish I could do something to take care of the firewood problem, but sorry to say, I'm helpless in that matter.

As I read the Old Testament in the morning and the New Testament at night, I constantly pray to God for your physical and spiritual well-being and our return together. I know He will grant us our wishes someday. As the saying goes, "Snail, take your time to climb Mount Fuji." There are times that we need to have that sort of patience.

The snow that lasted all day on the 17th was over by the next day, and the weather has become clear. With the dark glasses on, which you kindly sent, and bundled in my heavy overcoat holding many memories for me, I went for a walk in the glittering snow recalling past winters.

We had all thought that we'd be out of this camp by mid-August, but my heart is filled when I see that it's time again for us to see snow.

I understand they will be fencing in your camp. They are removing the access wire fences at our camp, and for all I know, these may be used there. I'm glad to hear that the food there is excellent. Since we're so few in number, we are able to do anything. On the day of the heavy snowfall of the 17th, the fishermen among us went to the river and caught fish that were used to make a dish called mixed *sushi*. The poor guard had to tag along too, and he told the fellows, "You crazy boys!"

It's too bad about Hiroshi, isn't it? I wonder if it's the same kind of an ailment as his brother's? This only makes one aware that health is everything. Let's both take care of ourselves.

Please thank Tsuneshi-san for me. Tell him that if I should be released I'll be bringing lots of stones with me. Give my best wishes to Akutsu-san, Itoi-san, Aunt, Cora, Doc, and the others who have been so considerate to us.

Sayonara, Iwao

P.S. I'm illustrating the cats' box:

It's laid on a gunnysack-covered concrete pad over a steam vent and weighted down with stones. When we are bringing back fish or meat from the kitchen for them, they would come to meet us halfway. They're bounding in the snow and enjoying themselves, uncaring about the snow that's going into their box.

Nov. 21, morning

[Translated from Japanese]

My dear husband:

I'll pick up the pen while Aunt is busy with laundry. It has been raining and snowing.

I've caught a slight cold but not enough to keep me in bed. Don't be concerned. Yesterday I received a letter from Mancini[a] saying that Ellen, their youngest daughter, will be getting married on December 12th. They're going to ask the people living at the house on 24th Street to leave and move into the place with their father. They said they're taking care of our things and Blacky and not to worry. Do you remember the love seat? The one we got through Saburo? They want to buy it. Shall we give it to them as a present or keep it for ourselves, since a feather-stuffed loveseat is hard to come by? I'll give you some time to think about it. Should we tell them that it's a keepsake and reject the offer? Also, should we send a wedding gift of five or ten dollars? Hurry and write back about what you want to do. They plan to reupholster and use it.

Our meals of late have been good. I've been enjoying toast and butter, coffee (we can have two or three cups although it will probably

---

a. The couple's former landlord.

be rationed soon), half an orange, and a soft-boiled egg. Yesterday, since it was Friday, for dinner we had fish (halibut) tempura, spinach, rice, tea, and bread pudding. Although lunch was light, hot cocoa was served. Recently we are having more rice than beans. I'm sure the cook is having a hard time of it.

Today Uncle should have come by. Wataru's frequent visits are comforting though the start of school on Monday has kept him busy. When I go down to the river he always accompanies me. . . .

Someone told me that your case should have already been decided and that you are keeping the news from me. Whatever the news, please don't hesitate to let me know what it is. Of course I believe that we will eventually be together, but even if the news bad, I won't go to pieces, so please tell me the truth. I'm resigned to face whatever the decision is.

Recently I've been receiving coal, and when I tell people how wealthy I've become, they laugh. Ishibashi-san is teaching me how to knit socks. Once I get good at this, shall I knit you a pair? Don't you have holes in your socks? If you need anything don't hesitate to ask. Mr. Yamagata's acquaintance in Ogden, Utah can get *senbei* [rice crackers]. Shall I send you some? We can order some Japanese food items. I tried ordering a few. We all continue to do well.

Take care. I pray for your return.

Hana

| 85

Nov. 24, 1942
[Translated from Japanese]

Dear Hanaye,

Thanksgiving Day is near. While there may be some bones of contention, in some ways we have a lot to be thankful for. How can we not be thankful that we're able to live every day with ample material provisions and kept from physical harm. There's nothing else for us to do but pray to God for our family's reunion.

It warmed up a bit and the snow on the ground has melted, but the snow on the mountains still remain. I've started reading Soseki's "Cat" from yesterday. It's a book that's funny no matter how many times one reads it.

Give my regards to everyone, and take care of yourself.

Iwao

| 86

Nov. 27, 1942

Dear Hanaye,

Yesterday was an overcast Thanksgiving Day. This was our banquet menu: turkey, cranberry sauce, celery, fruit salad, chicken soup, pumpkin pie, rice, and pickled vegetables . . . the preceding eight items. With full stomachs, we gave thanks for such plentiful fare.

It's snowing heavily today. It's deep enough to cover one's boots and won't pack even when you grab a handful and squeeze it. It reminded me of skiing.

Changing the subject, according to a public announcement from Washington, there's a possibility that internees may be able to join their families. In other words, those internees that have applied for and received approval, it seems, will be allowed to live with their families at a family camp.[a] My status hasn't been resolved yet; of course, if I'm paroled, I'd be transferred to the center, but even if I'm not, there's still chance for us to be reunited.

I think I should be prepared to apply for a family domicile. Should my request be granted, we'd be relocated to a designated family camp somewhere. Wherever that might be, there can't be any objection to being together, is there? What do you think? I'd like to get your opinion, and if you have no objections, you and I would make separate applications for a change in venue. I'll be waiting for your answer. After I hear from you, we'll work on the details of your application.

It must be a scenery of white everywhere at your camp. Is it cold in your room? Please wear enough clothing to keep yourself warm and take care not to catch a cold.

a. In November 1942 the INS opened a camp at Crystal City, Texas, for German, Italian, and Japanese internees and their families. The camp remained in operation until 1947.

209

Give my best regards to Aunt, Cora, Doc, Yamaoka, and the others.
Sayonara, Iwao
P.S. Two-foot-long icicles are hanging from the barrack eaves.

| 87

My dear wife,

Thank you very much for your ever-interesting letter. As to the life insurance, you'd better see the receipt you should have received from the company last May, or ask Doc to write a letter & find out. Regarding the love-seat, I like to keep it for the same reason as you stated. Therefore I suggest you will write him something like this: "We like to keep it, because it reminds us the whole history of our life in Seattle, but you may use it as you like, etc. . . ." As for the wedding present, you may send 5^{\underline{00}}$ or 10^{\underline{00}}$, whichever you think correct. Socks & heavy stockings are supplied by the Government, so you needn't bother yourself about sending them, & you'd better keep senbei cookies & foods for yourself.

Regarding my status, I'm not hiding anything from you. Really I haven't received any notice from the officers here yet, but it is over a month now since I had my status inquired, so I think I'll do so again within a few days unless I hear something. It's almost a year now since we were separated, & I'm proud of you—a woman of such physical weakness, could stand such a strenuous ordeal as never before experienced in your life. But I'm quite sure our Heavenly Father will never forsake us. Let's pray to God with all our heart so that we may be allowed to live together pretty soon.

May God protect you all the time & make you strong physically & spiritually!

Your loving husband, Iwao Matsushita
P.S. The following is a Haiku poem I composed yesterday:

> [line in Japanese characters]
> (Translation) I called "Kitty, Kitty!"
> She rolled in the snow,
> what a lovely kitten!

live together pretty soon .
    May God protect you all the time + make you strong
physically + spiritually !
                        your loving husband.
                        Iwao Matsushita

(Letter #87)

    P.S. The following is a Haiku poem
        I composed yesterday :-

        キリと呼べば 雪にころがる 仔猫かな
        (Translation)
        I called " Kitty, Kitty ! "
        She rolled in the snow,
        what a lovely Kitten !

Dec. 4, 1942

[Translated from Japanese]

My dear husband,

I received your English and Japanese letters. It sounds like you had a wonderful Thanksgiving Day feast. I got a high fever that day, and Uncle insisted that I enter the hospital. Immediately the following day the fever went down, and since there was no danger of it developing into pneumonia, I returned home Saturday afternoon.

Getting to the bath is a job because our shoes get stuck in the swampy mud. When the ground is frozen it's fine, until the sun comes out. When it snows or rains, we have to swim through the mud to get anywhere. . . .

The hospital is comfortable, steam heat keeps the rooms warm. Mrs. Ishibashi is kind enough to visit me daily with Summy to see how I am doing. She has even prepared *udon* twice. With no soy sauce to be found anywhere, making noodles is a chore, especially since she has to run back and forth to the laundry room to get water. I'm really grateful to her.

For two or three days, Aunt brought rice to me from the cafeteria, but the road is bad and it was hard for her. It's now been eight days since I've fallen ill. I wanted to reply sooner but got behind in writing. . . . Last week someone came to ask me about whether I wanted to move. When I told them it sounded like a good opportunity but I couldn't really make a decision until I had heard from you, they told me to write down the reasons I didn't want to consider moving. I wrote that I didn't want to be interviewed when I was in no position to decide. . . .

I asked Uncle to send the insurance money, and I sent the letter to Mancini as you requested along with five dollars. I also sent fifty cents to pay for Blacky's license. Shigeko (Tamaki) sent a fruitcake which I haven't forwarded to you because I sense that you may arrive here soon. I'll send it when I'm well enough to walk to the post office. I await your immediate homecoming. . . .

A man (he was quite old) from our block named Abe was out looking for greasewood when he got lost. He was found three days later, but it was too late. . . .

It's nearly Christmas. Reflecting on last year, I feel as though this year's will be a much happier Christmas. Last year I didn't even feel as though I were alive. *Senbei* can no longer be sent through the mail probably because the censors are getting to be very strict. . . . [a]

Cora is working nights at the hospital so we need to let her sleep in the afternoons—it's trying, but she's a sweet girl.

Hana

| 88

Dec. 7, 1942
[Translated from Japanese]

Dear Hanaye,

On this anniversary date, it was decided that I'm to be interned. It was quite unexpected and regrettable. You'll probably be terribly disappointed having waited a lonely year with hopeful expectations, but please don't cry. Keep your chin up. Let's think of the families of soldiers who are fighting in the heat of the tropics or in the cold snow, what they must be feeling.

There are fortunes and misfortunes in this world. The Bible says, "One shall be taken and one will be left behind." We can't expect that all things will be meted out fairly. Eight out of ten who have been sent here are to be interned, so that's a small consolation, but I can't blame you for being disappointed when in fact there were some that were released. When I compare my circumstances with those that were released, I can't help being very perturbed.

You, as well as a host of others, know that I haven't done anything that would harm America. I stand before God innocent of all guilt. It's said that a setback is sometimes a blessing in disguise. The fact that I couldn't be released to go to Minidoka may be God's divine will, and we won't know whether it'll be for the best until later. As in the hymn, "Where He leads me I will follow," let us accept His command and pray that His blessings will be upon us.

The reason for my internment, according to the Attorney General, was that I was "potentially dangerous to the public safety." I am keenly disappointed that the sincerity of my love of America in my appeal had

a. Military police detachments were ordered to inspect incoming and outgoing parcels. Mail was not censored at WRA centers.

not been accepted. Since there's no use dwelling in the past and "crying over spilt milk," let's consider some future options.

(1) Rehearing. This is held if, at the initial hearing, you were not able to fully state your case, or if substantial evidence has been uncovered and submitted to the Hearing Board with an affidavit of an influential individual who can vouch for your character and background, *and* if the Board deems your case has sufficient merit to warrant a rehearing. Generally, unless you have extremely convincing evidence, permission for a rehearing is usually denied. In fact, there's a case where an appeal made several months ago have never been acknowledged.

I've had my say in my first hearing, so I've nothing else to add. I felt so good after the hearing, it was like the sky clearing. At this date I've nothing to submit, and the only affidavit I can probably get is from Mr. Griffin, so I don't think I have a chance going this route. I heard, though, that there've been some that have gone to your camp as a result of a rehearing. Do you know anything about it?

(2) Reconsideration. This isn't a formal procedure, but there's been a case where a wife of an internee had an important American friend write a convincing affidavit saying that while her husband is interned he is of no use to the United States, but he would be useful should he be released. She petitioned Washington, and as a result her husband's sentence was rescinded and he was paroled. I'm thinking about doing the same. Especially in my case, the Hearing Board had recommended release but the Attorney General had stated that the evidence at his disposal warranted internment. Now, I don't believe any evidence exists that would be detrimental to me. Even if there were thought to be, I'm sure it could easily be explained. However, there may be a matter of interpretation. For example, if I picked up a stone unthinkingly for no reason, and that was construed as my intent to throw it, there's no defense. Accordingly, I wonder if we shouldn't make a direct appeal to the Attorney General with a joint petition from you and me, and possibly one from an American friend.

(3) To request a transfer to a family camp. This has to be done in any case if my internment status is changed to parole and I am not permitted to return to the center. According to your letter I received

today, there's already an inquiry being done at your camp, so we should definitely submit our request without delay.

If the plan doesn't agree with you, the problem is whether to go with (2) and ask for a rehearing and make an effort to be released to the center, or seek one of the other options.

For myself, I can't bear to be stigmatized as "potentially dangerous," so I propose to petition for a rehearing and at the same time request our joint tenancy. The point is we need to be together as soon as possible. You may know of families in your camp with internment returnees who can relate their experience, or you may have good ideas of your own. Please give this careful thought and give me your reply. I doubt if the internees left here will be suddenly be transferred to another site.

A couple, three days ago, we had a visit from an official from the U.S. State Dept. asking us about our treatment. I told him I'm most distressed by being separated from my family. He said, "Please be patient and bear it awhile, we're already working on that problem."

There's been a disturbance at the Arizona's Poston Relocation Center, and there also was an ugly incident yesterday at California's Manzanar Camp. We're saying how troublesome those camps were, and we'd be better off in a family camp.

This letter will take the place of three, so you won't hear from me the rest of this week. Please give my thanks to Doc for all he's done for us. I'm deeply indebted to him. Our reunion was postponed, but I feel I can see the sunshine behind the dark clouds. Let's take care of our health and pray to God that we can be together again soon. You mentioned the people who have been so kind and helpful while you were ill. Please give them my personal thanks and regards.

Sayonara, Iwao

| 89

Dec. 17. 1942

[Translated from Japanese]

Dear Hanaye,

I sent you a parcel today. Though it's Christmas, being in camp, there's nothing I fancy as presents that I can get. Please accept the package as a token from my heart.

(1) Model sailboat. A seaman from California made this for me. He made it using scrap wood he gathered in the camp, and you can see his painstaking craftsmanship in the sail he whittled so thin from a piece of wood. The rudder handle is carved from the handle of an old toothbrush. My friend even made me a box to mail the boat in. If you find it hard to remove the boat from the box, you can take off this piece, and that should make it easier. The box may be useful for repacking, so it'll be best to save it.

(2) A round buoy. An Italian person made this, and it's a frame to put a picture in.

(3) This heart-shaped stone was made from the stone that I got from the Missoula River the month after you were transferred to Minidoka (Sept. 16). I shaped and polished it with great effort. It had lain on the black cover of my English Bible on my desk every day until I carved an *H* a few days before sending it to you. If you could let it rest on your Bible as I did, it'll surely make the stone happy. Our hearts are like this stone . . . without blame.

Let us pray that the war will end soon and "Peace on earth and blessings to mankind" will again prevail. I'm awfully sorry that you already had to spent two lonely Christmases. Please stay in good health. I know that the Lord will answer our prayers one day and the sun will also shine.

Sayonara, Iwao

P.S. On the 18th Shigeko-san sent me a book, *Washington Is Like That*. She's a commendable young lady.

Dec. 23, 1942

[Translated from Japanese]

Dear Hanaye,

Did you receive my lengthy letter of Dec. 7 concerning my internment? Since I haven't heard from you I'm worried that you might have become ill from despair. I'll be awaiting your reply. I mailed you a parcel again on the 18th, and it's supposed to be your Christmas present.

Shigeko-san sent me a book and a snapshot of her and Kayama Iku-chan. I wrote thanking her for her concern and care for you and also for the recent present of the book and candies.

Is there any talk of a family camp there? If there is, please send me the details. I've already submitted our request.

It's been rather warm lately, so the snowdrift would melt and become sludgy and then freeze again. Dr. Koike writes me quite often. Please give him my regards.

Remember, health above all. I'm hale as usual.

Iwao

| 91

Dec. 26, 1942

[Translated from Japanese]

Dear Hanaye,

Yesterday was really a White Christmas. The snow that had fallen the day before had accumulated and transformed the world around us as pretty as a Christmas card. The two trees in the mess hall were decorated with cotton, red paper, apples, oranges, and other things, and we were able to enjoy a Christmasy mood. Just as the meal we enjoyed on Thanksgiving Day, there was more food than one could eat at one sitting.

My friends at the barrack put up a tree for me on my desk, and all decorated like the ones in the mess hall. I'm writing this letter besides that tree.

We sang "Silent Night" to the words of my own composition, which follows:

1. The snow falls silently,
   O'er Lolo's peak, camp grounds too,
   Silently, ever deeper it falls.
2. The trees, the fences, roofs too,
   Where'er I look, is virgin white,
   'Tis Christmas greeted by snow.
3. Silently and white the snow falls,
   Reverently, we greet this Yule,
   The night passes silently.

217

4. O, Prince of Peace,
   Who was born in Judah's town,
   Save this discordant world, we pray.

Last Christmas I held some expectations, but I've none of that this year, and there have been only two Christmas cards from Shigeko-san and Koike-san.

I'm very worried since I haven't heard from you in a while. Are you down with a cold? It must be terribly inconvenient. When I imagine that you are being reticent as usual, I can hardly bear it. Please, for my sake, gird yourself and be strong. God will someday answer our prayers. I read the Bible every night and pray that the Lord's strength and kindness will enrich you abundantly. Please give my regards to everyone.

Sayonara, Iwao

Dec. 30, 1942, noon

[Translated from Japanese]

My dear husband:

I received two of your letters and one postcard. I cannot apologize enough for not writing for so long. I've become very weak from illness, though when I told this to Uncle he did nothing, as usual. I've been coughing without letup until today. I'm fine now, but it's been a month since I've been able to sleep without coughing. I'm sure I've been a nuisance to others, but in the past few days I've improved considerably, so please don't worry. My suffering from illness may be part of God's plan, but I feel so worthless around healthy people who aren't sympathetic and just can't comprehend how I have to whip and push myself to live each day despite this illness. It pains me that when I pick up the pen I can't even finish a letter to you. I'm writing now because I feel rather settled today. I'm sorry I haven't written sooner, but communal life at the camp doesn't allow me to write when I want. I feel guilty, please forgive me. I still can't believe you are interned. I want to get my apologies and this letter off to you quickly.

I heard that it would be beneficial to find someone who knows you well even if it is not someone well known. Uncle is out of the question, so I'll try to find someone from whom we can seek help.

I've been inquiring around about your internment camp. I worry that impediments will arise in trying to correspond with the outside if I move to your camp and am given the same treatment you receive. I want to consider this a bit longer. After a request for a transfer, decisions take two to three months, but I don't want to ask for a transfer until after the hearing decision. There is nothing I can do about the fact that I may have to continue living alone. . . . I must also consider the possibility of your coming here or our being forced to repatriate to Japan together. If I'm outside at that time, I can take care of things and we can return to Japan. It's important to consider the various possibilities. I want to see you as soon as possible, but I also want to go on to a new camp only after investigating its regulations regarding family.

Just as it was when you were at the Seattle Immigration Station, where you could see a visitor for only five to ten minutes once a week and had to speak in English, there are times now when it's easier to communicate by letter, although in New Mexico or Louisiana, English letters take five or six weeks to arrive. Important news is apparently sent by telegram. At night, unable to sleep, I lie in bed thinking about what to do but am still at a loss. Let me know how you feel about the situation.

It was a lonely Christmas. I spent it crying. Seeing happy families gathering together brought a lump to my throat. I imagine you spent a lonely Christmas too. This year's was more sad and lonely than last year's or any I've had. Thank goodness for Summy's family and the Takases who treat me like their own child. . . .

Recently I've been taking my knitting over to Ishibashi's or Takahashi's. I thought I might be able to receive a small single room since my nerves are so weak, and I asked Uncle to get the signature of the head doctor. I'm hoping that as a sick person I may get a room, though with Uncle involved who knows? At any rate I've been in hellish pain since November 26. I know I shouldn't be telling you all of this, but I'm writing because I've decided that I'm ok now. . . .

Hanaye

92

Dec. 31, 1942
[Translated from Japanese]

Dear Hanaye,

Today is the final day of this year. I've been waiting anxiously for over three weeks to receive your reply regarding some important matters I mentioned in my letter of December 7. I'm very worried. I received the candies a few days ago. Having gotten the package, I assume that you must be all right, and now I'm wondering whether my letter had gone astray. According to Koike-san's letter, it seems that my letter did reach you. Have you gone again into a spell of no writing, or have you given up in despair? I'm terribly concerned.

I received a reply from Washington regarding my request to be transferred to a family camp. It said that I'll be notified one way or the other pending completion of preparations. I've got my appeal and other documents ready to be filed with the Attorney General, but without a word from you, I'm at a loss about what step I should take. It's another matter if you are taking action from your end, but still without any reply, I can't help being worried.

It rained a lot last night so I thought the snow would be melted, but much to my surprise, everything is still covered with snow. Did you get the model boat, buoy, and stone I sent?

I pray that the new year will bring us new hope, and the Lord will bless you with good health and comfort you.

Please pass my best regards to Koike-san, Tsune-san and family, Aunt, Cora, Yamaoka-san, and the others who've been always kind and thoughtful to us.

Sayonara, Iwao

93

Jan. 2, 1943
[Translated from Japanese]

Dear Hanaye,

I spoke at length with superintendent Fraser[a] yesterday, concerning

---

a. Bert Fraser was the officer in charge at Fort Missoula.

my situation. He agreed that there were grounds for a review of my case and suggested that I petition Washington for such a review. I told Mr. Fraser that was my intent but was waiting to hear from you.

He was of the opinion that, since there shouldn't be any objection on your part to hasten our reunion, it was best to write to Washington right away. While that too was in my mind, I have delayed doing so because I thought that in order to present our case most effectively we needed to set up the following procedures and get your ideas for a better course of action. But time is of the essence, so I will go ahead with the petition and hope you do the same without delay:

(1) Write to Griffin-san (Grace and Eldon), who sent you an affidavit for our first hearing, and ask them to write you another one. Include this with your personal petition and mail them together to the Attorney General. I've enclosed the drafts of the letters to be sent to the three persons. Of course, you may revise the letters as you see fit. Mail the letters by airmail and enclose airmail stamps with each letter for return mail purposes.

(2) Wait ten days to hear from the three. If you receive replies from all of them, it's well and good; if not, gather whatever is available and mail them with your personal letter to Washington. I've enclosed the draft of that letter. It goes without saying that you may edit the letter any way you wish.

(3) Make two carbon copies of the original letter to Washington. Airmail the original, and send a carbon copy by regular mail on the next day. It'll be best to retain copies from the three also. All this is a precaution in case the mail doesn't get through for some reason or other. The second copy is for you to retain in safekeeping. To be sure that the letter to Mr. Biddle is properly composed and free from misspellings, have Cora or another Nisei friend type it neatly for you.

(4) As soon as your affidavits arrive and your letter to Mr. Biddle is ready for mailing, please let me know when you would be mailing them off so I can mail my petitions at about the same date. I'm sure it would be more convenient for the recipient

to receive our petitions together than having them dribble in piecemeal.

My draft to Mr. Biddle has no paragraphs, but I'm sure that a Nisei will know how to fix that properly. A day faster means the reply will come a day earlier. That's what I'm counting on.

Sayonara, Iwao

| 94

Jan. 5, 1943
[Translated from Japanese]

Dear Hanaye,

I received your letter after I mailed my letter dated on the 2nd. As I had surmised, you haven't been too well. This has been my biggest concern all this time. If I were only there you needn't feel any imposition on others. When I think of this I'm really sorry for you, but you know it's impossible for me to fly there to you. There's no other recourse but for you to be of stout heart, hope in the future, and live each day bravely. I pray to God every morning and night for your health and well being.

It breaks my heart when I think how difficult it is for you in a communal setting among so many different types of people. When you're ill, don't hesitate to ask Doc for help. He writes to me quite often.

Superintendent Fraser persuaded me to write to Washington without waiting for you. I took his advice and mailed my letter yesterday since I had everything ready to go. Therefore, as soon as you receive the affidavits mail them off to the Attorney General without waiting to notify me. If the affidavits are not forthcoming by the end of ten days, you need to look around for someone who'd be willing to vouch for us. I don't think a Japanese person would do. Can you ask Mr. Kawasaki if he knows anyone in his company? I don't want to involve more people if I can help it, but the situation is such that I don't think we have a choice.

222

The rumor about a family camp is silly, isn't it? No one knows for sure what'll happen, but the rationale may be that keeping families apart negatively reflects on the U.S. from a humanitarian perspective. I can't imagine that the American government would spend a huge amount for such a foolish project as the rumors suggest. If in one of a thousand chances that should come about, we can always negotiate with the authorities to revise the plan. But I can't see it happening at all.

I've no intention of going to Japan, nor have I asked to be repatriated. Being interned doesn't necessarily mean repatriation for us. Even if it should come about that we must return to Japan, there's no way we'll be able to settle our estate in wartime. It's best not to think about such things.

In the Old Testament, Joshua 1:9, it says: "Be strong and of a good courage; be not afraid, neither be thou dismayed; for the Lord thy God is with thee whithersoever thou goest."

I believe this verse will give you courage and strength.

Our New Year's meal consisted of: for morning, *ozoni*,[a] evening, mixed flavored rice, rice balls, grilled fish, teriyaki chicken, fish cake made from the whitefish caught from the Missoula River, bamboo shoots, orange, beer, fancy eggs.

It's getting late so I'll quit here. Please give my regards to everyone. Please take care of yourself. I'm 100% OK, so don't worry.

Sayonara, Iwao

| 95

Jan. 9, 1943

[Translated from Japanese]

Dear Hanaye,

I'm told there is a family camp already in existence in Crystal City, Texas. There, I understand, the families will board. An official here has told us that the rumor that married couples in a same camp would be segregated is utterly ridiculous, and he asked that we inform our families of the fact.

Did you receive the papers I sent you? Did you mail the letters to the three? As I mentioned previously, I've already mailed my letter to Washington. Please do the same as soon as possible.

a. Soup of selected vegetables and *mochi*.

Dr. Koike sent me a greasewood cane. It was such an unusual item that the camp officials and my colleagues gathered around and made a big fuss over it. I also received the Minidoka *Irrigator* and read Doc's article about the Idaho mountains in the Christmas issue. But it seems to me there's no more scenic place than here. For the past couple of days the ice-fog has been so beautiful, and unlike ordinary snow it forms an icy bloom on every exposed surface. I often wish I had a camera to record this scenery.

Tomorrow is my birthday.

Cold greetings my birthday in Missoula.

Iwao

| 96

Jan. 14, 1943
[Translated from Japanese]

Dear Hanaye,

How is your condition? Try not to be concerned about anything and live each day without care. Did you receive my package I sent before Christmas? I didn't let you know about it in advance, so I'm worried that it might have been lost.

Several days ago the Spanish vice-consul from San Francisco was here and interviewed us. The Spanish government is acting as an intermediary between Japan and the United States. According to him the family camp in Texas is just about completed. He plans to visit your camp too and may inquire about you because I told him about us.

The winter in Montana isn't as cold as last year. I'm still in my B.V.D.'s. The fellows admire me for being so robust. Yet when the temperature nears the freezing point, I do feel a bit cold. The temperature is above freezing today for a change, so everybody is saying it's warm. I feel that about 35 degrees is just about right. The fact that there's no wind makes it easier to withstand the cold, I'm sure. It must be warmer at your place than here, isn't it? Do be very careful that you don't slip when there's a freeze.

Please give my best to Aunt, Tsune-san family, Doc, Cora, Yamaoka-san, and the others.

Alone in a makeshift furrow
I gaze at the ceiling.

We leave and enter the barrack
reading a thermometer.

When sun shines and snow flowers
scatter, it is three o'clock.

With ink brush I draw
winter mist of the Missoula mountains.

Iwao

Iwao to Hanaye, January 18, 1943. Note occasional use of difficult-to-translate words in English.

97

Jan. 18, 1943
[Translated from Japanese]

Dear Hanaye,

A few days ago a cold snap greeted us rather suddenly. The winds that were absent of late also blew, stinging our faces as we trudged to and from the mess hall. Fortunately, the winds quit after a day. It is, of course, below freezing and the [illegible] left near the window froze from the air that seeped through the cracks. The window panes in the bath-washroom area are frosted by beautiful leaf designs. Our living area, on the other hand, is heat regulated, so we're able to do anything.

The snow turned to slush the other day, froze again, making the ground a sea of ice. It's too cold even for snow to fall. It's quite a job to keep from slipping on the ice while going to the mess hall.

Several days ago, one of the fellows shared some sea bass he had received from Spokane. I ate my fill of that sashimi with gusto. That was the most delicious sashimi I've had since the ones I ate last year of yellowfin tuna sent from Seattle. Besides, the leftover Kikkoman shoyu [soy sauce] really gave me a feeling of being on the "outside."

I've heard that a few hundred people were sent to the family camp from Wyoming[a] on the 15th. Has anyone from your camp gone?

I am praying every day for your spiritual and physical well-being. Please give my regards to those with whom you share your ward and others who have been so solicitous.

Sayonara, Iwao

P.S. A baby whitefish I caught in the river is swimming like a guppy in a jar on my desk. Snapdragon's in it too.

98

Jan. 20, 1943
[Translated from Japanese]

Dear Hanaye,

Following a spell of bitter cold when it got as low as minus 16 degrees, the temperature rose to 28 degrees above today. I don't particularly feel

a. Heart Mountain Relocation Center.

the cold, but the snow flurries are a pain in the neck. Words to a song came to me as we used to walk gingerly over the "sea of ice" to get to and from the mess hall. The tune is from an old song called "*Oi toko souda yo*":

Watch it, you'll slip!
Hate to see you fall;
Take it slow and easy.

It's slippery as can be,
It's a sea of ice, you know;
Walk as slow as you can.

Didn't I tell you so!
You went and fell.
Does your bottom hurt?

No wonder you slipped;
It's a sea of ice, you know.
Sparkling in the daylight.

There you go again!
Didn't I warn you?
Watch out, it's dangerous.

Don't be in a dither
Ole man of white,
You gotta be alive to tell the tale!

How have you been feeling lately? I'm very concerned. As I've mentioned many times, try to relax and don't dwell on the past. Please have patience and put your hope in the future as you face each day. I remember you in my daily prayers that the Lord will make your daily life a joyous one.

Have you heard from Washington? I'm sure we'll get a response soon. Even if, by chance, things don't turn out as we hoped, take heart that the sun's already risen in the form of a family camp. It shouldn't be long now for the sun to shine on us too.

Please give my regards to everyone.

Sayonara, Iwao

227

99

Jan. 23, 1943
[Translated from Japanese]

Dear Hanaye,

I heard from Wakamatsu-san that it's gotten down to minus 5 degrees at your camp. We're speculating that there might really be a problem with the firewood situation.

We've had heavy snow for the past two or three days, but it's not that cold, as the temperature is in the teens. The snow on the rooftops melts from the warmth of the barracks, forming icicles on the eaves.

I hear from Koike-san quite often. He seems to be having problems with colds and a sore back, but appears to be lighthearted about it. I wish some of that easygoing nature could rub off on you. As usual I'm in very good shape. I try to live a purposeful life by reading and writing and studying English every day.

Please give my regards to everyone. I pray for your health.

Sayonara, Iwao

Jan. 26, 1943
[Translated from Japanese]

Dear Hanaye,

I have learned that you've been doing well lately. I'm really relieved. I worry about you every day wondering how you're faring—whether you're in bed with a cold again.

At last Sunday's dinner we had *sushi* and rice balls with whitefish caught from the Missoula River. I always think about you when I eat *sushi*, wishing I could send you some. I don't think you'd be able to taste anything like this in Idaho.

I heard from the Alien Enemy Control Unit which is under Attorney General Biddle's supervision. It was in response to my petition I sent earlier. The letter requests that I apply for a rehearing of my case. In my circumstance, however, a rehearing is not going to do any good. I plan to appeal again to the AECU. As I've mentioned before, there have been cases where wives have been successful in having their spouses released without any rehearings by making direct personal appeals to the

Attorney General. I'll hold up on my letter to the AECU until I hear from you how you feel about writing to Mr. Biddle.

I've been reading Kenjiro Tokutomi's *New Spring* again, which I've enjoyed a number of years ago. I never tire of it no matter how many times I read it. In it there's one called "The Hundred and One Song." Do you recall it?

Let's take on our daily lives with renewed spirit. I'm hale as ever even in this minus-20-degree weather. My regards to everyone.

Sayonara, Iwao

P.S. I received a query from the State Department asking whether I desired to return to Japan. I replied in the negative. The officials here have asked for your name and address, so I expect you'll be asked the same question. I thought I'd let you know my response so yours would be the same. Of course, I'm speaking of a wartime situation.

Jan. 26, 1943, 8 a.m.

[Translated from Japanese]

My dear husband:

I received your letter yesterday. . . . I am slowly putting on weight. Thanks to Dr. Mitsumori and Ishibashi, who lives with Dr. Shigaya, I'm feeling much better. Everyone has helped me so much in getting through this illness. . . .

Thank you for the model ship and stone. I'll keep it forever. I've put it carefully away since our place is so full of Aunt's things that we can't even walk a straight line in the room—it's practically a storage room. . . .

I sent you a box of chocolates. Did you receive them? I also put a registered letter in the mail.

The other day I saw the Spanish consul-general. He knew about you. Also, Dr. Kitagawa translated for me when I talked to people from Washington, D.C., about you. Yesterday, I received a reply from [Eldon] Griffin who is no longer at the University of Washington. And Bruno's reply arrived. . . .

Lately I feel as if I'm about to fall into a big hole, but I find some comfort in attending the Episcopal church sermons. I never see the Methodist priest around. I go to Ishibashi's after lunch every day. His wife works as a dishwasher. I'm learning how to knit. I hate to barge in on them every day, but Aunt is disagreeable of late, forcing me out of the house. I'd like to move to a different place. If I'm too tolerant I'll go crazy. Cora's boyfriend went to a Detroit college, and she's looking very lonely. I understand her feelings completely.

Two or three days ago there was a meeting for internee families about Crystal City, Texas. Mr. Sander explained to us that the houses there are duplexes for two families. In the middle of three rooms is a bathroom and other facilities to be shared by both families. Each family cooks for itself using an oil stove, cooking ingredients and foodstuffs are provided. If we move there, I have to resign myself to receiving the same kind of treatment as you. All letters and parcels are checked, and all money is to be put away. Permission must be given for any use of money, one must live on a determined amount of money, and cards are used for dealings with outside people. Visiting hours are set, so that contact with the outside is not free as it is here. Once you move in, there's no getting out, and since the living situation is even more confining for those with children, families with kids of child-rearing age are discouraged from living there. Those in the middle of hearings should wait until the hearing is over to move. Correspondence is severely limited.[a]

After discussing the situation with everyone, I still have not signed up to go there, although it sounds as if you have. I think we should think about it a little longer. According to Mr. Sander, one may . . . cancel a request to be moved to that camp. At the end of this month there is a group going to Texas, but I won't be going. I may appear callous, but it won't be too late to decide about going after your hearing. How do you feel about it? The camp can accommodate one or two thousand people. At this point, one thousand are scheduled to make the move, and there is a chance that we may not get in if we wait too long to decide, though I think it's better to finish the hearing first. Think about it, and if you feel that I should go immediately I will. . . .

The Okumura family has returned. Tae passed away, so they've been living with little Henry, a six-year-old. They seem so lonely. Yamamoto has been ill in the hospital for three months but has since improved. I see Mrs. Wakamatsu from time to time. She's doing much better now.

a. All mail was subject to the same censorship at this INS camp as at Fort Missoula.

I received a Christmas card from Mr. Wakamatsu. Please give him my thanks. Occasionally I run into Hayasaka. . . .

I've given up trying to do anything. I've been having insomnia that keeps me up for two to three nights at a time thinking about things.

I'm sorry not to have wished you a happy birthday during my illness. Uncle Koike is still acting strangely—a hopeless case.

Last week thanks to the efforts of Ishibashi's friend Fujimoto, my trunk finally arrived. Uncle should've been the one dealing with it. The lid of the trunk was stamped with the names Koike and Matsushita, so I really needed Uncle's help or risk it getting lost. I finally asked Fujimoto to help. . . . The transportation costs were $25. I'm at my wits' end with Uncle, who is so unconcerned with my situation that he won't even write letters for me. I can ask Kawasaki, but his place is too far away to get there very often. Besides Uncle there aren't many people who can write English.

My head and hands are shaking. I can't write any longer. I thank God for his blessings and put down my pen.

Hana

Jan. 30, 1943

[Translated from Japanese]

Dear Hanaye,

I was very glad to receive your four-page letter dated the 26th. Whenever I see your letter, I can't help feeling hopelessly inadequate for not being able to be there to see you through all the anxieties. Although there are people to whom I owe my thanks for looking after your welfare, I've not written because I sense many are wary of having any correspondence from this camp. Can you please give them my regards and thanks?

I was relieved that you've received the model boat and the heart-shaped stone. Thanks for the candies. I wrote you an acknowledgment on December 31 (#92), but there probably was a backlog in the mail.

I think it's best to go ahead and mail your letter to Washington together with the affidavits you managed to obtain thus far. Let's figure our next course of action after we hear from Washington.

Thank you for the detailed information about the family camp. It may not be much of a problem for us without any children, but since our aim is to be together in a center, let's wait and see what transpires. If my turn comes around, I'll request that it be reconsidered. You can also wait until a move becomes imminent.

You needn't be concerned about money, so please take care that others are not strapped with any bad debts. I don't smoke, and most of my daily needs are met by the rations. There's really nothing to spend money on. This past year I've spent $7.50 for a trunk and $5.00 for a dictionary. The other expenses were mostly for postage. But even that's free now. It's more than anyone deserves.

After reading Tokutomi-san's *New Spring*, I've just now come to realize the similarities between us and the author and his wife—the fact that they were married at twenty-seven and twenty-one years of age, that they loved the mountains and hiked together a lot, and that they didn't have any children. It's been my long-time ambition to write a memoir like his.

In applying the author's theme to our lives, I feel that we are now at the stage where we are undergoing a "promotional examination." I've also learned the scripture verse that says, "All things are possible to those who believe in the Lord." Let's take heart and do our very best. As the saying goes, "Do the best you can and leave the rest to Providence." Let's not be discouraged and give it our best effort until we can go no further, then leave the rest to God.

I know how bothersome living in a center can be. We've heard from people who left here for other camps, and they say there's no place like Missoula. The mail is on time, food is good, and the scenery is great.

Your letter was a lengthy one. Even I would probably get numb in my head and writing hand! I suggest you write in installments. That'll be easier on you, and the censor, too.

I pray that God's grace you will continue to keep you healthy and give you spiritual comfort.

Sayonara, Iwao

Feb. 2, 1943

[Translated from Japanese]

Dear Hanaye,

Inasmuch as Washington's response to your petition indicated that our reunion in Idaho would be unlikely in the near future, I think that the our next move, as was suggested to me by Washington, is to submit all the documents through the Seattle Hearing Board for resubmission to Washington.

Since the Hearing Board recommended my release at the original hearing, I can't see that another hearing would improve my status, and if one is needed for formality, I have no idea when that will take place or when a decision will be rendered. It may take another year. As long as the verdict is not for my release or parole, we'd be back to step one.

On the other hand, if this is to be our last chance to enter a family camp, we should be ready to decide whether to risk a hearing with its uncertainties, and lose our place in line, or go ahead to enter a family camp.

This is not to say we should abandon all attempt for a hearing, because we may still be able to do that from the family camp. I know of a person who had deferred his request for a hearing because of the family camp problem. He says he's taking whichever route will reunite his family.

No doubt a wife will be accorded the same treatment as her spouse in a family camp. Letters will probably be censored (but this is exactly what we have here), and any money will have to be deposited in an account and limited to a five- or ten-dollar withdrawal every ten days. This too is the same here. Receiving visitors will probably require the same restrictions as we do now. Not that I expect many to visit us.

Aren't the folks at your camp more afraid of the inconveniences and lack of material things? I would think that the joy of a family reunion would override any such concerns. We can weather any hardships if we're together, helping and consoling each other. Because I'm in Missoula I'm able to correspond freely, and in Japanese, but the people in the southern camp[a] aren't so fortunate. They must be hoping to be with their families   **233**

a. Probably the Santa Fe camp in New Mexico.

at the earliest opportunity. I don't know what our future holds for us. However, please let me know your feelings about a family camp so I can be prepared to make a quick decision if we're given a sudden choice of two options. If it's like what you've reported, the quarters may be better than the center's, and we all feel that it may also be better in other aspects too. I'll stop for now. Please give my regards to everyone.

Iwao

P.S. "Spring is Close" (Kenjiro Tokutomi):

Those separated shall meet again; the dead shall live; the departed shall return. That season is certain to come. To doubt this is like saying there won't be a Spring after a Winter. Spring will come, Spring is close. Even though the rustling of the dry oak leaves bespeaks the cold, aren't there the plumes of warm air rising in the paddies?

(a song)
As long as you wait Spring will come;
Spring arrived even whilst I was in reverie.

| 103

Feb. 4, 1943
[Translated from Japanese]

Dear Hanaye,

Mr. Ito told me I must be at my desk for at least twelve hours every day. He was impressed and said he couldn't continue such a routine for very long.

I get up at 7 a.m. and listen to the radio. I have breakfast at 8 a.m., complete the house chores and I'm at my desk by 9 a.m. at the latest. I begin the day by reading the Bible and by the time I go to bed around 11 p.m. it's been fourteen hours. Say that two hours are spent away from my desk for meals, walks, and other activities, indeed, I will have spent twelve hours right at my desk.

I read the Seattle and Spokane papers, read English and Japanese books, teach those who come for English lessons. There's not a moment that I can say that I'm idle. There's a daily radio program at 3:15 p.m. to 3:45 p.m. called "Mother and Dad" that I enjoy listening to while lying on my cot with my eyes closed. This is the only time that I lie in bed during the day.

This program features hymns, old American melodies, and hillbilly music that so engross me that others who kiddingly complained that they can't concentrate on their reading or writing have now come to admire me.

There are those who play poker and *hana-fuda* [card game], but I've abstained from them. Nevertheless, I'm treated nicely and referred to as *sensei* by everyone. When I suffered a stomach disorder due to the extreme cold and lack of exercise, folks were very solicitous of me, and the cook made gruel and soup especially for me. I got well in no time by watching my diet and going on daily walks. Once I let slip that I'd like fresh celery, and lo and behold, when celery became available in the kitchen, folks made sure that I got the best part of the stalk.

Try not to catch a cold. Relax, be aware of your health, and strive to make each day an enjoyable one. I'm praying for you every day. My best to everyone, especially to Tsune-san.

Sayonara, Iwao

| 104

Feb. 9, 1943
[Translated from Japanese]

Dear Hanaye,

How have you been? I've been very concerned. As for me, I'm fine. It's not as cold as it was last year, and all's well here. Please let me know if anything has happened. I pray that you'll able to enjoy each day with good health and happy anticipation. My regards to all.

Sayonara, Iwao

| 105

Feb. 16, 1943
[Translated from Japanese]

Dear Hanaye,

Koike-san informed me about your situation. If I'd been there I wouldn't have let you go through all that hardship. I'm really sorry. I know you'll be lonesome at times, but I pray that it'll be good for your physical and mental health. Don't hesitate to see the doctor when you're not feeling well.

The envelopes addressed to us are labeled "Free," but given the uncertainty of our status, continue using a stamp when writing to us. For the rest of this month the Japanese-language censor will be assigned to another duty, so if you have any urgent matters please write to me in English. After March 1 it'll be back to normal. Have you heard from Washington yet?

The weather was so gorgeous yesterday afternoon that I accompanied the fishing bunch to the Missoula River. What contrast of sceneries there is between summer and winter along the river. The trees were bare, but their ice-covered branches were beautiful against a background of cloudless blue sky. The dead weeds and brush were also coated with frost, and the blossoms formed by the ice needles were so pretty they made me want to pluck them like flowers for my vase.

The river is lined with large poplars, some of them gnawed so much I'm afraid they may fall in a windstorm. I'm amazed at the little creatures when I see the dams they have built.

I can hear the gentle whir of the reels as the fishermen cast their lures into the water. As I sit on a piece of board the February sun beams, and while my breath forms a white vapor, my face is bathed in warmth.

The Italians' mangy wire-haired dog always tags along with us. He's lame and hops along as he goes. The other day he emerged from a brush with a blue-neck duck in his mouth. We'll be getting duck soup soon, I'm sure. The fishermen didn't have much luck but still ended up with five or six squaw fish. The catch will probably end up as fish cake or in a miso soup. Folks are occupied with three days a week of fishing and another three days of movies. I saw Sonja Henie and Tyrone Power in *Second Fiddle* the other day. I also saw *In Old Chicago*. The younger folks are making a skating rink by grading an ice patch between two barracks. I wonder how it will turn out.

Please give my regards to Koike-san. I'm sure we're indebted to Tsune-san and his family for their kind assistance to you. Please pass on my sincere thanks and regards to them. Mrs. Hayasaka has mentioned that she runs into you occasionally at the center. I pray for your health.

Sayonara, Iwao

March 4, 1943

My dear wife,

March 9th, being your birthday, I sent to you yesterday, a package containing 50 fig bars, one can of peanuts, some green tea & 2 packages of cigarettes—the ones which you sent to me some time ago & I didn't smoke them. Please celebrate your birthday with these things with Wataru's folks. This is all I could do now. I am enclosing herewith a birthday card which I made myself with flowers I preserved last summer from the camp ground.

Yesterday, being Hinamatsuri [girls' festival] we celebrated it with dinner, consisted of maze-zushi [rice mixed with fish and vegetables], spinach sprinkled with goma [sesame seeds] and manju [dumplings]. We missed girls very much.

It may take some more days before the Japanese censor comes back, so please write in English when you have important things to tell me in a hurry.

Wishing you many happy returns of your birthday, & God bless you all the time.

Best regards to Doc. and Sam's folks.

Your loving husband, Iwao Matsushita

| 108

March 9, 1943

My dear wife,

Today, being your birthday, let me offer to you my hearty congratulation & I trust you duly received my humble presents & had a happy birthday party with Wataru & his folks. I wrote Wataru the other day, thanking him & his folks for all kindnesses they have given you & will render in the future. Doc. writes me often, telling me about your condition.

How do you feel now? I am kind of worrying about you. Every morning & night I never fail to pray God so that you will be healthy & happy & we will be allowed to live together as soon as possible. Have

237

---

a. Letter 106 was a printed Christmas card with no personal message.

trust in God & be given strength from Him so that you can brave a "lonesome road".

Have you heard from Washington yet? Our Japanese censor is still away. I'll let you know as soon as he comes back. Last Sunday night we again enjoyed comedy drama performed by Italian detainees. Around this time last year we had a sea of mud, but this year we still have freezing weather.

Please take good care of yourself & don't hesitate to ask Doc. to help you when you are in trouble.

Yours ever, Iwao Matsushita

| 109

March 15, 1943

My dear wife,

According to Doc's letter, you received only candy & nothing else. After being inspected by the officer here, I packed the package & tied it myself, so there shouldn't be any mistake on this end, & as it was not insured, it was impossible to trace the missing articles. However, the officer said he would inquire at the post office in Missoula. I think there's something wrong elsewhere. For your information I packed the parcel this way: [diagram]

How did you receive on your side?

If you haven't received an answer from Washington D.C. 30 days after mailing, you'd better ask them if they received yours. I received their answer to my letter 3 weeks after I sent it.

We made a boat for fishing & launched her on the Missoula River last Saturday, & named her "Señorita", which means a "miss" in Spanish.

We still have snow & ice on the ground, & it still freezes & snows sometimes, but Spring is coming!

Your loving husband, Iwao Matsushita

| 110

March 18, 1943

My dear wife,

I'm glad to know by Doc's letter that it was a mistake on your part about the package & you received all that I sent to you for your birthday, & I trust you enjoyed them with Wataru's folks & others.

238

Mr. Wakamatsu sent to you a box of candy yesterday, and it seems that he wishes to express his thanks toward me by doing so. I thanked him already & when you receive it, please let me know & you'd better thank his wife too.

Yesterday afternoon I was taken out to the town of Missoula for the first time & enjoyed two hours of shopping in a beautiful town.

As my money is getting lower I am drawing out 30\underline{^{00}}$ today by check & another payment for my life insurance is due in May, so will you please let me know how much balance we have in Bank of California's check a/c?

Well, I hope your health is much improved & enjoying every day with kind friends.

Your loving husband, Iwao Matsushita

| 111

March 23, 1943
[Translated from Japanese]

Dear Hanaye,

I'm thankful I can write again in Japanese now that the Japanese censor is finally back.

It was a quite sudden decision, but Hayasaka-san will be moving to your center. Although I personally don't relish taking over his duties as the group leader,[a] I'll do my best if it'll help the others.

Springlike weather suddenly came upon us last night, and the snow has begun to melt, making large pools that we have to detour around.

I received a letter from Kanazawa-san, whom I haven't heard from in several months. He said he saw you at church and that you looked fine. I was relieved to hear that. Please take good care of your health and try to enjoy each day.

Well, I'll stop here for today. When you're feeling well, please write me even if it's only a short note.

Please give my regards to Tsune-san and his family, and to Doc too.

Sayonara, Iwao

a. Spokesman for the Japanese contingent at Fort Missoula.

March 31, 1943
[Translated from Japanese]

Dear Hanaye,

I've kept myself very busy lately because of the influx of people. The Italians entertain us with beautiful concerts from time to time. Mr. Wakamatsu mentioned reading in a letter from his wife that she was very happy to have gotten together with you. Mr. Wakamatsu was impressed with your letter of thanks written in excellent English. He was very impressed, saying it certainly bespoke an educator's wife. I demurred, but he remained impressed.

According to some who have seen the family camp in Texas, the scenery cannot compare to Missoula's, but there are groves of orange and grapefruit trees, and the living quarters are far superior to any others. I don't know when and where we'll be together, but one thing seems to be certain. That is, the Family Camp is not such a bad place.

Have you heard from Washington? Please give my regards to Doc and Tsune-san and his family. Take care of yourself.

Iwao

113

April 3, 1943
[Translated from Japanese]

Dear Hanaye,

It's been one year and four months since we've seen each other, so I'm enclosing my picture I've asked the authorities to take of me. The photo is untouched, so I may look a little unprepossessing. But there's no mistaking my latest self. I've lost some weight, but this life is different from the outside world.

I haven't been able to do any studying on my own or write letters when I want to because of the extra duties I've assumed. I want to write to Doc and Tsune-san, but please tell them what I've said.

The snow has melted from the mountains surrounding our camp, and I can even hear the meadowlarks' call. The days have gotten longer, so we can play baseball after dinner.

I'm praying for your good health. I'm doing fine.

Sayonara, Iwao

| 114

April 8, 1943
Mrs. Hanaye Matsushita
2-12-D
Hunt Branch
Twin Falls, Idaho[a]

Dear Wife,

I wish to show you the picture of where we live.[b] Ask somebody from here for details.

Yours ever, Iwao Matsushita

| 115

April 15, 1943
[Translated from Japanese]

Dear Hanaye,

We had a second boat christening on the Missoula River last evening. I chose the name Minnehaha from Longfellow's narrative poem "Song of Hiawatha." We also had our dinner at the riverside, and we had a great time. When I saw how superbly the beavers had felled large trees and trimmed the branches as if with hatchets, I felt I wanted to see them in action. I saw huge anthills teeming with several hundreds of ants, rowed a boat, and spent an enjoyable two hours.

I believe the premium for West Coast Life is due on May 2. If you haven't already heard from them, please pay the required amount. May's premium should have the dividends and loan interest deducted from it. If we don't remit the sum within thirty days, there may be complications later, so please make the payment as soon as possible.

a. Hanaye had moved to new, solitary quarters at Minidoka Relocation Center in February 1943.
b. Picture postcard

I received a letter from Tsune-san. Is he hurt? Since I'm not in any position to look in on him, please give him my well wishes and take care of him.

The last few days have been virtually like summer. It's warm and the wild flowers are again carpeting the ground.

Health is first. Let's pray that we can live together again soon.

Iwao

| 116

April 22, 1943

[Translated from Japanese]

Dear Hanaye,

Easter is here again this year. It's somewhat different this year with new faces in our midst. The natural changes that are taking place around us, seasonal changes, the spring flowers don't move me as much since I saw them all last year.

When will we be able to celebrate Christ's resurrection together at another place? I haven't been in the mood this year to compose any Easter song. I'm so busy every day as the mayor before I realize it a day is over, a week passes, then a month.

We have to have our option ready in case we hear from Washington, but have you had any news from them? Did you follow up with a second letter? I've asked Koike-san to help you, so if you have urgent matters that need to be communicated don't hesitate to ask him to do so in English for you as often as the situation requires. He'll understand.

I've heard from Hayasaka-san and others that you're well, but I'm still concerned about you. Hide-san sent me some chocolate from Denver the other day. He mentioned that he hasn't written you for a long time too. He's been very busy. Tsune-san sent me an interesting letter, but I haven't answered him yet. Please give him regards. And to his family, too.

I pray every morning and night for your health and that each day will be a happy one for you. I pray that with Easter you will gain your strength anew.

242   Sayonara, Iwao

P.S. This yellow buttercup was the first flower to bloom in our camp grounds.

May 1, 1943

My dear wife,

As the Japanese censor is away again, I write this in English. I received a card from Mr. Ihashi, informing me that he saw you at the farewell meeting for Kanazawas. Wataru-san sent me Easter cards & eggs, making me happy in this monotonous life. Our life here is same as before, but as I have to do Mayor's duty, which became more complicated since Mr. Hayasaka left, my mind is always occupied by numerous things, forbidding me leisure time to compose poems as before. But everybody should do something to make our life here as comfortable as possible, helping each other, some do barbering, some cooking, etc. I don't fail to pray to God every morning & evening so that your health will be improved & the day will come soon when we can join in happiness. I trust you are doing same. Please give my best regards to Doc., Wataru-san & his family. May God bless you always.

Your loving husband, Iwao Matsushita

P.S. I trust you paid my insurance premium.

May 9, 1943, Mother's Day

[Translated from Japanese]

Dear Hanaye,

I'm enclosing the pictures [see page 59] taken on April 14, the day we christened the "Minnehaha."

1 Just shows what the scenery around the river was like. Those are pines on the opposite banks. The boat is not shown.

2 This is the entire party. You probably can spot me in the center wearing dark glasses and a black tie. Wakamatsu-san is standing left of the large tree and wearing a white hunting cap and a dark shirt. He's looking down.

3 This shot was taken so the name Minnehaha could be seen. I'm at the right of the boat. The white bark of the aspens . . .

243

a. Letter 118 is either missing or Matsushita erred in his numbering.

the beautiful slopes of the mountain in the background . . . in winter the lure of skiing beckons strong.

4 This is the picnic ground. Here's where we ate delicious sandwiches and rice balls. The fellow on the extreme left with the cap is the camp guard. I'm in his shadow so you can't see me. Mount Mitton can be faintly seen beyond the forest.

5 That's "Shiro," a white dog that follows around. She had a litter a few days ago.

6 This is a scene of the river taken from a different angle. That's me peeking from behind the Caucasian fellow. You can still see snow left on the mountains in the background.

I sent three pictures to Wataru-san, but please show him the rest. I didn't send any to Koike-san so show him the pictures too.

Please give my regards to Wataru-san's family, the Reverend Kitagawa and the others to whom we're indebted for their kindness.

May God bless you and look after you and make every day a joyous one.

Sayonara, Iwao

| 120

May 13, 1943
[Translated from Japanese]

Dear Hanaye,

For some reason I mistook the anniversary of your coming to Idaho as May 15 or 16. But while I was wrapping some items I wanted to send you, I realized that you went to Puyallup from Seattle on April 28 and it wasn't until August 15, 16 that you'd gone to Idaho. I've given a lot of thought about what to get you. And since they're already packaged, I'll mail them:

2 boxes of Kleenex (something you've always used, and I thought they may be useful)

1 small tin of pineapple . . . label is off but there shouldn't be any mistake.

Some hard candy (you sent me these)

A chocolate-colored stone pendant I made in remembrance of your relocation from Seattle to Puyallup last year. On the back is inscribed S-P 4-28 1942. *S* is for Seattle, *P* for Puyallup. The arrow shows you went from Seattle to Puyallup on the date shown. It took quite a bit of effort engraving it with a piece of pointed steel.

I've also enclosed another pendant shaped like a finger. If you wax it, it'll show its luster. Both are covered with candy wrappers, so watch out and don't bite on them. After you've removed the stones, please give Mrs. Ishibashi the candies.

Please thank Wataru-san for the picture taken with the Reverend Kitagawa. Thank the Reverend for me too.

Did you receive the photographs? Keep well! My regards also to Koike-san.

Sayonara, Iwao

| 121

May 19, 1943
[Translated from Japanese]

Dear Hanaye,

Please thank Koike-san for the book I received. I forwarded a petition to the Attorney General in Seattle and also requested a favorable response to your letter as well. See Missoula's scenery. Aren't the slopes near the town ideal for skiing? We're surrounded by these mountains. They don't look too high, but they are around 8,000 feet.

My regards to Wataru-san.

Iwao

| 122

May 21, 1943
[Translated from Japanese]

Dear Hanaye,

I mailed you a can of candies from Wakamatsu-san yesterday. He asked me to send it since he didn't want you to be concerned about writing a thank-you letter or anything like that. He's probably done this to repay me for the favors I've done for him. Please thank his wife.

The matter of moving to a family camp for Wakamatsu-san may be decided fairly soon. Our final status is yet unclear, so I haven't made any definite request to that effect, and it seems nor did you. If it becomes obvious that being transferred to a family camp is the only way we can be reunited, there's no choice but to take that course. I have made that known to the authorities six months ago.

The weather has been pleasant for some time, but the last four or five days have been like summer, and it's become uncomfortable in the barracks. Soda pop is selling well.

Please give my best to Wataru-san's family, Hayasaka-san, the Reverend Kitagawa, Koike-san, and the others. My prayers are with you always that each day will be a joyous one.

Sayonara, Iwao

| 123

June 10, 1943
[Translated from Japanese]

Dear Hanaye,

I have been so swamped with work from morning to night I haven't even had time to bathe. I'm also bothered that I can't have my set morning and evening times for Bible reading. When I think that what I'm doing is for the good of the people here I can't help but exhort myself to do the best I can with sincerity and honesty as the mayor.

I suppose I should be thankful for the opportunity to be able to observe and study human relations, but being a nature lover, the more I witness the unseemly side of human behavior, I have the urge to run off into the hills and commune with the birds and animals.

I believe that no matter how ill-natured a person is sincerity would someday win him over. I'd like to experience what the saying says, "Love will be the final victor." I'm resolved to keep Christ in me and march forward bearing the cross. By the grace of God I hope to be of service to this large family with virtue and respect. Those that have been together with me up to this time are very understanding and in any situation amenable to my suggestions. I hope to be as helpful to the newcomers too.

I mailed you a doll yesterday. A dentist friend made it from plaster shaped in a mold and painted. I received a snapshot from Wataru-san the other day. I was relieved to see you well. Please stay in good health until we can be together again. Hide-chan sent me a photo of himself on horseback. He appears to be enjoying it and wants to show us the mountains of Colorado.

Please give my best wishes to Wataru-san's family, Hayasaka-san, Rev. Kitagawa, Koike-san, Doc, and the others.

My intestine seems to be shrinking from problems and a busy schedule.

Sayonara, Iwao

| 124

July 5, 1943

[Translated from Japanese]

Dear Hanaye,

According to my record I haven't written you since June 10. I surprised even myself. I've got a pile of laundry that has been collecting for three weeks. That's how busy I've been lately.

It's become quite a chore to be a head of a huge "family." I'm constantly at the people's call for all sorts of favors. So I'm never without a memo pad and pencil in my pocket. Recently I've finally managed to find time to take a fifteen-minute walk before breakfast, but I spend the rest of the day in the office communicating with headquarters and taking care of business for the internees. There are as many varied opinions as there are different places where the people are from. This is no easy job. I think Hayasaka-san picked the right time to leave here. I'm not one to lose my temper, but there have been folks who made me angry a time or two.

I'm doing my best to run things to see that the people get what they want. But I can't help praying that we'd get permission soon to live together.

I can't hope to recapture the leisurely feeling I had a year ago when I used to rejoice at seeing wild flowers in bloom or write a verse after watching the beautiful skies. I'm asked to give a speech at all sorts of occasions: baseball opener, start of a judo class for the Italians, an Italo-Japanese variety show, etc.

247

Fortunately, it's not a chore for me to give an address in English, but still the preparation for an occasion takes up much of my time. Besides, an English school has been started and I devote several hours a week teaching. On the other hand, I welcome these diversions as means of getting away from the other drudgery.

I think I've lost some weight after things got so busy, but I haven't had time to weigh myself. I have to punch new holes in my belt from time to time. My friend told me to take it easy or I'll ruin my health, but I've managed to stay fit and I'm doing fine. It must be my spirit that's keep me going.

How I long to be with you soon and to talk about old times with Wataru-san! A year, seven months sure is a long time.

When we found out about the drowning of Tada-san's son,[a] Wakasugi-san and I sent a telegram.

Koike-san sent me some new stamps. Please thank him for me. Please give my regards to Wataru-san and his family and to the Reverend Kitagawa. My best to Hayasaka-san too. Take care of your health. Pray that we can be together even a day sooner, that my health will hold up, and that with the Lord's help I will be successful in discharging my duties.

It's 8 p.m. but the sun is still bright. It'll be light until 10 p.m. I was all alone in the office writing this.

Sayonara, Iwao

| 125

July 19, 1943
[Translated from Japanese]

Dear Hanaye,

I sent you some dried fish today. My friend caught and dried the fish he caught from the river. There should be a mix of trout and whitefish. I've thought of sending some to Mrs. Ishibashi too, so please contact her and perhaps you can partake of the fish together.

There's a baby bluebird perched on the telephone on my desk. I've been feeding it flies and insects, so it's contentedly perched on one foot and opening and closing its eyes. What lovable creature it is. I've come to abhor the ugliness of the human world. This bird who innocently

248

a. In the irrigation canal running through the Minidoka Relocation Center.

trusts me without qualm must be close to God. I'm always wishing I could be in a position to commune with the birds and animals as friends. I like to think that the bluebird is bringing me happiness in the near future.

It seems that a lot of Seattleites have returned to the center from the south. My case always appears to be on hold. I guess we just have to be more patient.

Sometimes I want to quit this thankless and stressful job as mayor and enjoy nature or study a favorite subject. However, I'm merely thinking of myself. I'm reminded that it is a precious experience to suffer for others, and at other times I keep hoping that everything will be finally be resolved. My every day is unsettling to me; I'm at agony to bear such days for long. I regret that my faith is not strong enough to permit me like the bluebird to leave everything in the Lord's hands.

Even while I'm bemoaning my plight, I pray and petition God that through Ishibashi-san, Rev. Kitagawa, Koike-san, and others around you, He will brighten up your daily life.

Please pass on my regards to these people. Let's pray that our day of reunion will come soon. Please take care of your health.

Sayonara, Iwao

P.S. It continues to be hot. It was 95 degrees indoors today, but it's cool in the mayor's office so I hesitate to return to the barracks.

July 21, 1943, afternoon
[Translated from Japanese]

My dear husband:

Today the dried fish you thoughtfully sent arrived in one piece. It must be mountain trout or salmon. Please give everyone my thanks. . . . And thank you for the candy and the "Jiminy Cricket." They're all very well done. . . .

I pray for green sagebrush to cover the brown mountains, but my prayers are being ignored, and the stifling days and months shamelessly drag on. Perhaps you are not aware of it, but since around this time last year, writing has been a real chore. My eyes flutter so that I can't write at all. It may be age, but it appears to be nerves, so I try to write when I feel calm. . . .

Mr. Morinaga, who lives in Block 2, is a very considerate person, opening my windows, etc., for me. Unfortunately I can't invite him to dinner to repay his kindness because single women in this camp have to be careful about rumors being spread about them. . . .

Moving begins on the 9th here too. People returning to Japan and those not very loyal to this country will be moved somewhere else.[a] Somehow I'm making it through these difficult days. . . . It's distressing that my nervous system is deteriorating so rapidly that it makes writing difficult. I'll work on collecting myself and writing to you. The stars were visible a short while ago. I usually head out to the bath around midnight. It's now around 12:05. I'll bathe and sleep, or if I can't sleep, rest. I pray for your health and that your work keeps you busy.

Hana

| 126

July 27, 1943
[Translated from Japanese]

Dear Hanaye,

There were several high officials of the Justice Department here yesterday, from Philadelphia and Washington. Being the mayor of this camp, I was asked all sorts of questions about the camp. They also conducted what amounted to a personal hearing of my case. The camp superintendent told me, "You haven't heard from your wife in seven months,"[a] and urged me to phone Hunt and speak to you directly. I politely declined his kind suggestion for fear that it may affect you emotionally.

At the hearing I asked that you be informed about what transpired. When I returned to my quarters, I received a phone call that there was a letter for me. That may be what is known as "coincidence," in English.

Getting your first letter in seven months was like rain from a clear sky. I gather you've received everything and really enjoyed them. I feel now it was all worth while and I'm very happy. My daily needs are being

a. To the Tule Lake Segregation Center, in northern California.

a. Actually, six months.

more than adequately met, and I'm deeply grateful for the improving conditions in this camp.

Koike-san sent me some stamps yesterday. He's been very thoughtful. Please thank him for me. Please give my regards to the Ishibashi family, the Reverend Kitagawa, and others.

The temperature is about 90 degrees every day.

I'll write again,

Iwao

| 127

Aug. 8, 1943

[Translated from Japanese]

Dear Hanaye,

I'm writing today for I'll be too busy to write later, since a bunch of Japan-bound people will be arriving in two or three days.[a]

For some reason, after I've become the mayor all sorts of changes have been taking place, and I've lost all sense of my former sense of tranquillity. There's no time for even my favorite studies, let alone writing verses.

I've been showered with all kinds of requests, complaints, and problems. There have been many times I wanted to quit this thankless job, but I realized that it was just a selfish wish on my part and someone had to do it. The knowledge that what I'm doing is for the good of the people is what keeps me going. Of course, when the folks lose confidence in me and ask me to quit, I'll be glad to step down. However, instead of asking me to quit, they have been begging me to continue. Until such time as I hear from Washington about the disposition of my case, I've told the people, I'll continue to work for them.

I've been told, "You're too concerned about others," "Don't work too hard," or "Just let it be," but being as I am, a "square," conscientious sort, I can't help thinking about others, nor can I ignore requests made to me. Since I'm not the type to be idle while others work, such advice would be for naught.

251

a. From other INS camps, who sailed to Japan on the *Gripsholm* on September 3, 1943.

Recently I dreamed for two nights about the goings on of the camp. That's how concerned I am about the camp. But that's not to say this place is in a turmoil. Folks who've joined us from all over say that this is the most well-run and livable camp they've been to. They talked about rival factions and improper conduct of the elected officer. I try to treat everyone equally and do my best to meet everyone's request. When there's any onerous chore to be done, I set an example by taking the initiative to do it. This is so I can stem any dissatisfaction in the bud and make this camp a comfortable place. Telling you all this won't amount to anything, but I just want you to know what my feelings are.

Several days ago I sent Mrs. Ishibashi Missoula's renowned dried fish (twenty-four each). I'm sure you've tasted some by now. Do you know what has become of our Sumimoto Bank savings account? My West Coast Life insurance will mature in May. I'm arranging for the cash payment to be deposited in my account with the Washington Mutual Savings Bank in Seattle.

Don't you think you should have your eyes examined? Old age may not be what's the problem. My eyesight is very good; I haven't used glasses since being interned. I've become skinnier and have had to make new holes in the belt. However, my appetite's good and I'm quite healthy. I'm a long way from being "all in."

Koike-san has been sending new stamps for me to enjoy. I received a postcard from Shigeko-san who is on a vacation on the East Coast. Please stay healthy until we meet again.

Sayonara, Iwao

| 128

Aug. 12, 1943
[Translated from Japanese]

Dear Hanaye,

The enclosed are the necessary papers for me to collect on my life insurance. On the bottom of the mimeographed form there is a place for you to sign. Also, on #2 of the supplementary papers there's a place for the policy date. I wrote May 2, 1923. If this differs from the policy, please make the change. After you've signed the form, please send the insurance policy and the papers to the West Coast Insurance Company of San Francisco. The deadline is September 4, so please forward the papers and the policy as soon as you receive this letter. I'm sure my policy is among other important papers you have with you, but if you can't locate it, consult the San Francisco office of West Coast Life and determine what you should do. Even though it's a bother, you need to do it right away, even if it means asking Koike-san to help you. I'm sure he won't mind at all. As soon as you've forwarded the papers, please let me know. If you can't, please ask Koike-san.

I'm very busy now that there are many more people. But I'm fine so don't worry.

The address of West Coast Life Insurance Co. is 605 Market St., S.F. Sayonara, Iwao

| 129

Aug. 21, 1943

[Translated from Japanese]

Dear Hanaye,

I've been resting awhile to recover from fatigue.

I met Mrs. Harue Yasui who was here on a visit from your camp. She'll no doubt contact you and give you a report on me.

I don't think my case will be resolved any time soon. There's nothing for us to do but to wait patiently. In the meantime let's both keep ourselves in good health.

In memory of your move from Puyallup to Minidoka (August 15, 16), I mailed you a package with a brooch I had made last year.

Doc sent me some new stamps. Please thank him for me. Say hello to Hiroshi-san, too.

Sayonara, Iwao

P.S. Did you send the insurance?

Sept. 7, 1943
[Translated from Japanese]

Dear Hanaye,

After hearing about you from Mr. and Mrs. Yorita, in detail, I was quite relieved that you are all right. I'm glad that you have those wonderful people as your neighbors.

I received a pencil stand made of greasewood, which I understand was crafted by Morinaga-san. Please thank him for me. The pictures and a new Bible from you arrived safely. Also, Yorita-san has sent me a necktie. Please thank him. I couldn't find anything appropriate here to send him, so could you get him something in return? Ask him about any detail about our camp.

Ishibashi-san sent back those dried fish I sent previously, all seasoned and ready to eat. They were delicious to everyone's delight.

I don't have the foggiest idea what the prospect for our reunion is. You're not in favor of a family camp, and apparently nothing can be decided without a rehearing, so there's no telling when anything concrete can take place. I guess there's no choice but to be patient and wait for the time to come. I plan to ask our camp superintendent for a rehearing, being that lots of people from other internment camps are being returned to their families.

We two arrived in Seattle twenty-four years ago. The latter part of November (this year) will be our silver anniversary. I fervently hope something can be done by then. They say, while there's life there's hope, so let's watch our health and wait for the day we can be together.

I understand Mitsumori-sans have been very helpful to you. Please send them my very best too.

It's already autumn.

Sayonara, Iwao

Sept. 20, 1943, night
[Translated from Japanese]

254 My dear husband:

I'm writing to you from Uncle Koike's. I'm sure you are keeping busy. How are you feeling? I was relieved to hear from Mr. Tomita's

wife's that all goes well. Thank you for the photographs and other gifts.
I also received the Bible. Please give Mrs. Tomita's younger brother my
deep thanks. . . .

My health has improved considerably. Last Wednesday, with the help
of the Reverend Kitagawa, Wataru Ishibashi left for school on the East
Coast. It will be good for Wataru, though I'm hopelessly lonely. I'm too
worked up to provide much more detail. The Ishibashis will be bustling
about with moving today and tomorrow. Mitsumori moved into my
building today. I'm exhausted. The Washington Mutual bank sent a
notice saying that they deposited the insurance money.

Mr. Yamagata sometimes visits. Aunt was ill, but is much better now.

Camp life is busy but without change. I borrowed a book from
Kitagawa but have had no time to read it. The Tsutagawa family returned
to Japan. . . . Hiroshi, who has been in the Tacoma mental hospital for
two years, is getting better and is taking care of other patients. He sent
me a sweet letter, which I may forward to you. . . .

Snow will soon fall in the mountains, which starts me thinking. . . .

Hanaye

| 131

Sept. 22, 1943

[Translated from Japanese]

Dear Hanaye,

Miss Howell[a] delightedly told me that she had met you. It seems that
she ran into Yorita-san in a five-and-ten store in Missoula, and he had
taken her to see you in Minidoka. Wasn't it a strange coincidence? I've
been so busy I haven't been able to attend every Bible class of hers, but
from time to time when I'm able to be in on her sessions, I can't help
being impressed by her zeal. Her fervor has given me strength to serve
the people here with equal zeal. I've probably told you this before, but
when I expressed my desire to resign from my position as the mayor,
the folks begged me to stay on, so here I am still on the job. When
the opportunity arises I am planning to resign. I'm up to my ears with

a. A lay Christian speaker who conducted bible study classes at several of the
internment camps and relocation centers.

problems that keep cropping up. There was a funeral for one of our sick inmates, and I had to officiate. I'm not able to keep up with all the things I'm asked to do. I suppose I ought to be thankful that I'm given this chance to study human behavior at close hand, but thanks to it I've lost quite a bit of weight.

I'll send you a recent photo so you can see how thin I am now. However, I'm all right as far as my health is concerned.

Saburo is here. He'll probably be here awhile. His wife is with her mother in Minidoka, I believe. Perhaps you've met her already.

Our supper yesterday was chicken . . . a half of a big one at that. The chickens were raised by the internees since this spring. They were so tender; we've not eaten such good stuff even when we were living outside. Pickles are made by the Japanese internees themselves too, and they're fresh and delicious.

I haven't heard from Koike-san for some time. Is he OK? Please send my regards to Yorita-san, Mitsumori-san, Morinaga-san, and others. Please take care of your health.

You might be getting some local mushrooms from Hayasaka-san. They've been test-eaten so they're safe.

Sayonara, Iwao

| 132

Oct. 9, 1943
[Translated from Japanese]

Dear Hanaye,

I mailed you a cigarette case yesterday. One of my friends made it by unraveling a potato sack and weaving the strands. It should be preserved as an internee art object, so please take good care of it. I rolled the cigarettes myself but naturally I don't smoke.

I've been notified that my rehearing will take place here next month. I think it'll take a month before I will know the result. We probably won't be able to celebrate our silver anniversary together. I'm very disappointed.

Of course we can't know now what the outcome of the hearing will be, but shouldn't we be prepared for the worst by making up our minds that we would go to a family camp if the results are negative? There are indications that the people who have already made up their minds to go to a family camp may realize their wish soon. If we dilly-dally there's no telling how long we'll be in this present situation. It's not good for a man and a wife to be separated like this for two years.

I'm finally resigning from the mayor's job after tomorrow. I've made it very clear that I won't reconsider, so I'm sure I'll be free of my responsibilities soon.

I heard from Koike-san yesterday. Please thank him for the stamps. It seems Wada-san has come from Tule Lake.[a] I pray that one day soon we can all get together and chat. Please take good care of yourself.

Sayonara, Iwao

| 133

Oct. 15, 1943
[Translated from Japanese]

Dear Hanaye,

I've finally resigned as mayor today. I feel a bit more relaxed for the first time in seven months. To get in the mood of things, I've begun making stone handicrafts.

Miss Howell told me she has sent you a postcard and has kindly offered her place for you to stay if you should come to Missoula. At noon every Tuesday and Friday she faithfully holds lectures for about two hours. Please ask Koike-san if he can write her a reply for you.

It's gradually becoming colder, and it's been below freezing since the day before last.

The other day we found clams in the river near the camp and tried them. They were OK. My friend made a batch into *tsukudani* [pickled kelp] so I'll be sending you some. The mushrooms I sent to Hayasaka-san came back to us flavorably seasoned. We can fish, pick mushrooms and, now, clams. I don't know what we'll discover next.

Please give my best regards to the Ishibashis, the Reverend Kitagawa, Morinaga-san, Mitsumori-san, Yamaoka-san, the Yoritas, and others. It's going to get cold, so please take care that you don't catch a cold.

Sayonara, Iwao

257

a. In the fall of 1943 this WRA camp was converted to a segregation center for "disloyals" whose status was determined by a loyalty questionnaire. Transfers of "loyals" at Tule Lake to other camps was necessary to make room for them.

134

Oct. 22, 1943

[Translated from Japanese]

Dear Hanaye,

It's being a week since I've quit the mayor's office. Since then I've been busy with stone craft. I've made ashtrays, ink stands, and flower vases, eight pieces in all. It takes quite awhile to finish even one piece. I'll send them to you later, a few at a time.

I'm happy, now that things are relaxed as they used to be. As usual I am teaching. I really appreciate Koike-san sending me stamps as they are newly issued. Please thank him for me.

Miss Howell is, as usual, earnestly giving Bible lectures. The mountaintops are quite white already.

Did you receive my photo, cigarette case, and seasoned clams I mailed the other day?

Koike-san wrote me about the diarrhea epidemic at your camp, and I was relieved to learn that you had gotten it too but have since recovered. I'm fine, as usual, with surprisingly good teeth and eyes.

As I wrote you recently, the hearing may take place in early November. We probably have to wait a month to learn what the outcome would be. I'm hoping the day will come soon when we can be together. Please give my regards to everyone, especially to the Yoritas next door.

Sayonara, Iwao

135

Oct. 30, 1943

[Translated from Japanese]

Dear Hanaye,

Yesterday I mailed you two of the stone handicrafts I made. Although the ones I've sent you before were made by a friend, I made these myself. So won't you hold them in safekeeping? Compare these with the previous ones and see how much care I have taken in making these. It took lots of work in matching the color and shape of each one. The ashtray is a small one for individual use. The flower vase is the one with the empty Alka Seltzer bottle. I'm completing them one after the other every day. I've already made fourteen pieces. I'm trying to make as much as I can while I'm in the mood. Day before last I made a cookie jar. It was a big one, and it took nine straight hours to finish it, giving me a backache to boot.

While I was the mayor, my mind was filled with nothing but camp business every waking and sleeping hour. But now, I'm only thinking about the designs for my stone wares. If your friends have any requests, I can make them according to their specifications and send them to you.

Miss Howell has been praying for you every day. I heard that it's already snowing where you are. Take very good care not to catch a cold; it would be terrible if it turned into pneumonia.

Please pass on my best regards to Koike, Mitsumori, Yorita, and Morinaga-sans, and the same to the Ishibashis and the Hayasakas.

Sayonara, Iwao

| 136

Nov. 6, 1943

[Translated from Japanese]

Dear Hanaye,

On the third my friends presented me with a certificate of appreciation and a commemorative gift. The certificate was really a magnificent one, about half the size of a drawing paper. It was like a Christmas card written by hand in old English letters using a variety of colors like red, blue, purple, gold, etc. The card was done by one of the internees who had done this sort of work professionally. I'm told there are perhaps only two or three people in the country that can write this way.

I had this person copy the 23rd Psalm for me once before, and everyone who has seen it marveled at his work. Christmas cards are made by photocopying his elegant calligraphy.

My gift was a Shaeffer desk pen, a truly beautiful one.

The surrounding mountains have gradually become adorned with snow, and the snow line is moving ever lower. There's occasional snow at the camp, but it is not heavy enough to accumulate.

259

I haven't lost my "stone-fever" yet. I'm keeping busy every day and hope to surprise you with a masterpiece when I have the chance.

Give my regards to everyone, and please take care of yourself.

> As I spend late summer
> with my stones
> mountains with their light makeup
> wait winter's coming.

Sayonara, Iwao

| 137

Nov. 11, 1943
[Translated from Japanese]

Dear Hanaye,

I mailed you three pairs of chopsticks and a cake platter yesterday. The chopsticks were made by a certain elderly reverend. He gave me three pairs so you could share a couple with your friends if you wish. The platter is one of the stone craft I've spent quite a bit of time on. It turned out a little interesting, if I may say so myself.

My rehearing scheduled for this month has been postponed, probably until next month. With all the delays I don't have any idea when we can be together, but let's take this as God's will and bide our time. I'm deeply disappointed that we can't celebrate our silver anniversary together later this month. But when I think of the people who are in more trying circumstances, I feel we must endure this disappointment, too. Let's keep our spirits up and stay healthy until our wishes are granted.

How is Koike-san? I'm happy to receive stamps from him so often. Being the way he is, he writes letters too brief to give me an inkling about how he is. Won't you drop in on him sometimes since he's along in years.

I expect Owada-san pays you a visit from time to time. I haven't heard from him since he was transferred from Tule Lake to your camp, but according to Wakamatsu-san's letter it appears so.

Please send my regards to Ishibashi-san, Yorita-san, Mitsumori-san, and others who are being so helpful to you daily.

It'll be getting cold, so take care not to catch a cold. I'll write again.

Sayonara, Iwao

| 138

Nov. 17, 1943

[Translated from Japanese]

Dear Hanaye,

I presume you received the chopsticks and the platter I mailed you a few days ago.

I received a letter from my brother in Japan yesterday. The letter was postmarked on November 27th, 1942, went to Geneva in February of this year, then it was date-stamped October 30th at the relocation center in Eden [Hunt], Idaho. You probably haven't seen it, since it is a year old. He wrote that everyone is safe, mother is comfortable and in good health, and he's praying that the Lord comfort us in our ordeal. He said to keep our hopes and faith alive.

Miss Howell says a prayer for you all the time. She stopped by yesterday to chat. She says she plans to persuade Mrs. Fujii to visit Missoula. If she is willing, Miss Howell will suggest that you come along. If you're inclined to do so, I think it's all right. Unlike the previous year, it's much easier now to have a visitation. However, I'll leave the matter up to you.

I heard that Mrs. Murakomi passed away, also Tatusa-san. Your health is of prime importance, so please don't overexert yourself. Don't hesitate to ask Koike-san if you have any problem.

Sayonara, Iwao

| 139

Nov. 26, 1943

[Translated from Japanese]

Dear Hanaye,

The following is what we had for dinner yesterday, on Thanksgiving Day:

two each large slices of dark and light meat turkey, stuffing, celery, two large olives, sweet potato, salad, soup, dessert, cranberry sauce.

All the food was heaped on my tray. At the table were bread, coffee, butter, and nuts. It was quite a meal!

It just so happens we received our ration of clothing on this day: two pairs of trousers, two woolen shirts, overcoat, winter hat, gloves, and belt.

The temperature was 27 degrees, but when you come across an absolutely cloudless day think of this verse:

> An over-generous ration of clothing this Thanksgiving Day
> A heaped tray while exiled this Thanksgiving day.

Last Sunday I started on making a fancy stone craft for our silver anniversary. It's practically done, but it will probably take two or three more days to put the finishing touches on it. It is supposed to be a powder box. I'll let you know when I'm ready to mail it to you.

I sent Koike-san a postcard yesterday. Please give my regards and thanks to the folks who've been helpful to you: Yorita-san, Ishibashi-san, the Reverend Kitagawa, Mitsumori-san, and others. Do you know Hiroshi-san's whereabouts?

It'll be getting cold soon, so take care not to catch a cold.

Sayonara, Iwao

| 140

Nov. 30, 1943
[Translated from Japanese]

Dear Hanaye,

Yesterday I sent you the powder box I promised you. When you receive it, please let me know via Koike-san. It took exactly eight days to complete. It's a white stone with a 25 inscribed on it to signify our silver anniversary. If you hold it away from you can see the number clearly. On the right side is my initial I in red (red stands for the color of garnet, my birthstone). On the left side is your initial H in greenish red, to simulate the color of February's birthstone, blood stone.

262   On the reverse side of the 25 an M is inscribed. I used green to represent the green of pine (*matsu*) and the mountains I love. I had a hard time coming up with a satisfactory combination of *IHM*. The finished

product didn't come out quite clear. Between the *I* and *M* and *H* and *M* are red and white stones. I'm sure you'll spot them right away since they're conspicuous.

The powder box wasn't quite up to my expectation, but I've put my heart and soul in making it, so please use it in that light. I'm sure you can find use for it, if not for powder.

I had a difficult time making the cover. Especially in smoothing the narrow edges, I had to hold my breath while I used a honing stone. As you can surmise, the edges are quite thin so please handle it accordingly. Since I've shellacked the entire surface, the box should be waterproof.

I meant to include an ashtray for you to give to Yorita-san, but the package exceeded four pounds,[a] and I didn't have enough money on me. I'll send it next week. Don't hesitate to put in your requests for anything.

I'm praying for your health.

Sayonara, Iwao

| 141

Dec. 7, 1943

[Translated from Japanese]

Dear Hanaye,

Today I'm mailing an ashtray (please give it to Yorita-san) and a vase (please give this to Koike-san). I let Koike-san know about it yesterday.

The snowfall in Missoula has finally gotten heavy enough to accumulate. It probably won't melt. It's warmer this year than last, perhaps because heaven took mercy on the many folks who've come from a warmer climate.

Miss Howell is wondering why she hasn't heard from Fujii-san. I told her she might have gone to school in the east. Whenever she's out here on Tuesdays and Fridays, she prays for you. She's such a kind and devout person.

As usual I'm busy with my stone craft. I made a totem pole, picture frame, and yesterday, I tried making a tray.

a. Internees were allowed free postage privileges on outgoing parcel postage packages weighing less than four pounds.

I received a Christmas card and a plaque with Christ's figure from the Prisoner Assistance Committee of the Episcopal church. I intend to send them a thank-you letter, but in the meantime can you personally thank the Reverend Kitagawa and Mrs. Ishibashi?

Did you get my silver anniversary gifts? Did they survive intact?

It'll be getting colder; please take care against catching a cold. I 'm in the best of health. Please give my regards to everyone.

Sayonara, Iwao

| 142

Dec. 18, 1943

[Translated from Japanese]

Dear Hanaye,

[CENSORED] I'm in very good shape so please don't worry. The people from the warmer regions are cringing from their first taste of a bitter cold winter. It's no problem for those of us who have already spent three winters.

My rehearing date keeps on being postponed, so I have no idea when the day will be. It's come to be that anyone left at this camp is considered very unlucky. Just yesterday I appealed to our camp superintendent if he couldn't do something about expediting my hearing. Since there are only a few people here requesting a rehearing, I feel our cases will just be set aside once again. Some may be wondering why, while there are people from the south that are returning in droves, none are returning from Missoula. The reason is as I stated above. It seems that if you're unlucky, hard luck keeps on plaguing you. I believe, though, luck will be coming my way one of these days.

I 'm very concerned that you're going through this cold period. Please take care not to catch a cold. When you're out of coal for the heater, let Owada-san know. I've also asked Koike-san to look in on you, so don't hesitate to go to him with any problems you have.

I mailed some stone ware to Yorita-san and Koike-san, but I haven't heard that the package reached either of them. If you're missing something that I have been sending you, please let me know.

264

I 'm working on my stones every day, as usual. Requests for my wares for Christmas gifts are keeping me very busy.

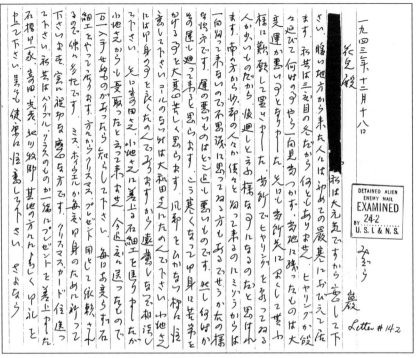

| Iwao to Hanaye, December 18, 1943. Note censor's cut out.

Miss Howell prays for you all the time. She's truly a kind, admirable person. Please send her a Christmas card at least. We of the Bible class got together and got her a present.

Please give my regards and thanks to the Ishibashi's, Yorita-san, Rev. Kitagawa, and others.

Take good care of yourself.

Sayonara, Iwao

| 143

Dec. 23, 1943

[Translated from Japanese]

265

Dear Hanaye,

Yesterday each one of us in the barracks received *tsukudani* and things from Yorita-san. I wrote him a thank-you letter, but could you thank him personally for me, too?

I mailed you a can of candy and a carton of Luckys today. These were given to me. You can give the cigarettes away a little at a time to anyone you know.

Miss Howell mentioned that she received a Christmas card from Fujii-san at Minidoka, but she wondered why she hadn't received an answer to her letter she sent previously. She prays for us at every meeting. Our Bible class chipped in ($10 each) and got her a sweater and a muffler. She also gave us presents in return. For knowing the Ten Commandments well, I won a desk pad as a first prize. I'll be singing "Silent Night" solo at our Bible class Christmas party tomorrow night.

Hiroshi-san sent me a Christmas card. Since I won't be sending any cards to Ishibashi-san, Hayasaka-san, Rev. Kitagawa, and the others, please give my best regards to the folks I've named and those who've looked after your welfare in my place.

I received a letter from Mrs. Kawasaki, whom I haven't heard from since Puyallup days. I wrote her right away. She said she's not able to visit you because of the distance.

Have a nice Christmas and New Year. There seems to be an epidemic of cold in the country, so please take good care. I'm OK, so far.

My third Nativity
in stockade ground.

Sayonara, Iwao

| 144

Dec. 28, 1943
[Translated from Japanese]

Dear Hanaye,

This Christmas has been unusually warm, and the night before, the rains turned the grounds into a swamp. By contrast, last year it snowed all day on Christmas and there was a foot of snow covering the ground. We're puzzled by the weather we're having.

Miss Howell couldn't attend the Christmas Eve party because of a cold, but it was a very nice party. We were amazed at the American minister from Missoula who sang carols and quoted Scriptures in Japanese. Miss Howell had taught him.

On Christmas day, together with Miss Howell, we visited our local hospital and ministered to the Italian and Japanese patients with carols and Miss Howell's wonderful storytelling.

Our turkey dinner was so magnificent it bordered on extravagance. Yet I was deeply disappointed not being able to celebrate Christmas with you this year as I had hoped.

I petitioned the District Attorney in Seattle today to expedite our reunion, since my hearing appears to have gone in limbo. If you could similarly petition the D.A. it may help our case very much. I've already contacted the Reverend Kitagawa, so please see him and send an appeal as soon as possible. You can't just sit and expect good things to happen, you know.

This will probably be my last letter for this year. Please greet the new year in good health.

> With a prayer for my beloved wife
> the year slowly ends.

I can't thank all of the folks—Ishibashi, Koike, Mitsumori, Morinaga, Yorita, Owada, Hayasaka, and others—individually, so please give them my best regards.

Sayonara, Iwao

| 145

Jan. 3, 1944
[Translated from Japanese]

Dear Hanaye,

The long awaited good news finally arrived from Seattle. You must have heard about my parole already. After two years since the subject came up, we're finally able to be together. I guess the petition to the Attorney General in Seattle was unnecessary after all.

Please have things ready to meet me. If this place isn't to your liking, I think it would be all right for me to go over there. I have few personal effects, so if it becomes necessary for me to relocate, this may work out, too. I'll leave the matter up to you. It'll probably be a week at the earliest before I can leave anyway. As soon as things are firmed up, I'll wire you right away.

Yesterday I had a request by Fukano-san to send him some stones from Missoula. Since regulations prohibit mailing raw stones, I'll see if I can bring them with me. Can you tell him that when you have a chance?

My regards to everybody.

Sayonara, Iwao

| 146
[Telegram]

JAN. 6, 1944

LEAVING HERE 10TH, MONDAY AFTERNOON. ARRIVING TWIN FALLS, TUESDAY NOON OR AFTERNOON.

IWAO MATSUSHITA

NOTES

| 1: Establishing Roots

1. In Kazuo Ito, *Issei: A History of Japanese Immigrants in North America*, trans. Shinichiro Nakamura and Jean S. Gerard (Seattle: Japanese Community Service, 1973), p. 51.

2. Seattle *Post-Intelligencer*, September 4, 1919.

3. Passenger and Crew Lists of Vessels Arriving at Seattle, Washington, 1890–1957, microfilm, roll 42, National Archives–Pacific Northwest Region (NA--PNR), Seattle.

4. U.S. Bureau of the Census, *Historical Statistics of the United States, Colonial Times to 1957: A Statistical Abstract Supplement* (Washington, D.C., Government Printing Office, 1960), Series C 88-114. According to 1940 Japanese government records, most immigrants came from Hiroshima-ken (72,484) and from four other prefectures: Kumamoto (65,378), Okinawa (57,283), Fukuoka (55,492), and Yamaguchi (41,788). These data were compiled by Yuji Ichioka and cited in *Pacific Citizen* (Los Angeles), November 11, 1983.

5. Iwao Matsushita passport, box 1, Iwao Matsushita Papers, University of Washington (UW) Libraries, Seattle.

6. Iwao Matsushita, 12 interviews with Carol Zabilski, Seattle, 1975–76, copies of notes in author's possession (hereafter Matsushita interviews).

7. Teruko Inoue of Fukuoka, Japan, eldest daughter of Matsushita's older sister, Toku, provided early biographical data on Iwao and Hanaye Matsushita by way of correspondence and interviews, Seattle, 1991–94. For Matsushita's professional biography, see box 1, Matsushita Papers.

8. Joseph M. Kitagawa, *Religion in Japanese History* (1966; New York: Columbia University Press, 1990) , pp. 177–261.

9. "My Father's Mission Work in Tonomi: Persecution at the Primary School," in "Life as a Fulbrighter, 1954–1955," by Teruko Inoue, undated, unpublished manuscript, in the author's possession.

10. For example, Matsushita's brother, Sekio, was a seminarian at Vanderbilt University; his niece, Teruko Inoue, came to the U.S. as a Fulbright scholar in 1954 and taught English in an all-girl's high school in Nagasaki until 1980.

11. Carol Zabilski, "Dr. Kyo Koike, 1878–1947: Physician, Poet, Photographer," *Pacific Northwest Quarterly*, 68 (1977):72–79.

12. Matsushita passport.

13. Reminiscence of Chiyokichi Kyono, quoted in Ito, p. 40.

14. Passenger freighters from Japan were common visitors during this period in both Seattle and San Francisco harbors. Many passengers of the era were picture brides on steamers arriving almost biweekly during busy seasons. Although comparable data for Seattle and Victoria/Vancouver are not available, 22 ships arrived at San Francisco in 1918 alone, bringing 524 new brides who had not yet met their husbands. From 1911 through 1919, 5,654 picture brides entered the U.S. at San Francisco. U.S. House Committee on Immigration and Naturalization, *Japanese Immigration Hearings*, 66th Cong., 2d Sess., 1921, Part 1, pp. 144–45.

15. Trachoma and hookworm were common ailments brought to America during the immigration period. Health examinations conducted in the home country failed to uncover all the problems. Examination by U.S. immigration authorities was strict and, although not often cause to return an immigrant to Japan, frequently resulted in a quarantine of days or weeks, during which there were repeated eye examinations and feces inspections. Checks for syphilis were routine. For details of the ordeals of immigrants, both leaving Japan and entering U.S. ports, see Tsurutani Hisashi, *America-bound: The Japanese and the Opening of the American West,* trans. Betsey Scheiner (Tokyo: Japan Times, 1989).

16. Matsushita interviews.

17. S. Frank Miyamoto, *Social Solidarity among the Japanese in Seattle* (1939; rpt. Seattle: University of Washington Press, 1984), table 5, p. 31.

18. Among the Japanese-owned businesses catering to the community were 282 hotels and lodging houses, 91 retail grocers, 44 laundries, 45 fruit and vegetable stalls in public markets, 73 restaurants, 10 clothing establishments, 5 banks, and 4 newspapers. *Japanese Immigration Hearings*, Part 4, pp. 1109–22.

19. Ibid., p. 1178.

20. U.S. Bureau of the Census, *Census of Population, 1920.*

21. *Japanese Immigration Hearings*, Part 4, p. 1354.

22. *Census of Population, 1920.*

23. Ito, p. 526.

24. An inventory of hotels provided by the hotel inspector for the state of Washington, dated July 9, 1920, listed S. Chesaro as manager of the Chesler [*sic*] Hotel. *Japanese Immigration Hearings*, Part 4, pp. 1353–54.

25. Matsushita interviews.

26. The average wage for Seattle Japanese was $116.49 at the end of 1930. No wage statistics for Mitsui or other workers have been found.

27. *Polk's Seattle City Directory,* 1920–24.

28. The Northwest American Japanese Association's occupational census of 1930 showed Seattle with 167 white-collar employees of 12 Japanese trading companies and banks, of which there were 56 male Issei and 9 Nisei. Eight years later, 67 Seattle Japanese were employed by importing and exporting firms. Roger Daniels, *Asian America: Chinese and Japanese in the United States since 1850* (Seattle: University of Washington Press, 1988), p. 161; John A. Rademaker, "The Ecological Position of the Japanese Farmers in the State of Washington," Ph.D. dissertation (University of Washington, 1939), p. 285.

29. Maurine Greenwald, "Working-class Feminism and the Family Wage Ideal: The Seattle Debate on Married Women's Right to Work, 1914–1920," *Journal of American History,* 76 (1989):124–25. For a study of working Japanese American women, primarily in the San Francisco Bay area, see Evelyn Nakano Glenn, *Issei, Nisei, War Bride: Three Generations of Japanese American Women in Domestic Service* (Philadelphia: Temple University Press, 1986).

30. The Seattle general strike of 1919 is detailed in Robert L. Friedheim, *The Seattle General Strike* (Seattle: University of Washington Press, 1964). For general histories of Seattle, see Richard C. Berner, *Seattle in the 20th Century,* 2 vols. (Seattle: Charles Press, 1991–92); Roger Sale, *Seattle: Past to Present* (Seattle: University of Washington Press, 1976). Also see Clarence B. Bagley, *History of Seattle: From the Earliest Settlement to the Present Time,* Vol. 1 (Chicago: S. J. Clarke Publishing Company, 1916).

31. For the most thorough study of Japanese exclusion in California to date, see Roger Daniels, *The Politics of Prejudice: The Anti-Japanese Movement in California and the Struggle for Japanese Exclusion,* 2d ed. (Berkeley: University of California Press, 1977)

32. Daniels, *Asian America,* p. 115.

33. Seattle *Star,* July 26, 1919. The *Star,* bannering itself "An American Paper That Fights for Americanism," ran front-page stories every day for a full month, detailing every move of the exclusionists. Interestingly, Seattle's other daily newspapers, the *Post-Intelligencer* and the *Times,* ignored the story altogether.

34. Daniels, *Politics of Prejudice,* pp. 92–105; Jeff H. Lesser. "Always 'Outsiders': Asians, Naturalization, and the Supreme Court," *Amerasia Journal,* 12 (1985):83–100.

35. Matsushita interviews.

36. *Japanese Immigration Hearings,* Part 4, pp. 1119–20.

37. Ibid., pp. 1110–22.

38. For details of Koike's artistic life and examples of his photography, see Koike materials in Special Collections Division, UW Libraries. Also see Zabilski, pp. 72–79; Robert D. Monroe, "Light and Shade: Pictorial Photography in Seattle, 1920–1940, and the Seattle Camera Club," in *Turning Shadows into Light: Art and Culture of the Northwest's Early Asian/Pacific Community,* ed. Mayumi Tsutakawa and Alan Chong Lau (Seattle: Young Pine Press, 1982), pp. 8–32.

39. Monroe, p. 9.

40. Kyo Koike, "The Seattle Camera Club," *Photo-Era*, 55 (1925):182.

41. Asakichi (Frank) Kunishige (1878–1960) and Koike were the same age, but Kunishige arrived in America 22 years earlier, in 1895. With more experience in America and having come at an earlier age, he was more receptive to new influences than his spiritual mentor, Koike, who stayed closer to the traditions of the old country. Kunishige was one of the few members of the Seattle Camera Club who had formal training in photography. He ultimately achieved greater acclaim than Koike, was praised for the fragile beauty of his tissue-paper prints of female forms and still lifes, and had three one-man shows during his lifetime. In 1971 the University of Washington's Henry Gallery exhibited 50 of his prints in a solo artist exhibit. See Monroe, pp. 8–32; Kunishige photos file, Henry Art Gallery Records, UW Libraries.

42. Iwao Matsushita photographs, Special Collections, UW Libraries.

43. "Nomura Exhibition," *Town Crier* (Seattle), July 15, 1933, pp. 9–10.

44. *Kenjiro Nomura: Retrospective Catalog* (Seattle: Seattle Art Museum, 1960).

45. *Kenjiro Nomura: The George and Betty Nomura Collection* (Seattle: Wing Luke Museum, 1991). For other examples of Japanese American artists' work influenced by the World War II incarceration experience, see Estelle Ishigo, *Lone Heart Mountain* (1972; rpt. Los Angeles: Communicart, 1989); *The View from Within: Japanese American Art from the Internment Camps, 1942–1945* (Los Angeles: Japanese American National Museum, 1994); Deborah Gesensway and Mindy Roseman, *Beyond Words: Images from America's Concentration Camps* (Ithaca: Cornell University Press, 1987); Miné Okubo, *Citizen 13660* (New York: Columbia University Press, 1946).

46. Berner, I, pp. 178–86.

47. *Japanese Immigration Hearings*, Part 4, p. 1118.

48. Calvin F. Schmid, *Social Trends in Seattle* (Seattle: University of Washington Press, 1944), pp. 99, 130–135; Miyamoto, 1984, table 1, p. 14.

49. Schmid, p. 133.

50. Henry Itoi, untaped interview with the author, Seattle, April 6, 1996.

51. *University of Washington Bulletin: Catalog, 1926–1927* (Seattle: University of Washington, 1927).

52. Monroe, p. 21.

53. In 1940, Matsushita's annual salary was $6,350, plus bonuses. The average annual salary for college teachers in 1940 was $2,906; net income for nonsalaried physicians was $4,441 and for nonsalaried dentists, $3,314. See *Historical Statistics*, Series D 728–34.

54. Undated Internee Report (copy), Matsushita Papers.

55. Daniels, *Asian America*, pp. 161–62.

56. Matsushita to Mitsui and Company, August 31, 1940, box 1, Matsushita Papers.

57. Thomas A. Bailey, *A Diplomatic History of the American People,* 8th ed. (New York: Appleton-Century-Crofts, 1969), pp. 733–37.

1. In *Poets behind Barbed Wire,* ed. and trans. Jiro Nakano and Kay Nakano (Honolulu: Bamboo Ridge Press, 1983), p. 13.

2. Bob Kumamoto, "The Search for Spies: American Counterintelligence and the Japanese American Community, 1931–1942," *Amerasia Journal,* 6 (1979):45–75. Intelligence gathering on Hawaii's Japanese population may have begun as early as World War I. See Gary Y. Okihiro, *Cane Fires: The Anti-Japanese Movement in Hawaii, 1865–1945* (Philadelphia: Temple University Press, 1991), pp. 102–28.

3. "Proposal for Coordination of FBI, ONI and MID," June 5, 1940, in *United States Naval Administration in World War II* (Washington, D.C.: Navy Historical Division, 1959), pp. 68–80. For a history of the ONI's role during World War II, see Jeffery Dorwart, *Conflict of Duty: The U.S. Navy's Intelligence Dilemma, 1919–1945* (Annapolis: United States Naval Institute, 1983).

4. Beulah Amidon, "Aliens in America," *Survey Graphic,* 30 (1943):58–61.

5. U.S. House, "Fourth Interim Report of the Select Committee Investigating National Defense Migration," Report 2124, 77th Cong., 2d Sess., 1942, reprinted in *American Concentration Camps: A Documentary History of the Relocation and Incarceration of Japanese Americans, 1942–1945,* ed. Roger Daniels, 9 vols. (New York: Garland Publishing, 1989), V, pp. 95, 230, 234 (hereafter cited as Tolan Hearings).

6. Kumamoto, pp. 58, 62. More than 300 Japanese clubs and organizations providing cultural awareness, entertainment, recreation, and intellectual stimulation were implicated in suspected espionage activities. It was enough to appear on a membership list of a suspected organization to have one's name placed on one of the ABC lists.

7. No reference to an overt surveillance of Matsushita could be found among FBI, INS, or other official documents relevant to him.

8. Lt. Commander Kenneth Ringle, a naval intelligence officer who had worked in both Japan and southern California and who developed a network of Nisei informants, estimated that no more than 3,500 ethnic Japanese in the entire country might act as saboteurs or espionage agents. Curtis Munson, a businessman providing intelligence through FDR's "ear," the journalist John Franklin Carter, drew similar conclusions, although he was "horrified" that so much damage might be inflicted on unguarded vital installations by small numbers of saboteurs. Peter Irons, *Justice at War* (New York: Oxford University Press, 1983), p. 23; Kenneth D. Ringle [pseud., An Intelligence Officer], "The Japanese in America: The Problem and the Solution," *Harper's Magazine,* 185 (1942):489–97; C. B. Munson, "Japanese on the West Coast," in Daniels, *American Concentration Camps,* I; Kumamoto, pp. 55–56.

9. Until 1940 the INS was part of the Department of Labor.

10. "Joint agreement between the Secretary of War and the Attorney General regarding internment of alien enemies, July 18, 1941," Papers of the U.S. Commission

on Wartime Relocation and Internment of Civilians, Part l: Numerical File Archive, reel 3, pp. 391–98 (hereafter cited as CWRIC with reel and pages).

11. Arrests of Japanese, German, and Italian enemy aliens carried out by the FBI on December 7 were made under authority of a blanket presidential warrant signed by Biddle permitting emergency arrests necessary to prevent "irreparable damage to the United States." Francis Biddle, *In Brief Authority* (Garden City, N.Y.: Doubleday & Co., 1962), p. 207; Morton Grodzins, *Americans Betrayed: Politics and the Japanese Evacuation* (Chicago: University of Chicago Press, 1949), pp. 232–33.

12. Don Whitehead, *The FBI Story: A Report to the People* (New York: Random House, 1956), p. 183. For Biddle's written confirmation of the verbal order, see "Instructions for the Director of the Federal Bureau of Investigation from the Attorney General," CWRIC 9:472.

13. City of Seattle, Annual Report of the Police Department, December 31, 1941. The report claims that on December 7 alone, 55 Japanese, German, and Italian aliens were arrested in Seattle. During the latter part of December, every dwelling and place of business occupied by Japanese was investigated and a personal history of each occupant over the age of 14 obtained.

14. J. Edgar Hoover, "Alien Enemy Control," *Iowa Law Review,* 29 (1944):396–408

15. Kumamoto, p. 62.

16. Takeo (Tom) Matsuoka, taped interview with author, April 16, 1992, Ridgefield, Washington.

17. Kenji Okuda (Okuda's son), taped interview with author, August 9, 1995. In 1953 Heiji Okuda received the Fourth Class Order of the Sacred Treasure from the Japanese government for service to the Japanese community. In 1956 he received the Fourth Class Order of the Rising Sun. See also Heiji Henry Okuda Papers, UW Libraries.

18. Monica Sone, *Nisei Daughter* (1953; rpt. Seattle: University of Washington Press, 1979).

19. Department of Justice, press releases, December 8, 13, 1941, February 16, 1942, cited in Grodzins, p. 232; FBI memoranda, CWRIC 9:474–81.

20. Seattle *Post-Intelligencer,* December 10, 1941.

21. The precise number of Seattle resident enemy aliens apprehended by the FBI during World War II has not been established. The data used here were extracted from news articles in the *Post-Intelligencer* and the *Times* of the period.

22. Memo, adjutant general to command generals, January 6, 1942, CWRIC 3:364. Because the Japanese language was largely unknown outside the Nikkei (Japanese) community, the INS likely insisted that communications be in English in order to enable the censors to read them. Censors' identification indicia may be found on surviving correspondence.

23. Kumamoto, pp. 66–67.

24. 1940 survey of Seattle Nisei, cited in *Pacific Citizen* (San Francisco), September 1941.

25. Bill Hosokawa, "The Uprooting of Seattle," in *Japanese Americans: From Relocation to Redress*, ed. Roger Daniels, Sandra C. Taylor, and Harry H. L. Kitano, rev. ed. (1986; rpt. Seattle: University of Washington Press, 1991), pp. 18–20.

26. Roger Daniels, *The Decision to Relocate the Japanese Americans* (Philadelphia: J. B. Lippincott Co., 1975), pp. 61–64. The Issei were prohibited from leaving their residential communities. The Department of Justice sealed off the borders of Mexico and Canada to "all persons of Japanese ancestry whether citizen or alien." See Roger Daniels, *Concentration Camps USA: Japanese Americans and World War II* (New York: Holt, Rinehart and Winston, 1972), p. 35.

27. Seattle *Times*, December 9, 1941.

28. Department of Justice, press release, December 10, 1941, cited in Grodzins, p. 233.

29. Los Angeles *Times*, December 8, 1941. Through January 4, 63 of 67 opinions written by the California press were favorable toward the Japanese in America. Grodzins, pp. 379–80.

30. Seattle *Times*, December 9, 1941; Seattle *Post-Intelligencer*, December 11, 1941.

31. *Northwest Enterprise* (Seattle), December 12, 1941.

32. Seattle *Post-Intelligencer*, December 8, 1941.

33. Council of Churches—Seattle Records, box 15, UW Libraries; Seattle *Times*, December 9, 1941.

34. Seattle *Post-Intelligencer*, December 9, 1941; Seattle *Star*, December 8, 1941.

35. Daniels, *Asian America*, p. 218.

36. Seattle *Post-Intelligencer*, December 20, 1941.

37. Memo, attorney general to commanding general, Western Defense Command, December 14, 1941, CWRIC 3:382.

38. W. F. Kelley "memorandum for the file," CWRIC 9:481.

39. Seattle *Times*, December 18, 1942.

40. Undated itemized list of detainee belongings, Fort Missoula File 1017/T, Enemy Alien Internment World War II, Records of the Immigration and Naturalization Service, Record Group 85, National Archives, Suitland, Maryland (hereafter cited as RG85 Suitland).

41. Yoshiaki Fukuda, *My Six Years of Internment: An Issei's Struggle for Justice*, trans. Konko Church of San Francisco and Research Information Center of Konko Churches of North America (San Francisco: Konko Church of San Francisco, 1990), p. 8.

| 3: Incarceration

1. In *Poets behind Barbed Wire*, p. 53.

2. Paul F. Clark, "Those Other Camps: An Oral History Analysis of Japanese Alien Enemy Internment during World War II," Masters thesis (California State University, Fullerton, 1980), pp. 7–8. An abridged 53-page version of this document may be found in CWRIC 4:192–244.

3. On December 19, 1939, the German liner S.S. *Columbus* was scuttled after failing to outrun a British blockade in neutral waters off Cape May, New Jersey. See New York *Times*, December 20, 1939.

4. Bert Fraser to W. F. Kelley, September 19, 1942, Fort Missoula File 1036/A, RG85 Suitland. The final contingent of 125 Italian seamen arrived at Fort Missoula on May 1, 1941.

5. John E. Allen and Marjorie Burns, with Sam C. Sargent, *Cataclysms on the Columbia* (Portland, Oreg.: Timber Press, 1986), p. 57.

6. Umberto Benedetti, *The Lifestyle of Italian Internees at Fort Missoula Montana, 1941–1943: Bella Vista* ([Missoula]: U. Benedetti, 1986).

7. Anonymous, handwritten census for the file, Fort Missoula File 1036/L, RG85 Suitland.

8. Visit of Spanish Embassy personnel, December 16, 1943, Fort Missoula File 1015/H, ibid.

9. Paul S. Kashino to author, July 7 and August 6, 1992. Kashino, a Kibei, was employed by the INS as a censor and interpreter at Fort Missoula. He also interpreted for the loyalty hearings at other INS camps.

10. Visit of Spanish Embassy personnel, December 16, 1943.

11. Visit of Swiss delegate for war prisoners, June 1942, Fort Missoula File 1016/F, RG85 Suitland.

12. *Great Northern Daily News* (Seattle), February 13, 1942. The *Great Northern Daily News* was a Japanese-language paper with an English-language section; Matsushita's poems appeared in the English section.

13. The attorney general's authority derived from the Alien and Sedition Acts of 1798, as amended during World War I, authorizing the president to restrict the rights of noncitizens by proclamation during wartime.

14. The U.S. rate was 10 cents per hour.

15. *Foreign Relations of the United States: Diplomatic Papers*, Vol. 1: *1942* (Washington, D.C.: Government Printing Office, 1960), p. 792.

16. Stimson to attorney general, January 17, 1942. CWRIC 1:145; U.S., *Department of State Bulletin*, May 23, 1942, pp. 445–47.

17. Collaer was superintendent until summer of 1942 when he was transferred to Crystal City, Texas, to organize the INS family camp there. By April 1943 he was at INS headquarters in Philadelphia and later served as acting assistant commissioner for alien control. After the war he was chief of the INS detention and deportation service.

18. Yahei Taoka to Nick Collaer, December 30, 1941, Fort Missoula File 1014/A, RG85 Suitland.

19. Quoted in Collaer to W. F. Kelley, December 30, 1941, Fort Missoula File 1013/L, ibid.

20. Ibid.

21. Fukuda, p. 40; *Foreign Relations of the United States*, Vol. 3:, *1943*, pp. 1050–55; Spanish Embassy to officer in charge, May 12, 1942, File 1016/F, RG85 Suitland.

22. P. R. McLaughlin to detainee spokesmen, April 20, 1942, Fort Missoula File 1021/H, RG85 Suitland.

23. Three deaths from natural causes, however, occurred at Fort Missoula during this period, in February, March, and April 1942. One case involved pneumonia accompanied by "advanced senile decay"; a second, heart attack secondary to pneumonia and senility; and the third, colon cancer. The ages of the patients are unknown. The Japanese government protested the deaths and demanded an accounting of invalids being taken into custody with no subsequent consideration to their ill health. The State Department's reply indicates that the patients were attended by Japanese physician detainees or, in the case of the cancer patient, by medical personnel at a Missoula hospital, as provided for in the Geneva Convention. In two instances family members and the Japanese spokesmen expressed gratitude for the treatment and courtesies extended during the period of illness. See *Foreign Relations of the United States*, Vol. 3: *1943*, pp. 1050–51, 1073–75. For additional instances of mistreatment of Japanese nationals in detention and internment camps, see John J. Culley, "The Santa Fe Internment Camp and the Justice Department Program for Enemy Aliens," in Daniels, Taylor, and Kitano, pp. 57–71; Tetsuden Kashima, "Mistreatment of Internees," ibid., pp. 52–56; John J. Culley, "Trouble at the Lordsburg Internment Camp," *New Mexico Historical Review*, 60 (1985):225–48; *Foreign Relations of the United States*, Vol. 5: *1944*, pp. 942–65, 1130–39.

24. At the start of the First World War, 4,000 crew members of German ships seized within areas under American sovereignty were interned as illegal immigrant enemy aliens. In addition, a small number of resident German enemy aliens were arrested by order of the attorney general and detained pending review of their cases by the Department of Justice. Eventually, 2,300 men were turned over to military authorities and interned at four army camps. See Joerg A. Nagler, "Enemy Aliens and Internment in World War I: Alvo von Alvensleben in Fort Douglas, Utah, a Case Study," *Utah Historical Quarterly*, 58 (1990):388–405.

25. Instructions to Alien Enemy Hearing Boards, Supplement 1, January 7, 1942, Fort Missoula File 1016/K, RG85 Suitland.

26. Ibid.

27. Kashino to author.

28. Arthur A. Hansen and Betty E. Mitson, eds., *Voices Long Silent: An Oral Inquiry into the Japanese American Evacuation* (Fullerton: California State University, 1974), pp. 109–22.

29. Other members of the Washington board were J. Speed Smith, a Seattle attorney, and Leslie Stone, an Orting banker. The board heard cases at the Seattle Immigration Station before traveling to Fort Missoula in January. The interpreter for the Washington hearings at Fort Missoula was a Nisei coed from Spokane. A second board for the Seattle District was announced on March 21, 1942; Judson F. Falknor, dean of the University of Washington Law School, was chair, and a Seattle

businessman, Andrew Steers, and a local attorney, Clifford Hoof, assisted. *Great Northern Daily News,* March 21, 1942.

30. Floyd Schmoe to American Friends Service Committee headquarters, February 2, 1942, box 15, James Y. Sakamoto Papers, UW Libraries.

31. Matsushita's hearing was originally scheduled for January 27, 1942: Notice of Hearing, Department of Justice, Alien Enemy Hearing Board, January 16, 1942, box 9, Matsushita Papers.

32. Anonymous memo to Thomas Cooley II, assistant to the director, Alien Enemy Control Unit, December 20, 1943, in Iwao Matsushita File, Records of the War Relocation Authority, Record Group 210, National Archives, Suitland (hereafter cited as RG210 Suitland).

33. Hansen and Mitson, p. 127; Herbert Nicholson, *Treasures in Earthen Vessels* (Whittier, Calif.: Penn Lithographics, 1974), p. 65.

34. Kashino to author.

35. Undated Circular No. 3589, Supplement No. 12, "Rehearing of Alien Enemy Cases," Fort Lincoln File 4290/P, RG85 Suitland.

36. Edward J. Ennis to internees and members of their families, undated, box 9, Matsushita Papers.

37. By the end of April, 82 Seattle detainees had received parole status. These were individuals against whom no information of subversion could be found and who convinced their board they were harmless. Family ties to the homeland or former membership in suspected organizations, however, barred their outright release. Early parolees returning to their prewar homes, mostly located in Washington, Oregon, and California, were required to report their activities to local federal officials on a periodic basis. Later parolees faced additional problems because evacuation of the coastal Japanese American communities had begun in earnest by the end of April 1942. Parolees found themselves in the paradoxical position of having just obtained their freedom from incarceration by the Justice Department only to be incarcerated by the army at one of the assembly centers. See U.S. War Department, *Final Report: Japanese Evacuation from the West Coast, 1942* (Washington, D.C.: Government Printing Office, 1943), pp. 153–66.

38. Justice Department, press release, May 3, 1942, CWRIC 1:210–211.

39. War Department, *Final Report,* table 50, p. 373. No detailed study of the assembly centers currently exists.

40. "Joint Agreement between the Secretary of War and the Attorney General regarding internment of alien enemies," July 18, 1941, CWRIC 3:391–398.

41. Telegram, P. R. McLaughlin to INS headquarters, April 10, 1942, Fort Missoula File 1017/T, RG85 Suitland.

42. Telegram, Bert Fraser to INS headquarters, August 2, 1942, ibid.

43. The Swedish liner S.S. *Gripsholm* made humanitarian voyages to Europe and Asia during the war, transporting repatriates and forwarding comfort packages and mail. It sailed to Asia in June 1942 and September 1943 carrying repatriating Japanese

(diplomats and renunciants) to be exchanged for North American civilians in Japanese custody. For a study of the special division of the State Department responsible for the negotiations with Japan resulting in the exchanges, see P. Scott Corbett, *Quiet Passages: The Exchange of Civilians between the United States and Japan during the Second World War* (Kent, Ohio: Kent State University Press, 1987). Unfortunately, an accounting of these negotiations from the Japanese government's point of view is not available.

44. Motosuke Hayasaka to Fraser, October 9, 1942, Fort Missoula File 1017/U, RG85 Suitland.

45. Fraser to F. H. Arrowood, November 17, 1942, ibid.

| 4: Stone Fever

1. In *Poets behind Barbed Wire*, p. 56.

2. Visiting clergymen held services for the inmates. A nondenominational graduate from the Federated Bible School held Japanese services twice weekly for the Christians.

3. Deanna Durbin was a favorite movie star among the Italians.

4. Kyo Koike letters, box 15, Matsushita Papers.

5. *Missoulian*, July 22, August 7 and 15, October 1, 1941; Program, box 10, Matsushita Papers.

6. Tom Matsuoka interview.

7. U.S. Immigration and Naturalization Service, *Monthly Review*, 2 (June 12, 1945):159–61.

8. By war's end the freeze on accounts in U.S. banks had lifted. Assets in Japanese banks were ultimately redeemable at approximately one cent on the dollar.

9. Lloyd Chiasson, "Japanese-American Relocation during World War II: A Study of California Editorial Reactions," *Journalism Quarterly*, 68 (1991):263–69; Grodzins, pp. 377–419.

10. Seattle *Post-Intelligencer*, February 7, 1942.

11. Tolan Hearings, pp. 11404–409.

12. *North American Times* (Seattle), February 26, 1942. In all, 40 state workers, 23 from the University of Washington, lost their jobs, as did 4 Seattle City Light employees. See Louis Fiset, "Redress for Nisei Public Employees in Washington State after World War II," *Pacific Northwest Quarterly*, 88 (1996): 21–32.

13. *Personal Justice Denied: Report of the Commission on Wartime Relocation and Internment of Civilians* (1983; rpt., Seattle: University of Washington Press, 1997), p. 49; Daniels, *Decision to Relocate the Japanese Americans*, pp. 113–14.

14. Seattle *Post-Intelligencer*, February 21, 1942.

15. The Seattle community was affected by six civilian exclusion orders (CEO 17, 18, 36, 37, 40, and 57), each defining specific geographic areas inhabited by up to 1,400 residents. The Matsushita residence was located within the boundaries defined by CEO 18. See War Department, *Final Report*, table 47, pp. 364–65.

16. On May 31, 1942, the Puyallup Assembly Center population reached its maximum, at 7,548. Included among the Seattleites were 151 Japanese from Alaska

and 1,054 from Pierce County, including Tacoma. "Evacuee Population Changes of Puyallup Assembly Center by Days: April 28, 1942—September 12, 1942," Box 15, General Correspondence, Puyallup Assembly Center, RG338, Western Defense Command, Fourth Army, WCCA and CAD, NA, Washington, D.C. War Department, *Final Report*, table 47, pp. 363–66.

17. *Great Northern Daily News*, April 17, 1942.

18. Ibid., April 17, 1942.

19. First published in the Seattle *Post-Intelligencer* on April 24, four days before the arrival of the first Seattle residents, the name was probably an army public relations gimmick.

20. Audrie Girdner and Anne Loftis, *The Great Betrayal: Evacuation of the Japanese-Americans during World War II* (Toronto: Macmillan, 1969), pp. 154–55. Although an in-depth study of the assembly centers does not yet exist, information may be found in many texts. See, for example, Michi Weglyn, *Years of Infamy: The Untold Story of America's Concentration Camps* (New York: Morrow Quill Paperbacks, 1976), pp. 79–82; Okubo, *Citizen 13660*; Sandra C. Taylor, *Jewel of the Desert: Japanese American Internment at Topaz* (Berkeley: University of California Press, 1993); War Department, *Final Report*, pp. 151–233; Charles Kikuchi, *The Kikuchi Diary*, ed. John Modell (1973; rpt. Urbana: University of Illinois Press, 1993).

21. Bill Hosokawa to Japanese-American Citizens League Headquarters, May 7, 1942, box 10, Sakamoto Papers.

22. Koike to Matsushita, June 9, 1942, box 15, Matsushita Papers. Koike surrendered his Kodak and a pocket camera to Seattle police on December 28, 1941. Although he returned to his avocation after the war, he never regained his enthusiasm or success.

23. Ibid.

24. Koike to Matsushita, November 3, 1942, ibid.

25. Koike to Matsushita, August 15, 1942, ibid.

26. War Department, *Final Report*, table 33, p. 282.

27. Most of the remaining relocatees came from the Portland, Oregon, area.

28. Minidoka *Irrigator*, September 10, 1942.

29. Koike to Matsushita, July 11, 1942, box 15, Matsushita Papers.

30. Anonymous memo to Thomas Cooley II, December 20, 1943. Numerous attempts through the Freedom of Information Act failed to locate either Matsushita's FBI or INS file, either of which may have provided actual details.

31. The value of Matsushita's deposits in Yokohama Specie Bank and Sumimoto Bank in U.S. dollars, on January 1, 1942. See Hanaye Matsushita Report to the Treasury Department, February 16, 1942, box 9, Matsushita Papers.

32. Koike to Matsushita, October 4, 1942, box 15, ibid.

33. The INS family camp at Crystal City, Texas, opened in November 1942.

34. Matsushita to Biddle, January 2, 1943, box 9, Matsushita Papers.

35. Matsushita to Koike, April 19, 1943, ibid.

36. Matsushita to Koike, February 10, 1943, ibid.

37. Matsushita to Koike., March 3, 1943, ibid.

38. Joseph M. Kitagawa (1915–92) became a leading theologian after the war, introducing the West to the religions of Japan during his 41 years on the faculty of the University of Chicago's School of Divinity. For details of his wartime experience in INS custody, during which he was ordained as a priest, and his incarceration at the Minidoka Relocation Center, see Joseph M. Kitagawa, *The Christian Tradition: Beyond Its European Captivity* (Philadelphia: Trinity Press International, 1992), pp. 119–137.

39. Matsushita to Koike, May 4, 1943, box 9, Matsushita Papers.

40. Eldon Griffin to Biddle, January 20, 1943, ibid.

41. Matsushita to Spanish Embassy, July 15, 1943, Fort Missoula File 1036/L, RG85 Suitland. So many internees sought repatriation that much of Matsushita's time was spent corresponding with the Spanish Embassy in Washington, D.C., for Spain represented Japan's interests in the United States under the Geneva Convention.

42. C. Harvey Gardiner, *Pawns in a Triangle of Hate: The Peruvian Japanese and the United States* (Seattle: University of Washington Press, 1981), p. 82.

43. One of the letters was from John B. Cobb, a former missionary in Japan, 1918–41, who was acquainted with Matsushita's brother. He knew Matsushita by reputation alone, which he conveyed to the U.S. attorney. Cobb to J. Charles Dennis, October 7, 1943, box 9, Matsushita Papers.

44. Matsushita to Fraser, December 3, 1943, ibid.

45. Matsushita to Dennis, December 27, 1943, ibid.

46. Anonymous memo to Thomas Cooley II, December 20, 1943.

| 5: Fields under Snow

1. Matsushita Papers.

2. U.S. Dept. of the Interior, War Relocation Authority, *The Evacuated People* (Washington, D.C.: Government Printing Office, 1946), table 1, p. 9.

3. Lester E. Suzuki, *Ministry in the Assembly and Relocation Centers of World War II* (Berkeley: Yardbird Publishing Co., 1979), pp. 194–207.

4. The discussion of resettlement is based upon U.S. Dept. of the Interior, War Relocation Authority, *WRA: A Story of Human Conservation* (Washington D.C.: Government Printing Office, 1946), pp. 81–85, 94–97, 132–54.

5. During early January 1943, WRA offices appeared in Chicago, Cleveland, Kansas City, Salt Lake City, and Denver, and later in New York City, Little Rock, and smaller localities.

6. Eventually, more than 4,300 students left the assembly centers and relocation camps for college. See Robert W. O'Brien, *The College Nisei* (Palo Alto, Calif.: Pacific Books, 1949).

7. Undated interview notes (Newell), RG210 Suitland.

8. For details of this and other relevant Supreme Court decisions, see Irons, *Justice At War*, pp. 307ff; and *idem*, ed., *Justice Delayed: The Record of the Japanese American Internment Cases* (Middletown, Conn.: Wesleyan University Press, 1989).

9. Matsushita's initial appointment was special relocation officer, CAF-9, $3,640 per year salary, in the Seattle area office, not to exceed three months. Telegram, Harold S. Fistere to H. L. Stafford, July 30, 1945, RG210 Suitland.

10. *Historical Statistics*, Series D 728–34.

11. Frank S. Barnett to J. Charles Dennis, February 13, 1942, RG210 Suitland.

12. Stafford to B. R. Stauber, June 21, 1945, ibid.

13. Edward J. Ennis to Matsushita, September 29, 1945, ibid.

14. The attorney general announced termination of the enemy alien parole system 51 days later. R. P. Bonham to Matsushita, November 19, 1945, box 10, Matsushita Papers.

15. INS Interim Parole Agreement, August 4, 1945, Matsushita File, RG210 Suitland.

16. Telegram, Stafford to Harold S. Fistere, August 6, 1945, ibid.

17. Carlos A. Schwantes, *The Pacific Northwest: An Interpretive History* (Lincoln: University of Nebraska Press, 1989), p. 332.

18. Report on activities of the United Church ministry to returning Japanese, October 22, 1945, box 15, Council of Churches—Washington—North Idaho Records, UW Libraries.

19. *Hokubei Hochi* (Seattle), October 26, 1992.

20. Dr. Paul Suzuki, one of the Issei evacuee physicians at the Puyallup Assembly Center, and his wife, Nobuko, broke the restrictive covenant in the Laurelhurst neighborhood in the early 1950s. Nobuko Suzuki, taped interview with author, Seattle, August 29, 1995.

21. U.S. Dept. of the Interior, War Relocation Authority, *People in Motion: The Postwar Adjustment of the Evacuated Japanese Americans* (Washington, D.C.: Government Printing Office, 1947), pp. 175–77.

22. For a summary of economic adjustments of the returning Japanese to Seattle, ibid., pp. 113–32.

23. Daniels, *Asian America*, pp. 293–94; Seattle *Post-Intelligencer*, August 30, 1945.

24. Seattle *Post-Intelligencer*, January 23, 1945.

25. Ibid., April 29, 1945.

26. For a discussion of race relations in Seattle during World War II, see Howard A. Droker, "Seattle Race Relations during the Second World War," *Pacific Northwest Quarterly*, 67 (1976):163–74, and Quintard Taylor, *The Forging of a Black Community* (Seattle: University of Washington Press, 1994).

27. In all, 6,837 Japanese Americans, including the Matsushitas, resided in Seattle in 1950, a number approximating the Nikkei prewar population (6,975 in 1940); *Census of Population, 1950*. Most residents had been at Minidoka, but as of 1947,

there were at least 616 new arrivals from other parts of Washington and other states; *People in Motion,* p. 256.

28. The entire message, translated, reads: "All our family are also all right. I believe it is cold in your area. Please guard your health. I hope you will confirm your religious faith with patience, lightness of heart, and vigorously. All of us in your homeland will pray to God for you. I am sending this letter to you via an exchange ship. Blessings for the Christmas season." Quoted in Louis Fiset, "Wartime Communication: Red Cross Key to U.S.-Japan Mails," *American Philatelist,* 104 (1990):228–34.

29. Allied censors had not yet permitted outgoing international correspondence for citizens, so this early communication was unusual. A serendipitous encounter between Teruko and her brother's prewar English teacher, now an American army officer sent to Fukuoka to evaluate war damage, resulted in this communication being forwarded through the U.S. Army post office. Teruko Inoue to Matsushita, November 18, 1945, box 1, Matsushita Papers. Inoue interview, March 15, 1992.

30. Matsushita interviews.

31. Box 2, Matsushita Papers.

32. Matsushita's transcripts and renewal letters of appointment to the University of Washington staff may be found in ibid.

33. Daniels, *Asian America,* pp. 283–84, 305–306.

34. Box 8, Matsushita Papers.

35. Brian Niiya, ed., *Japanese American History: An A-to-Z Reference from 1868 to the Present* (New York: Facts on File, 1993), p. 70.

36. Certificate of Naturalization, box 1, Matsushita Papers.

37. Box 14, ibid.

38. *Japanese American History,* pp. 189–91; Seattle *Times,* May 7, 1989.

39. Inoue interview.

40. East Asia Library, University of Washington.

41. Ito, p. 952.

42. Inoue interview.

| 6: Censored

1. Justice Department detainees and internees were actually permitted to write letters up to 24 lines in length. The Japanese government allowed its citizens to write postcards containing up to 200 Japanese characters. See Fiset, "Wartime Communication," pp. 228–30.

2. Ibid., 230.

3. See, for example, Fukuda; Takeo Ujo Nakano, *Within the Barbed Wire Fence: A Japanese Man's Account of His Internment in Canada* (1980; rpt. Seattle: University of Washington Press, 1981); Kikuchi, *The Kikuchi Diary.*

4. What little has been written may be found in the philatelic literature. See, for example, Steven Roth, *U.S. Censorship of International Civilian Mail* (Lake Oswego, Oreg.: La Posta Publications, 1991).

5. Kashino to author. Kashino worked for the Yamacho Company in Seattle until the attack on Pearl Harbor, when the FBI shut down the business. The firm bought domestic lumber and logs and did business with Mitsui and Company, where Kashino first met Matsushita.

6. N. D. Collaer to detainee spokesmen, January 7, 1942, Fort Missoula File 1025/A, RG85 Suitland.

7. The Italian-speaking censor arrived at Fort Missoula in December, nearly a month before the Japanese censor was hired.

8. P. McLaughlin to C. Locatelli, March 23, 1942, Fort Missoula File 1021/F, RG85 Suitland.

9. INS camp populations declined in the spring and summer of 1942 as detainees had their hearings and were paroled or sent to army installations as internees of war. Military jurisdiction affected the protocol for censorship of internee domestic mail: English-language correspondence passed through the hands of local army base personnel who censored the mail before forwarding it to local post offices for placement in the mail stream. Native-language correspondence, on the other hand, was forwarded, unread, to the POW Unit at the New York field station, for examination by the appropriate censor. Thus, for more than a year, the POW Unit handled both the international and the native-language domestic mail of internees.

10. Regulations Governing the Censorship and Disposition of Prisoner of War and Interned and Detained Civilian Mail, July 3, 1943, p. 31, and June 14, 1944, pp. 30–33, Fort Missoula File 1025, RG85 Suitland.

11. Earl G. Harrison to officers in charge, January 16, 1943, Fort Lincoln File 56125/26-A, ibid.

12. This observation comes from surviving INS internee correspondence. First-class mail of the period often bore receiving dates applied by postal workers with circular date stamps at the post office authorized to deliver the mail to the addressee.

13. In several cases, the postmark date does not match the (earlier) date on the letter.

APPENDIX

Tables

1. Japanese Population of Seattle from 1890 to 1940

YEAR	TOTAL	FOREIGN–BORN	NATIVE–BORN	PERCENT OF TOTAL POPULATION
1890	125	125	—	—
1900	2,990	—	—	3.7
1910	6,127	5,749	378	2.6
1920	7,874	6,011	1,863	2.5
1930	8,448	4,448	4,000	2.3
1940	6,975	2,876	4,099	1.9

2. German, Italian, and Japanese Aliens Living in the Contiguous United States in 1940

NATIVE COUNTRY	U.S.	WASHINGTON STATE	SEATTLE
Germany★	314,105	2,932	1,085
Italy★	690,551	3,914	1,469
Japan★★	47,305	5,683	2,876

★ Department of Justice estimates
★★ 1940 Census

3. Estimate of Seattle Resident Enemy Aliens Arrested, through March 15, 1942

DATE	JAPANESE	GERMAN	ITALIAN
Dec. 9, 1941	116	28	2
24	13	39	6
Feb. 22, 1942	103	—	—
Mar. 8	20	—	—
15	12	1	—
TOTAL	264	68	8

BIBLIOGRAPHY

| Manuscripts

Council of Churches Seattle Records. University of Washington Libraries, Seattle, WA.

Council of Churches Washington North Idaho Records. University of Washington Libraries.

Inoue, Teruko. "Life as a Fulbrighter, 1954–1955," in the author's possession.

Koike, Kyo. Photographs. Special Collections, University of Washington Libraries.

Kunishige, Asakichi Frank. Photos File. Henry Art Gallery Records, University of Washington Libraries.

Matsushita, Iwao. Papers. University of Washington Libraries.

Matsushita, Iwao. Photographs. Special Collections, University of Washington Libraries.

Okuda, Heiji Henry. Papers. University of Washington Libraries.

Papers of the U. S. Commission on Wartime Relocation and Internment of Civilians, Part 1: Numerical File Archive.

Passenger and Crew Lists of Vessels Arriving at Seattle, Washington, 1890–1957, microfilm, roll 42, National Archives-Pacific Northwest Region, Seattle.

Records of the Immigration and Naturalization Service, Record Group 85, National Archives, Suitland, Maryland.

Records of the War Relocation Authority, Record Group 210, National Archives, Suitland, Maryland.

Records of the Western Defense Command, Fourth Army, WCCA and CAD, Record Group 338, National Archives, Washington, D.C.

Sakamoto, James Y. Papers. University of Washington Libraries.

| Articles, Books, Dissertations, and Theses

Allen, John E., and Marjorie Burns with Sam C. Sargent. *Cataclysms on the Columbia.* Portland, OR.: Timber Press, 1986.

Amidon, Beulah. "Aliens in America," *Survey Graphic* 30 (1943):58–61.

Bagley, Clarence B. *History of Seattle: From the Earliest Settlement to the Present Time,* vol. 1. Chicago: S. J. Clarke Publishing Company, 1916.

Bailey, Thomas A. *A Diplomatic History of the American People.* 8th ed. New York: Appleton-Century-Crofts. 1969.

Benedetti, Umberto. *The Lifestyle of Italian Internees at Fort Missoula Montana. 1941–1943: Bella Vista.* [Missoula]: U. Benedetti, 1986.

Berner, Richard C. *Seattle in the 20th Century.* 2 vols. Seattle: Charles Press, 1991–92.

Biddle, Francis. *In Brief Authority.* Garden City, N.Y.: Doubleday and Co., 1962.

Chiasson, Lloyd. "Japanese-American Relocation during World War II: A Study of California Editorial Reactions," *Journalism Quarterly* 68 (1991):263–69.

City of Seattle. Annual Report of the Police Department, December 31, 1941.

Clark, Paul F. "Those Other Camps: An Oral History Analysis of Japanese Alien Enemy Internment during World War II." Masters thesis, California State University Fullerton, 1980.

Corbett, Scott. *Quiet Passages: The Exchange of Civilians between the United States and Japan during the Second World War.* Kent, OH: Kent State University Press, 1987.

Culley, John J. "Trouble at the Lordsburg Internment Camp." *New Mexico Historical Review* 60 (1985):225–48.

———. "The Santa Fe Internment Camp and the Justice Department Program for Enemy Aliens." In *Japanese Americans: From Relocation to Redress* ed. Roger Daniels, Sandra C. Taylor, and Harry H. L. Kitano, pp. 57–71. Rev. ed. 1986; reprint, Seattle: University of Washington Press, 1991.

Daniels, Roger. *Concentration Camps USA: Japanese Americans and World War II.* New York: Holt, Rinehart and Winston, 1972.

———. *The Decision to Relocate the Japanese Americans.* Philadelphia: J. B. Lippincott Co., 1975.

———. *The Politics of Prejudice: The Anti-Japanese Movement in California and the Struggle for Japanese Exclusion.* 2d ed. Berkeley: University of California Press, 1977.

———. *Asian America: Chinese and Japanese in the United States since 1850.* Seattle: University of Washington Press, 1988.

Daniels, Roger, ed. *American Concentration Camps: A Documentary History of the Relocation and Incarceration of Japanese Americans, 1942–1945.* 9 vols. New York: Garland Publishing, 1989.

Daniels, Roger, Sandra C. Taylor, and Harry H. L. Kitano, eds. *Japanese Americans: From Relocation to Redress.* Rev. ed. 1986; reprint, Seattle: University of Washington Press, 1991.

Dorwart, Jeffery. *Conflict of Duty: The U.S. Navy's Intelligence Dilemma, 1919–1945.* Annapolis, MD: United States Naval Institute, 1983.

Droker, Howard A. "Seattle Race Relations during the Second World War," *Pacific Northwest Quarterly* 67 (1976):163–74.

Fiset, Louis. "Wartime Communication: Red Cross Key to U.S.-Japan Mails," *American Philatelist* 104 (1990):228–34.

————. "Redress for Nisei Public Employees in Washington State after World War II," *Pacific Northwest Quarterly* 88 (1996):21–32.

Foreign Relations of the United States: Diplomatic Papers. Washington, D.C.: Government Printing Office, 1960.

Friedheim, Robert L. *The Seattle General Strike*. Seattle: University of Washington Press, 1964.

Fukuda, Yoshiaki. *My Six Years of Internment: An Issei's Struggle for Justice*, trans. Konko Church of San Francisco and Research Information Center of Konko Churches of North America. San Francisco: Konko Church of San Francisco) 1990.

Gardiner, C. Harvey. *Pawns in a Triangle of Hate: The Peruvian Japanese and the United States*. Seattle: University of Washington Press, 1981.

Gesensway, Deborah, and Mindy Roseman. *Beyond Words: Images from America's Concentration Camps*. Ithaca: Cornell University Press, 1987.

Girdner, Audrie, and Anne Loftis. *The Great Betrayal: Evacuation of the Japanese Americans during World War II*. Toronto: Macmillan, 1969

Glenn, Evelyn Nakano. *Issei, Nisei, War Bride: Three Generations of Japanese American Women in Domestic Service*. Philadelphia: Temple University Press, 1986.

Greenwald, Maurine. "Working-class Feminism and the Family Wage Ideal: The Seattle Debate on Married Women's Right to Work, 1914–1920," *Journal of American History* 76 (1989):124–25.

Grodzins, Morton. *Americans Betrayed: Politics and the Japanese Evacuation*. Chicago: University of Chicago Press, 1949.

Hansen, Arthur A., and Betty E. Mitson, eds. *Voices Long Silent: An Oral Inquiry into the Japanese American Evacuation*. Fullerton: California State University, 1974.

Hisashi, Tsurutani. *America-bound: The Japanese and the Opening of the American West*, trans. Betsey Scheiner. Tokyo: Japan Times, 1989.

Hoover, J. Edgar, "Alien Enemy Control," *Iowa Law Review* 29 (1944):396–408.

Hosokawa, Bill. "The Uprooting of Seattle." In *Japanese Americans: From Relocation to Redress*, ed. Roger Daniels, Sandra C. Taylor, and Harry H. L. Kitano, pp. 18–20. Rev. ed. 1986; reprint, Seattle: University of Washington Press, 1991.

Irons, Peter, ed. *Justice Delayed: The Record of the Japanese American Internment Cases*. Middletown, CN: Wesleyan University Press, 1989.

Ishigo, Estelle. *Lone Heart Mountain*. 1972; reprint, Los Angeles: Communicart, 1989.

Ito, Kazuo. *Issei: A History of Japanese Immigrants in North America*, trans. Shinichiro Nakamura and Jean S. Gerard. Seattle: Japanese Community Service, 1973.

Kashima, Tetsuden. "Mistreatment of Internees." In *Japanese Americans: From Relocation to Redress*, ed. Roger Daniels, Sandra C. Taylor, and Harry H. L. Kitano, pp. 52–56. Rev. ed. 1986; reprint, Seattle: University of Washington Press, 1991.

Keene, Donald. *World within Walls: Japanese Literature of the Pre-Modern Era, 1600–1867*. New York: Holt, Rinehard and Winston, 1976.

Kenjiro Nomura. *Retrospective Catalog.* Seattle: Seattle Art Museum, 1960.

———. *The George and Betty Nomura Collection.* Seattle: Wing Luke Museum, 1991.

Kikuchi, Charles. *The Kikuchi Diary,* ed. John Modell. 1973; reprint, Urbana: University of Illinois Press, 1993.

Kitagawa, Joseph M. *Religion in Japanese History.* 1966; reprint, New York: Columbia University Press, 1990.

———. *The Christian Tradition: Beyond Its European Captivity.* Philadelphia: Trinity Press International, 1992.

Koike, Kyo. "The Seattle Camera Club," *Photo-Era* 55 (1925):182.

Kumamoto, Bob. "The Search for Spies: American Counterintelligence and the Japanese American Community, 1931–1942," *Amerasia Journal* 6 (1979).

Lesser, Jeff H. "Always 'Outsiders': Asians, Naturalization, and the Supreme Court," *Amerasia Journal* 12 (1985):83–100.

Miyamoto, S. Frank *Social Solidarity among the Japanese in Seattle.* 1939; reprint, Seattle: University of Washington Press, 1984.

Monroe, Robert D. "Light and Shade: Pictorial Photography in Seattle, 1920–1940, and the Seattle Camera Club." In *Turning Shadows into Light: Art and Culture of the Northwest's Early Asian/Pacific Community,* ed. Mayumi Tsutakawa and Alan Chong Lau. Seattle: Young Pine Press, 1982.

Munson, C. B. "Japanese on the West Coast." *In American Concentration Camps: A Documentary History of the Relocation and Incarceration of Japanese Americans. 1942–1945,* ed. Roger Daniels. Vol 1. New York: Garland Publishing, 1989.

Nagler, Joerg A. "Enemy Aliens and Internment in World War I: Alvo von Alvensleben in Fort Douglas, Utah, a Case Study," *Utah Historical Quarterly* 58 (1990):388–405.

Nakano, Jiro, and Kay Nakano, eds. and trans. *Poets behind Barbed Wire.* Honolulu: Bamboo Ridge Press, 1983.

Nakano, Takeo Ujo. *Within the Barbed Wire Fence: A Japanese Man's Account of His Internment in Canada.* 1980; reprint, Seattle: University of Washington Press, 1981.

Nicholson, Herbert. *Treasures in Earthen Vessels.* Whittier, CA: Penn Lithographics, 1974.

Niiya, Brian, ed. *Japanese American History: An A-to-Z Reference from 1868 to the Present.* New York: Facts on File, 1993.

O'Brien, Robert W. *The College Nisei.* Palo Alto, CA: Pacific Books, 1949.

Okihiro, Gary Y. *Cane Fires: The Anti-Japanese Movement in Hawaii. 1865–1945.* Philadelphia: Temple University Press, 1991

Okubo, Mine. *Citizen 13660.* New York: Columbia University Press, 1946.

Personal Justice Denied: Report of the Commission on Wartime Relocation and Internment of Civilians. 1983; reprint, Seattle: University of Washington Press, 1997.

Peter Irons. *Justice at War.* New York: Oxford University Press, 1983.

Polk's Seattle City Directory, 1920–24.

"Proposal for Coordination of FBI, ONI and MID," June 5, 1940, United States Naval

Administration in World War II. Washington, D.C.: Navy Historical Division, 1959.

Rademaker, John A. "The Ecological Position of the Japanese Farmers in the State of Washington," Ph.D. dissertation, University of Washington, Seattle, 1939.

Ringle, Kenneth D. [pseud., An Intelligence Officer], "The Japanese in America: The Problem and the Solution," *Harper's Magazine* 185 (1942):489–97.

Roth, Steven. *U.S. Censorship of International Civilian Mail.* Lake Oswego, OR: La Posta Publications, 1991.

Sale, Roger. *Seattle: Past to Present.* Seattle: University of Washington Press, 1976.

Schmid, Calvin F. *Social Trends in Seattle.* Seattle: University of Washington Press, 1944.

Schwantes, Carlos A. *The Pacific Northwest: An Interpretive History.* Lincoln: University of Nebraska Press, 1989.

Sone, Monica. *Nisei Daughter,* 1953; reprint, Seattle: University of Washington Press, 1979.

Suzuki, Lester E. *Ministry in the Assembly and Relocation Centers of World War II.* Berkeley: Yardbird Publishing Co., 1979.

Taylor, Quintard. *The Forging of a Black Community.* Seattle: University of Washington Press, 1994.

Taylor, Sandra C. *Jewel of the Desert: Japanese American Internment at Topaz.* Berkeley: University of California Press, 1993.

The View from Within: Japanese American Art from the Internment Camps. 1942–1945. Los Angeles: Japanese American National Museum, 1994.

U.S. Bureau of the Census. Census of Population 1920, 1950.

———. *Historical Statistics of the United States, Colonial Times to 1957: A Statistical Abstract Supplement.* Washington, D.C.: Government Printing Office, 1960.

U. S. House Committee on Immigration and Naturalization. Japanese Immigration Hearings, 66th Cong., 2d Sess., 1921, Parts 1 and 4.

U. S. House. "Fourth Interim Report of the Select Committee Investigating National Defense Migration." Report 2124, 77th Cong., 2d Sess., 1942, reprinted in *American Concentration Camps: A Documentary History of the Relocation and Incarceration of Japanese Americans. 1942–1945,* ed. Roger Daniels. Vol. 3. New York: Garland Publishing, 1989.

U. S. Interior Department. *People in Motion: The Postwar Adjustment of the Evacuated Japanese Americans.* Washington, D.C.: Government Printing Office, 1947.

U.S. War Department. *Final Report: Japanese Evacuation from the West Coast, 1942.* Washington, D.C.: Government Printing Office, 1943.

U.S. War Relocation Authority. *The Evacuated People.* Washington, D.C.: Government Printing Office, 1946

———. *WRA: A Story of Human Conservation.* Washington D.C.: Government Printing Office, 1946.

University of Washington Bulletin. Catalog, 1926–27. Seattle: University of Washington, 1927.

Van Valkenburg, Carol. *An Alien Place: The Fort Missoula, Montana Detention Camp, 1941–1944.* Missoula, MT: Pictorial Histories Publishing Co., Inc., 1995.

Weglyn, Michi. *Years of Infamy: The Untold Story of America's Concentration Camps.* 1976; reprint, Seattle: University of Washington Press, 1995.

Whitehead, Don. *The FBI Story: A Report to the People.* New York: Random House, 1956.

Zabilski, Carol. "Dr. Kyo Koike, 1878–1947: Physician, Poet, Photographer," *Pacific Northwest Quarterly* 68 (1977):72–79.

PHOTO CREDITS

Chapter opening photographs by Iwao Matsushita are courtesy of the Special Collections Division, University of Washington Libraries: 1, "Mountain Lake," 17503; 2, "Autumn Clouds," 17499; 3, "Lake Wilderness," 17578; 4, "Skyline Trail," 17501; 5, "The Mountain That Was God," 17500; 6, Untitled, 17579; 7, "Ice Coral," 17580.

Pg

6. Teruko Inoue Collection.

8. Matsushita Papers, University of Washington Libraries.

11. Special Collections Division, University of Washington Libraries, UW 17495.

13. Special Collections Division, University of Washington Libraries, UW 17514.

16. Special Collections Division, University of Washington Libraries, UW 17494.

17. Special Collections Division, University of Washington Libraries, UW 17515.

18. Teruko Inoue Collection.

20. Special Collections Division, University of Washington Libraries, UW 17498.

21. Special Collections Division, University of Washington Libraries, UW 17492.

22. Special Collections Division, University of Washington Libraries, UW 17516.

22. Special Collections Division University of Washington Libraries, UW 17087.

22. Special Collections Division, University of Washington Libraries, UW 17517.

23. Teruko Inoue Collection.

23. Special Collections Division, University of Washington Libraries, UW 17507.

35. K. Ross Toole Archives, Mansfield Library the University of Montana, 84–247.

41. Special Collections Division, University of Washington Libraries, UW 17508.

49. Montana Historical Society.

55. Special Collections Division, University of Washington Libraries, UW 17509.

57. Montana Historical Society.

59. Special Collections Division, University of Washington Libraries, UW 17512.

66. Seattle Post-Intelligencer Collection, Museum of History and Industry 28081.
67. Special Collections Division, University of Washington Libraries, UW 12209.
70. Special Collections Division, University of Washington Libraries, UW 14753.
75. Special Collections Division, University of Washington Libraries, UW 17096.
77. Special Collections Division, University of Washington Libraries, UW 17496.
78. Matsushita Papers, University of Washington Libraries.
92. Matsushita Papers, University of Washington Libraries.
93. Special Collections Division, University of Washington Libraries, UW 17489.
96. Special Collections Division, University of Washington Libraries, UW 17490.
96. Matsushita Papers, University of Washington Libraries.
102. Matsushita Papers, University of Washington Libraries.
108. Matsushita Papers, University of Washington Libraries.

The Letters: Matsushita Papers, University of Washington Libraries.

INDEX